Also by John L. Locke

The Child's Path to Spoken Language

*The Emergent Lexicon: The Child's Development
of a Linguistic Vocabulary*

Phonological Acquisition and Change

The

Why We

De-Voicing

Don't Talk to

of

Each Other

Society

Anymore

John L. Locke

SIMON & SCHUSTER

SIMON & SCHUSTER
Rockefeller Center
1230 Avenue of the Americas
New York, NY 10020

Designed by Jeanette Olender
Manufactured in the United States of America

1   3   5   7   9   10   8   6   4   2

Library of Congress Cataloging-in-Publication Data
Locke, John L.
The de-voicing of society : why we don't talk to each
other anymore / John L. Locke.
p. cm.
Includes bibliographical references.
1. Conversation analysis—Social aspects. I. Title.
P95.45.L63   1998
302.3′46—dc21   98-14921   CIP
ISBN 0-684-84333-1

Acknowledgments

This book has traveled. Some of the ideas about social talking first bubbled to the surface several years ago during a sabbatical at the Sub-Department of Animal Behaviour (Department of Zoology) at the University of Cambridge. These early thoughts found their way into a short article, "More Than Words Can Say," published in *New Scientist*. When I returned to "real life" at the Massachusetts General Hospital and Harvard Medical School in Boston, I sketched out some of the main points of the book, and further conceptualized and wrote it after relocation to my new academic home, the Department of Human Communication Sciences at the University of Sheffield in England.

I am indebted to some fine libraries. The Widener Library at Harvard and the University of Cambridge Library are chief among them. I regularly used the library at the University of Sheffield and, because I frequently visit my parents in Marquette, Michigan, availed myself of the excellent resources of the Olsen Library at Northern Michigan University.

I am also indebted to some fine people. Pat Millington, my secretary at the University of Sheffield, shielded me from competing activities. Annie Brown lent helpful contemplation and enthusiastic support to many aspects of my thought and writing. Tom Dickins, Mick Perkins, Michael Studdert-Kennedy, and Anne van Kleeck read the entire manuscript and suggested a number of helpful changes. Robin Dunbar, Marc Hauser, and Barry Keverne read chapter 2, and my interpretation of the primate literature is the better for it. I also wish to thank Steven Pinker for his personal comments on aspects of linguistic evolution. Outside the workaday academic realm, I was privileged to have the assistance of four "senior" scholars. Donald Wayne made editorial suggestions, informed by over a half-century of successful writing. His wife, Helena, offered knowledge of the life and literature of Bronislaw Malinowski—her father. My parents, Edward and Lillian Locke, gave encouragement, and not just that; at the age of ninety-one my father read the entire manuscript, locating eight errors.

For Barbara Callan,
who wanted the world,
and Annie Brown,
who got it

Contents

*If our friends are worth having,
nothing that we give them can be good
enough for them, and the best thing
that we can give, either in our life or
in our talk, is only ourselves.*

ERNEST DE SELINCOURT,
"The Art of Conversation"

Preface

In writing this book I relied on instincts acquired during several decades of empirical research in human communication science. These instincts steered me through the relevant scholarly literatures in biological and cultural anthropology, sociolinguistics, ethology, social psychology, sociology, and developmental and cognitive neuroscience, as well as business, economics, and government. These are the kinds of activities one expects of a university professor. But I also did some other things.

One thing I did was watch people informally and reflect on what I had learned from a lifetime of doing so. Ordinary life, if we treat it as such, is an Institute for the Study of Human Communication. The labs are street corners, dinner tables, cocktail parties, offices, public parks, university campuses, airplanes, and commuter trains—in short, wherever two or more members of our loquacious species are found.

I also read newspapers and magazines from around the English-speaking world. You will find a number of end notes that document articles from these sources. At first glance these notes may seem out of place, intermixed as they are with scholarly references. But these more public items reveal the emergent experience of contemporary people captured journalistically in the middle of their first reactions to community fragmentation, automatic bank tellers, telecommuting, and social isolation; to answering machines, electronic mail, and loneliness. Use of this material allowed me to document ongoing social and cultural phenomena, many of which are too recent to be described elsewhere.

You are a talker, and you live in much the same world I do. As you read the chapters, I invite you to reflect on your own social-vocal experience. Doing so, I believe, will confirm, enrich, and qualify in your own terms the observations and proposals that follow.

John L. Locke
Cambridge, England

Note to Readers
To avoid awkwardness of expression, I have used "he," "him," and "his" in a few places where pronouns of either gender would be appropriate. No disrespect is intended toward female readers.

And After Voice

Our species began to talk tens of thousands of years ago. But hundreds of millennia earlier, our evolutionary ancestors were already expressing themselves vocally while consorting with familiar members of their group.

If we were able to spend a day observing these near-humans, intercepting them just before they began to speak, we would see them clumped together in small congregations and hear the sounds of chattering, scolding, shouting, and laughing. These vocal communicants were exploiting an inherited capability for "close calls"—the intimate resonances of their ancestors, the great apes—for ways to signal personal intentions. And to good regulatory effect, for they secured for themselves and for us, their grateful progeny, new ways to promote and maintain friendships, cool off warring parties, scold and praise, gossip and argue, warn and appease, joke and show off. And when they did so, the voice assumed an exceptional commitment: primary publicist of each being's identity, feelings, character, and intentions.

We moderns are more like our evolutionary ancestors than we might care to admit. Like them, we use our voices to resolve disputes. Like them, we seek to convey amicable intentions to strangers, develop new friends, and gain admission to potentially helpful groups. But we humans would also like to be listened to. We need to be heard.

Most of us are pretty transparent, of course. Our looks and sounds express our feelings, even, as we are wont to say, "betray" them. But for

the most part, humans are culturally disallowed from conveying personal and emotional information without talking. Anyone who gener-
ates a range of facial expressions and vocal variations while not uttering
words is likely to be socially rejected, if not hospitalized or arrested. It
is not enough to want to send these personal messages. We must have
"legal" opportunities to expose our selves, and talking provides these
now, just as social sound-making did so many thousands of years ago.

But a funny thing happened just a century or two into the present
millennium. Our personal voices began to fade. The seeds were sown
when tiny tribes of humans gave way to large and diverse cultures that
had fewer pieces of shared information and a greater need to exchange
impersonal facts. The process continued when we developed quicker
ways to transmit messages and to conduct economic and personal business. Our appetite for information exploded when improved travel and
mass communication multiplied the number of things we need to know
about to compete and feel safe.

As we approach the new millennium, many of us modern crave men
have acquired the things we need and are now burrowed into a socially
detached style of unassisted living. We require no personal favors or
coalitions to meet our personal responsibilities. Social talking is a way
to kill time, and in complex, fast-paced societies, much of the spare time
is already dead. Warmly personal chats with friends are thus being
replaced by coolly efficient "info-speech" with strangers.

At one time the relationship was primary and the message almost
incidental. Now, the exchange of information is too often the reason for
speech, the personal relationship relegated to a position of secondary
importance. Indeed, where our ancestors enjoyed the company of small
groups, members of progressive societies are becoming monadic, foraging in the vicinity of other people but feeding mainly on themselves.

Our great-grandparents lived very differently. They could see and
hear their communicants. Messages were wrapped in blankets of feeling.
Voices moved, faces flashed. From an averted gaze, a grin, or a catch in
the voice, our great-grandparents knew when other people were ill at
ease or saying something not quite true. They knew from the tone of
the voice, set of the jaw, and focus of the eyes when their associates
"meant business."

How times have changed. We great-grandchildren trade thoughts on a daily basis with people we do not know and will never meet. The social feedback mechanisms that were handed down by our evolutionary ancestors—systems that were designed and carefully tuned by hundreds of millennia of face-to-face interaction—are rarely used nowadays, and there is a potential for miscommunication and mistrust as never before in human history.

We feel it when we shop. People are more and more wary of products and services. When our grandparents were newly married, they knew the people they were dealing with. Social monitoring systems were in full operation. Talk mattered. Reputations were at stake. A spate of unsatisfactory negotiations could ruin a businessman. Now, slander suits —once common in colonial America—are down. A person's public image matters less than in the past. Not knowing the person in charge or even who that is, and lacking the personal assurances of any credible party, purchasers now require legal guarantees and contracts. The confirmatory handshake, once as trusted as it was facile, is long gone.

Intimate talking, the social call of humans, is on the endangered behaviors list. Even when we're with friends, many of us try to avoid chatting and gossiping, disdaining these forms of verbal conduct and the people who indulge in them. But there are lots of people these days with a new form of locked-in syndrome, people who long for an aimless chat with a dear old friend—not a "conversation" over e-mail but a vocal chat, complete with eye movements and gestures and the possibility that either party could touch or embrace, console or congratulate the other.

As never before we are faced with discrepancies, growing by the year, between the ancestral environments that molded us and the modern ones that confront us on a daily basis—a deepening conflict between biology and culture. Increasingly we go it alone, underexercising evolved faculties for social communication. Sending few messages about ourselves, we get back few reactions from others. We thus night-sail blindly into uncharted social waters, dissociated from the usual ways of knowing where we are going and what we might be becoming.

Many of us are beginning to develop the symptoms of an undiagnosed social condition, a kind of functional "de-voicing," brought on by an insufficient diet of intimate talking. Years ago we were warned that "automation," now a delightfully quaint word, would take away our personhood. Aided by the widespread distribution of computers, automation has now reached socially objectionable levels. Several years ago the First National Bank of Chicago began the latest trend in impersonal banking—teller rationing. Customers are now charged $3 each time they attempt to speak to a human being at the counter. It's just the tip of a rapidly surfacing iceberg.

If you are autistic, welcome to the voiceless society. It was tailor-made for you. If you enjoy typing "I L-O-V-E Y-O-U" to a faceless stranger, a blissful future lies ahead. But if, like the rest of us, you need to share yourself with others, to enjoy the intimate company of close friends, and to be deeply understood, you may have already begun to miss the sound of social calls. You may be de-voicing.

ONE

The Articulate Heart

When a person realizes he has been deeply heard, his eyes moisten. I think in some real sense he is weeping for joy. It is as though he were saying, "Thank God, somebody heard me. Someone knows what it's like to be me."

David Myers, *The Pursuit of Happiness*

When Philip awoke from the surgery, his first reaction was that he must not have died because he was *aware*. He could see and feel and hear things. And if he was alive, he would see his wife and children again. In a few days he would be back home, resting, perhaps lying in the sun. Life would resume.

But it wouldn't be his old life. For what Philip never really banked on was the fact that while he could still hear and understand what others said to him, there would be no more responding in kind. For when the surgeon removed his cancerous larynx, Philip's voice went with it. Forever.

They had discussed this in advance. It was mostly a blur now, but Philip could remember talking with several medical specialists, each telling him something about the operation and the recovery process. One had mentioned the voice part, but it really hadn't made sense. How can a surgeon take away your . . . your *personality?*

This book is about a loss of voice. But it is not about the kind that occurs when physical disease destroys the vocal organs of a single individual. Rather, what we will witness here is a new and pernicious kind of social de-voicing—manifested most specifically and painfully as a loss of opportunities for intimate talking. And it is creeping, soul by soul, through the entirety of progressive societies.

It is important that we understand the etiology as well as the effects of this vocal deficiency on our personal lives and culture. To do so we must cast a glance backwards in evolutionary time and consider the ways in which our ancestors may have benefited from the capacity to create and maintain sociality through vocalization. We will also look at how our own present-day alliances were built up by previous social interactions. And we will see how these alliances now elevate trust, confidence, and personal security—resources that oxygenate the human psyche and enervate a range of cultural institutions. Before we plunge headlong into these issues, though, we need to think about the way personal identities are created and maintained.

Who We Are

Each of us cares how we are perceived and judged. It has never been otherwise. The earliest humanoid forms lived in small bands under precarious conditions. Food and other resources were scarce, and competitors were many. So were predators. Survival required cooperation. Early humans were thus heavily dependent on one another. To thrive, each of these social beings had to be able to recognize the other members of his small band, to read their intentions, learn their habits, and recall which owed, and which were owed, personal favors.

Who we are is conveyed by our possessions as well as our behaviors. Anthropologist Polly Wiessner learned a great deal about this in the 1970s while studying the !Kung, a hunting and gathering people living mostly in southern Angola, Botswana, and Namibia. She found that !Kung arrowheads displayed two kinds of personal information. One identified the language and possibly the dialect of the arrow maker, as well as the band to which he belonged. The other kind of information was about the man who made the arrow. These personal facts mattered to the !Kung, who reacted anxiously when Wiessner showed them some arrows of neighboring tribes. If they happened upon an animal that had been felled by one of these other arrows, tribe members said, they would worry because a stranger might be lurking about, one who might prefer their territory to his own.

Although Wiessner's immediate interest was projectile points, she drew attention to a larger generalization about self-presentation and public relations: competition between people accentuates differences in style. That's right—style. Ordinarily one equates style with fashion, with clothing and jewelry. Most of us have closets with skirts and ties of a dated length and width, kitchen cupboards with fondue pots and blenders. Surely these artifacts of yesteryear convey little about who we truly are or ever were, reveal little more about our underlying motivations in living life as we do. But there is a deeper meaning and significance to style, and it flows from the urge we were hoping to satisfy—to be understood in a particular way—when we acquired our personal belongings.

We residents of progressive societies are superficially unlike the !Kung. Except for the odd archer, arrowheads play no role in our lives, nor do we manufacture the objects that we use. But we are authorities on socioeconomic stress, and we have at least as much need for style. So we buy distinctive identities, showing off our purchases when we put on our clothes, walk out the door of our residence, and drive away in our car.

Martin Clarke, a professor at Leeds University in England, has found that automobiles say a great deal about the image we are seeking. "Your car locates you in our socioeconomic system," said Professor Clarke. "If you know the car, you know the person." The windows and bumpers of automobiles may also broadcast our personal views and philosophy. Not long ago, two professors drove around suburban Washington, D.C., in an attempt to classify bumper stickers. The messages, they found, either expressed affection for athletic teams, radio stations, and universities, or attitudes toward social issues and politics. There were strong correlations between the racial profile and economic status of neighborhoods and the content of stickers on the cars that were parked there.

Some of the loudest personal broadcasts are expensive and therefore must be justified to ourselves and our friends. So we play mental games.

We claim that our BMW, Rolex, and Montblanc "work better" when we drive, tell time, and sign our names, but in reality these objects are visual displays. They call attention to our existence, not just our nature. And the benefits are direct and immediate, because these displays are omnidirectional; even when others aren't looking, we still see ourselves using these things.

These *things*. Clothes, cars, and houses, like watches and pens, are acquisitions. They help us to be seen as a person who is sexy or daring or living well. But who is the underlying *person* who has these attributes? A car is unable to tell anyone that we are introspective; a house cannot disclose that we are young or witty. Clothing usually says little about our mood, which changes more often than we can dress ourselves. Cars cannot truthfully declare that we are educated or courteous. Things are thus powerful, but unreliably so, and that is their allure.

What there is to be known about us *is* transmissible, of course, and for this we owe a great debt—not to objects that we purchase like a suit of clothes or manufacture like an arrowhead, but to something that comes into the world with us. Something that moves and behaves with us, reflecting where we've been, are at the moment, and might be seeking to go in the future. It adorns and dogs each of our articulate steps. This rich source of personal information is our voice.

The voice is often thought of as a vehicle for speech, and with good reason—one is unlikely to win elocution awards by mouthing or whispering words. But the voice carries useful information all by itself, even when the mouth is relatively still, as in the sustained *aaahs* we produce for physicians or the *uuuhs* we utter while formulating our next thought. Even this motionless voice tells stories about us, many that we want told, some that we would prefer to keep private. The act of speaking, as we will see, gives up additional facts on its own.

As I will discuss, there are at least seven broadly different aspects of our selves—most of them linked to what would otherwise be private experiences and personal secrets—that are made public by our voices.

The Physical Self

When we use our voice, people acquire a great deal of information about us even if we would prefer that they did not. Most obviously, they learn about our physical nature. Listeners usually can guess from a voice on the telephone whether it belongs to a child or an adult, a male or a female, a young adult or a very old person. With some accuracy they can also tell whether a voice belongs to a large or a small person. This connection between body size and pitch is implicitly understood, and if the occasion requires, people may lower their pitch to seem bigger and more powerful than they really are. On the telephone an aging woman may raise her deepening pitch to avoid sounding like a man.

Although there are many connections between faces and voices, it is impossible to guess which go with which. A person can be, at one and the same time, euphonious and ugly. When leafing through a magazine, you may have come across a picture of a favorite radio broadcaster and were shocked to discover that a Paul Newman–sounding personality had the face of Ichabod Crane. Back in the fifties, some radio people couldn't make the transition to television, just as some silent film stars had to drop out of the acting profession when talkies came in.

Emotionality

When people talk, their voice is automatically influenced by feelings. And the voice conveys them. Not just anger and contempt, not merely fear and happiness, but sadness, surprise, love, astonishment, doubt, amusement, and indifference. Anxiety heightens breathiness and raises vocal pitch. Depression enhances nasal resonance. Shyness softens amplitude. Joyfulness animates vocal pitch. Frightened talkers may select words that disguise their fear, but when listeners hear breathiness and elevated pitch, they perceive apprehension. The deceptive talker may say all the right words, but when they're uttered hesitantly or with unsteady gaze, watchful listeners become doubtful.

Emotions are conveyed through the actions of a central nervous system, the evolution of which began not thousands of years ago but millions. For this reason the voice of the squirrel monkey, a *very* distant cousin, and the human voice are activated from comparable areas of the brain. The areas are as deep as they are old. Dissociated as they are from the higher cortical areas where vocal images are consciously experienced, the resonances that say so much about our feelings cannot be described in words. Emotions thus creep into the voice without first consulting the conscious mind. The talker, cordoned off from the command center of his species' most expressive system, is unable either to access or convincingly manipulate its inner workings. Social talking thus has a heart of its own.

It's a heart that's hard to fake. In Stanislavski's school of "method acting," the thespians, unable to turn on tears mechanically, attempt to develop empathy for the person portrayed—hoping this will trigger emotions "analogous to those required for the part"—or bring to mind an extremely sad event from their own previous experience. Feelings associated with that experience are thereby aroused and are expressed more or less naturally.

The imperfect controllability of vocal communication is paradoxically responsible for its greatest benefits. Listeners do not merely need to hear the talker, they also need to interpret him. From their standpoint the value of social talking begins where the control of it wanes.

Emotional transparency benefits the talker, too, at least if he's honest. If a person carries his vocal cards too close to his vest, if people can't "read" him, they're unlikely to invest much time or energy in a relationship with him. They may even find it "spooky" to be around such a person. Transparency also directly helps the talker when, in monitoring his own voice, he discovers from affective cues embedded therein what he himself is feeling. He hears an "edge" to his voice even before he is able to conclude from other clues that he is "edgy."

How we look matters, too, of course, but our facial and bodily architecture are more stable than our moods. They vary little from day to day and certainly do not change between breakfast and lunch. But our voice and speech work differently. They freely fluctuate with emotional changes that occur in a single conversation, in the uttering of a single sentence or even midway through a word.

If we must acquaint ourselves with these properties of the voice, the learning curve is a short one. Within a few hours of birth the heart rate of neonatal chimpanzees is differentially affected by divergent cries of their species. And the effect cuts across primate groups. Human children and adults require no instruction to glean the emotional content from monkey vocalizations.

Emotional displays are among the first stimulations that humans experience. The young of our species receive their maiden exposure to vocal emotion several months before birth. In the uterus, despite noisy listening conditions, the lower frequencies of the mother's speech and song can be heard, even learned, by the fetus. These frequencies, as it happens, are saturated with the inks and dyes of human feeling.

The infant's own expression of emotion may begin almost this early. Nearly three months before its birth, the fetus begins to hear. When loud sounds occur near the mother's abdomen, ultrasound imaging reveals a telltale facial expression by the fetus, a clenching of its eyes. Prenatal emotion may also be expressed by a kick or, incredibly, a howl. Once, in the middle of a delivery, a Scottish obstetrician thought he heard the cries of a baby. They were heard, he later recalled, "by two doctors, three midwives, and the patient. All were startled, and the operator looked about the labour room in his incredulity, to make sure that a nurse had not carried in a baby." Moments later the cries were traced to the fetus, vocally empowered when membranes ruptured and air whooshed into the birth canal.

When we speak, we do much more than turn on our larynx. We pronounce words with a particular rhythm and rate of speed, and with a degree of articulatory force. These oral gestures embed additional information in the speaking voice. Fold these articulatory characteristics in with our seemingly inexhaustible supply of pitches and resonances, and the scene is set for a serious analytical challenge. Which of all the hums and buzzes reveals our true feelings, the ones that may even escape our own notice? The answer is that they all do to some extent, but studies indicate that emotions are revealed mainly by the lower frequencies of the voice. These are the ones you hear when someone is speaking unintelligibly in an adjacent room. And with these lower sounds we can infer levity and sorrow from laughing and sobbing, even when words and thoughts are nowhere to be found.

In laboratories, too, electronic filtering of the upper frequencies of speech renders conversation unintelligible without obscuring the speakers' emotions. This tells us that the oral movements responsible for high-frequency "hissing" sounds such as *s* and *sh*—important constituents of words—convey more information about those words, hence thoughts, than feelings. By contrast, the deeper vocal resonances supplied by vocal chambers in our head and neck say a great deal about feelings. Evolution, in her wisdom, gave us a low-frequency band for emotions and gently laid speech across the top.

Cambridge psychologist Nicholas Humphrey claims that the stimulation arriving at our ears, eyes, and skin all combine to tell us who we are, and this sensory smorgasbord includes our own voice. If you have lived alone, you already know something about this, at least implicitly. On any given day you may have been unaware that you were beginning to feel a certain way until you talked for the first time. Then you heard the first clues in your voice, and suddenly you knew that you must be sad because you heard sadness, strident because you heard stridency. Just as sonar tells bats where they are in physical space, your own vocal feedback system tells you where you are in emotional space.

These sound-feeling relationships in the voice are not arbitrary and need not be learned. If you visit Istanbul, you will instantly recognize that a taxi driver is unhappy with his tip from the rush of speech that ensues, although you may not know a word of Turkish. Indeed, experiments reveal that even where language is perfectly comprehensible, listeners still consider tone of voice more reliable than words. If a speaker's tone conflicts with his words, listeners tend to believe the voice and doubt the words.

Self-identity

The voice tells many other things about people besides their physical and emotional nature. It helps answer a question about identity: which of all our friends and acquaintances is *this* person? Until we find out, we cannot know what to do or say. If you're like me, when you receive a letter, you skip to the end to establish authorship before seriously beginning to read it. If someone phones, your first priority is to identify the caller. If people physically approach from a distance, you look for familiar visual contours and perhaps a recognizable way of walking. If unseen, people may be identified by their smell, for better or worse, a feature that can now be measured in perceptual units called "olfs."

Our ability to distinguish and recall faces is almost limitless. If you went back for any of your high school reunions, you may have discovered this. In one study it was found that up to thirty-five years after graduation, alumni could still recognize over 90 percent of their former classmates regardless of the class size. This is why it is rare to mistake a stranger for an acquaintance; when you walk down the main street of an unfamiliar city, it is not with the expectation that you will be flooded with familiar faces that cannot be "placed."

Imagine living in a world in which you recognized no faces. Brain-damaged people with a condition known as prosopagnosia do precisely that. So do those with Capgras syndrome, an impairment in which the face recognition center in the cortex apparently becomes disconnected from the emotional association store in the underlying limbic system. This drives a wedge between the affected person and his relationships. Recently, two neuroscientists in San Diego, William Hirstein and Vilayanur Ramachandran, described a thirty-year-old Brazilian man who developed Capgras syndrome following a head injury. Since the old feelings of recognition were gone, the man thought all his friends were impostors. When shown photographs of himself, he thought that he was an impostor, too.

Our voice-recognition system isn't nearly as good. On the telephone we occasionally have to ask callers to identify themselves, but we recognize the same people when they stand before us. In one experiment, volunteers were unable to recognize more than 70 percent of famous Americans from two-second snippets of their voices, and they only had to mark the correct name on short lists. In a more appropriately designed study, one of the world's most eminent phoneticians, UCLA's Peter Ladefoged, was able to identify twenty-four of twenty-nine voices of personal friends and family members from half-minute speech samples. How the rest of us would do on such a task is anyone's guess, but voice identification usually falls well below face recognition ability. Of course, until recently at least, we have usually seen and heard those who spoke to us, and with the two sets of cues, we are usually able to identify people almost perfectly.

The police have long been interested in the identification of people from their voice. Unfortunately, the prospects of nabbing a criminal from audio recordings are not good. In *The Acoustics of Crime*, Harry Hollien, a voice scientist at the University of Florida, summarized the problem: "Simply put, we are not at all sure that you will always produce speech that is more like your own than it is like anyone else's, no matter how you talk, no matter how you feel, no matter what the speaking conditions."

Authorship even less naturally falls out of written language. Even discrimination of handwritten samples is difficult—witness the trouble experts had with "Hitler's diaries" a few years ago. And if the author of typed samples wishes to remain anonymous, we're even more likely to be left in the dark. But we may be able to determine if it is the same person who wrote some other work, the creator of which we do know. In a recent book, Jill Farringdon offers a method of determining authorship that takes into account such verbal habits as the number of words in a sentence and the number that are short or begin with vowels. When combined in a single analysis, these measures produce a sort of linguistic fingerprint. A similar method was used by a professor at Vassar to unmask the anonymous author of *Primary Colors*, the critically acclaimed fictional account of the 1992 American presidential race. The analysis was reliably performed, but the person who was "fingered" denied authorship. Then an unrelated analysis showed that scribblings on the original manuscript matched the suspect's handwriting. Ensnared by the consistency of both his expository and cursive styles, the author finally confessed.

The Biographical Self

To fully understand the *biographical* person, we need to know where he is in social and cultural space. This requires that we mine the deposits of social class, education, and geography from the voice, extract the veins of group affiliation. We do this because in evolution, membership in a group was indispensable to survival. The benefits to our ancient ancestors, the hominids, would have included protection against predators, defense of resources, foraging efficiency, and improved care-giving opportunities—benefits that also accrue to modern apes and monkeys.

Although the environmental playing field has shifted for us modern humans, the mere possibility of group exclusion provokes anxiety, a consequence we make every effort to prevent.

This is why one's standing *within* a group is so important. Social status is heavily dependent on verbal behavior. Members of any sub-group, whether a family or other natural class, develop ways of speaking that distinguish them from larger, potentially absorptive groups. In the United States, a particular affectation has spread from the teenagers of San Fernando Valley in California—the inventors of "valley speak"—to younger members of that set and to those who live elsewhere. In "up-talk" there is a tendency to raise the pitch of the voice at the end of declarative statements or to add "okay" with a rising tone, as in a question. This tends to convey self-doubt or a form of politeness, as if asking, "Do you understand what I'm saying?" But of course widespread propagation will eventually kill present forms of uptalk and force valley speakers to come up with new ways of displaying their membership in the "in group."

The relevance of verbal behavior to group inclusion and, therefore, social status is freely recognized in most progressive societies. In *My Dinner with Andre*, the key figure in the film, Andre, observed that one of the reasons a director friend gave up the theater was that "he just thought that people in their lives now were performing so well that performance in the theater was superfluous. We live in a world in which fathers or single people or artists are all trying to live up to someone's fantasy of how a father or a single person or an artist should look and behave." One of the goals of psychotherapy, according to psychiatrist Arnold Ludwig, is to give patients "a more satisfactory life story," or get them to turn the page in the one they've been writing.

Ironically, the disposition to present or "show" one's *self*, seemingly an act of individuality, is usually supported by a deeper motivation to be accepted by a group. To be accepted one must talk, and do so in a way that pulls one closer to the group. The likely result is an inoffensive, almost content-free type of talk. It is a voice sample and therefore a personality sample, an audition for friendship.

If our own talking can help to make us, the talking of would-be detractors has the potential to break us. Laws have been passed specifi-cally to prevent irresponsible talk. Fines and jail time await those who lower a person's position in business or the community with malicious gossip, a behavior outlawed by the statutes on slander.

The Psychological Self

When we speak, it is thoughts and words that consume our attention. Our intention may be to say something about our job, a garden we are thinking about planting, some problems experienced by our child, a business venture that succeeded beyond our wildest dreams, or last summer's vacation. But the message taken from our remarks—perhaps the *only* one that will be remembered six months later—may be that we are ambitious, naive, insecure, or in possession of an overly inflated sense of our own worth. Thus, regardless of what we believe we are infusing into the stream of speech, what has effectively been said is what our listeners take away. "A glance, a few spoken words," said S. E. Asch a half-century ago, "are sufficient to tell us a story about a highly complex matter."

When we talk, our wish is usually to strike others as we appear to ourselves. Adolescent boys want to appear masterful and manly, and are therefore embarrassed by spontaneous breaks into falsetto voice. We feel compelled to apologize when we have "a frog in our throat," a stuffy nose, or laryngitis. Perhaps we're afraid listeners will think we've changed or are trying to change into the person we now sound like.

It is also true that the reactions we get from others reflect the person we sound like to them. Nearly a century ago, Charles Cooley said that we learn that we are humorous, trustworthy, or intelligent when others respond to us as though we had such traits. When we interact with others, we and they find out who we are at the same time. A steady stream of evaluative reactions over a period of years produces a stable, heavily layered self-concept.

As a speech and language pathologist, I occasionally did voice therapy. I discovered the tendency of some patients to cling to their voice even when it was completely wrong for their sex or body size, or for their age group or profession. It was still *their* voice, and although it hurt to vocalize as they did, they didn't want a clinician to take it away. The strength of this link between voice and self is revealed in an unlikely place—the word "personality." It comes from the Latin word *persona*, which in ancient Roman theater referred to an actor's mask and specifically to the mouthpiece through which the *sona*, or sound, passed. Since the mask identified the character and his fixed facial emotion, the actor's voice had total responsibility for mood variations and personality. Over time, the word *persona* came to mean the actor himself and eventually any person or "personality."

With this etymology there should be little wonder that voice quality influences personality judgments. Several years ago Miron Zuckerman and his associates at the University of Rochester reported that a group of college students with highly attractive voices had more pleasantly rated personalities than students with less attractive voices. As might be expected, they observed a similar effect for facial attractiveness, but the vocal effect was stronger. When personality is involved, a pretty voice is better than a pretty face.

Research in a different laboratory confirmed Zuckerman's findings and also revealed a sex difference. In vocally attractive males, the attributes of strength, assertiveness, and dominance are conveyed by the voice. In females, an attractive voice is associated with warmth, honesty, and kindness.

Talking is virtually the only way to send or receive information about our psychological self. To demonstrate our earnestness, friendliness, sincerity, and sense of humor, we have no choice but to talk. And these attributes will be revealed as much by how we look and sound while talking as by any factual information that we may convey with words.

Listeners want information about our honesty. In fact, there's a commercial market for it. A Voice Stress Analysis device is now being sold in London that rates the truth value of people's oral statements based on "micro tremors" in their voices. One prominent public relations executive, caught in an ostensible lie, averred in self-defense that "even machines make mistakes."

For years British television was reluctant to let viewers see the psychological self of controversial Sinn Fein leader, Gerry Adams. They could watch him on television and hear his words, but the voice belonged to a "stunt speaker," a vocal stand-in supplied by the BBC. Broadcasters apparently feared that Adams's voice would be more inflammatory than his words and facial expressions.

When it comes to political campaigns, the candidates' personas are paramount. Many of the things that are said sound good enough, but we want to know if the aspirants mean what they say and if they'll still mean it in six months. We want to know if they share our values and will be steady and rational in a crisis. We thus ask the voice about the candidates' deeper values and character.

The impact of a person's looks while talking first became clear when John Kennedy debated Richard Nixon in the 1960 presidential campaign. Polls taken immediately afterward showed that Nixon had won in the opinion of those who heard the debates on the radio, and that Kennedy had won according to those who saw and heard the debates on television.

Self-display being so important, it is not surprising that candidates might wish to change theirs, but this can be a serious mistake. Jimmy Carter tried it by relocating the part in his hair. Gerald Ford tried it by switching from a two- to a three-piece suit. These alterations raised questions that a sitting president shouldn't have to answer.

Some years before he ran for president in 1983, Gary Hart did some switching. For one thing, he listed his birth date as November 28, 1937, even though he was born one year earlier. Further digging revealed that he had also changed his surname from Hartpence to Hart. His inability to explain these events later made people suspicious of his character. Who is he really, they wondered. What is he hiding? *Newsweek* called him secretive and mysterious. Then, disastrously for the senator, it was discovered that he had also changed his signature. That was the penultimate straw. People were not surprised when newspaper reporters caught Hart in a romantic liaison with a beautiful model after he had consistently denied involvement in such activity.

The reaction to Hart's cursive flexibility could have been predicted. Script has always been intimately associated with self, for reasons that are unavoidable. An eminent graphologist declared more than a century ago that "in using his pen a man acts unconsciously, as the current of his blood impels him; and there, at all times, nature flows unrestrained and free." Perhaps Hart watchers concluded that the senator's nature flowed a little too freely.

Friends come to know us by any identifying signs we give them. Twenty-five years ago I switched from an old manual typewriter to an

IBM Selectric. A friend to whom I regularly wrote complained that he missed the letters that were out of alignment or only partially formed, confessing that in his mind these irregularities had come to be "me." Now some e-mail users think it is good to get rid of all kinds of personal information. If our identities are concealed, they say, interpersonal business can be conducted in a more egalitarian fashion. Communications will be more fair when we don't know who we're dealing with. But of course no one set out to invent a medium of communication that would have this effect. Loss of self is an unintended consequence, and the egalitarian "benefit" a clever post hoc rationalization.

Our Physiology

The way we speak is also influenced by our physiological status. For example, listeners are likely to know from our sound-making whether we are ill or exhausted or drunk. You may recall the *Exxon Valdez*, the ship that went aground in Prince William Sound in March 1989, causing the biggest accidental oil spill in history. The skipper, Captain Joseph Hazelwood, was found not guilty of the charge that he had operated the *Valdez* while under the influence of alcohol. But analyses conducted in the laboratory of Dr. David Pisoni at Indiana University suggested that Captain Hazelwood's speech one hour after the accident was markedly different from recordings made nine hours later and the day before (when presumably he was sober). Specifically, he misarticulated several different consonant sounds and spoke with a reduced rate, lower vocal frequency, and increased pitch variability—findings consistent with, but not proof of, intoxication.

The Vocalyser, another device now being marketed in England, supposedly can tell whether a person has had too much to drink from the way he says "one, one, two, eight, nine." If motorists want to know if they've had too much alcohol to operate a motor vehicle, they dial a 900 number, utter the digits, and find out if they're fit to drive. The police are also interested.

The Relational Self

When I was at the University of Illinois in the mid-seventies, several graduate students and I wanted to study the way four-year-old children talked when no adults were perceptibly present. We invited into a test room pairs of children who were only slightly familiar with each other. Then we retreated to an adjacent room with a one-way observation window. Although our immediate interest was verbal fluency, we were struck by an unrelated phenomenon on our audiotapes—the frequency with which one child would say untimidly to the other, "Do you want to be my friend?"

This is something we all want to know, although adults usually don't blurt out such a question. Instead, we engage in what may seem to be insignificant palaver, including the infamous, "Do you come here often?" If the other person responds in kind, we either have our answer or know that we are about to get it, for during the ensuing verbal exchange we will scan all concomitant nonverbal behaviors to see if the other person does indeed want to be our friend.

There is another relational effect embedded in voice and speech, layered in so deeply that it often escapes our notice. Communication scientists call it "convergence." It involves a subtle gravitational process whereby certain of a person's behaviors, especially vocal ones, drift toward those of an interacting person. In the typical case, one of the parties, often the subordinate one, unconsciously mimics the pitch, rate of speaking, loudness, vocal quality, or some aspect of the other party's word pronunciation.

Under the glare of U. S. Senate lights and fear of imprisonment, President Nixon's lawyer, John Dean, converged. He did it lexically. Analyses of transcripts from the Watergate hearings showed that Dean's word choices were influenced by the lexical patterns of his interrogators. When they used rare words in their questions, he used rare words in his answers. If more familiar words were uttered, Dean gamely followed suit. Statistical analyses showed that he changed the frequency of his words, to paraphrase a Hollywood starlet of yesteryear, as easily as some men change their shirt.

Larry King, the talk show host, has been caught in the act of converging. He did it vocally. Acoustic analyses of a number of programs reveal that when King "pitched" his questions, his own vocal frequency drifted toward the average pitch of veteran newsman Mike Wallace and President Bush—two of the highest ranking guests in an independent evaluation. The pitch of lower-ranking guests such as Dan Quayle drifted toward King's own pitch. There was a general trend for lower-ranking individuals to converge with higher-ranking (dominant) persons.

I first discovered converging tendencies in myself as an American midwestern teenager. When talking with southerners, I had trouble hanging on to my own, less drawled way of speaking. Easterners gave me other problems with specific words. In my dialect, "aunt" rhymes with "pant," but occasionally I encountered easterners who pronounced it to rhyme with "want." I can remember thinking that if I continued to say the word my way, it would appear that I was correcting the speaker, whereas if I said it the other person's way, he might think either that I was mocking him or was phonetically "up for grabs." I found myself not wanting to say the word at all and would refer to "my father's sister" if I could. If I didn't converge, at least I could avoid going a separate way.

The Who System

If our identity is of paramount importance to our fellow human beings, we must have efficient person-recognition systems, and we do. Our brain's *Who System* is hundreds of millennia old and extremely reliable. All the major bugs have been worked out. Sad people do not look or sound happy to us, and we are rarely uncertain whether a visibly angry person sounds joyful. We even know when a sad person is trying to seem happy.

We are able to learn the different appearances of people effortlessly, but even under threat of death we would be hard pressed to memorize the distinctive appearance of as many trees. The reason for this superior person system is that our evolutionary ancestors could not function effectively without telling all possible strangers (potential foes) from dozens of acquaintances. They also needed to participate in coordinated group activities. Those who were good at these things were more likely to survive and pass on their genes, leaving us, the grateful progeny, with efficient Who Systems.

One of the reasons we can risk these assumptions about evolution is that nonhuman primates, our distant cousins, are very sensitive to facial and vocal displays. And little wonder. Monkeys have brain cells that are dedicated to faces. Some neurons respond more vigorously to upright and intact faces than to inverted or experimentally rearranged faces. Other cells are tuned to direction of eye gaze, facial orientation, specific parts of the face, emotional expressions, and a variety of movements. In view of the generally close connection between facial and vocal activity among primates, one might expect that monkeys have voice-sensitive neurons, too, and as it turns out, they do.

Like those of monkeys, our own brains contain socially specialized mechanisms that are dedicated to faces and facial activity, and to voices and vocal activity. This set of neural and cognitive specializations forms the basis of the human Who System. And there are gross anatomical similarities—both monkeys and humans experience emotion primarily in the right cerebral hemisphere. Damage to that area often impairs both the expression and the interpretation of emotion, yet leaves related functions alone. These right-hemisphere-damaged patients are recognized by their monotone voices and flat facial expressions, as well as their tendency to miss the humor in jokes and the point to stories. Right-hemisphere patients also tend to interpret figures of speech literally, such as "kick the bucket" or "shake a leg," phrases that are more common in casual conversation than serious discourse.

We do not, perhaps even cannot, deactivate our Who System even when a person's identity is irrelevant. This fact has emerged from psychological experiments in which learners were to remember lists of words. Much to the astonishment of investigators, the learners also recalled the actual sound of the speaker's voice up to several weeks after the experiment was over. But this is predictable: the brain mechanisms supplied by evolution spring to life whether their owners (or experimenters) direct them to or not. The vocal variations that distinguish nice or warm people from nasty or cold people were important to our ancestors. This made them grist for Darwin's mill, and they are therefore salient to us, their progeny, whether serving in laboratory experiments or attending a wedding reception.

Say and Display

Knowing about the expressive capacity of the voice is no license to go around moaning and murmuring to everyone we would like to know us better. In most cultures it is unacceptable to parade a conversation's worth of vocal and facial emotions before a person to whom we are *not* talking. The sight of such a thing would certainly be grounds for asking the waiter to change one's table in a restaurant!

To display vocal emotions we must follow an important rule: talk. This requires a suitable topic and some appropriate words. But a topic can be a theoretical red herring, deluding us into thinking that the desire to exchange information about the topic was the *cause* of the conversation.

If we are to express ourselves personally—to show that we are honest or loving or trustworthy—talking is the least that we must do, but for many intents and purposes it will be all that is needed. For as soon as we begin, our words unleash a rich flow of "nonverbal" behavior, and it is in this flow that personal cues reside. Nonverbal behaviors do not merely accompany speech like so much spare baggage, they are our species' preferred mode for the transmission of personal information. While it is true that vocalization enables us to talk, the display of our selves through the voice may be the primary reason for conversing, a motive likely to be unknown even to the participants themselves.

What would be left over if verbal information were drained from our speech? "For anyone who regards *language* as the canonical form of human communication," said the English physician and opera director Jonathan Miller, "the answer would probably be 'Not much is left over.' " But in reality, he said, "eliminating words and sentences exposes a level of communication of unsuspected richness, one in which human beings express their true meanings."

Most of us view ourselves as complex and interesting individuals whose character and views were built up over the entirety of our lives. It may therefore be ego-deflating to know that complete strangers can, in fact, learn a great deal about us in several seconds, as S. E. Asch said. In a study conducted at Harvard by Nalini Ambady and Robert Rosenthal, volunteers evaluated a number of attributes of university instructors from just three two-second clips of silent videotape of their classroom teaching. Over a dozen attributes, from optimism and confidence to enthusiasm and warmth, proved to be highly correlated with independent ratings of the instructor's teaching ability. Essentially the same level of prediction was achieved in a second study of high school teachers, using evaluations of the school principal as the criterion of teacher effectiveness. As startling as these findings may be, there is nothing about them that is biologically anomalous. If our ancestors couldn't tell friends from foes with several seconds of nonverbal behavior, there probably wouldn't have been any survivors generations later to prove it in a Harvard psychology lab.

The Eyes Have It

Much of the communicative richness of which Jonathan Miller wrote cannot be phonetically transcribed or even tape-recorded. It is "a way without words," and much of that way involves visual monitoring of the face and body. The eyes are literally the focus of most of it. "As soon as a strong current of mutual admiration begins to flow," said Robert Louis Stevenson, "the human interest triumphs entirely over the intellectual, and the commerce of words, consciously or not, becomes secondary to the commercing of eyes."

The role of eye gaze is unveiled at an early age. Infants begin to track eye movements in the first few months of life, and they notice what others are looking at. At some point they infer that what people view while talking is related to their words. This is a monumental advance, for it allows infants to "look up" the meaning of their first words.

Face reading is so natural that we tend to miss all the *work* accomplished when glances are cast. Consider as simple a thing as conversational turn-taking. When a speaker and listener exchange roles, the speaker usually ends his utterance by looking directly at the listener with a sustained gaze. The listener then looks away as he himself begins to speak. The speaker's glance at the listener signals his readiness for the listener to respond, and the listener's turning away indicates that he has accepted the "offer."

The eyes can also be extremely menacing. Primates avoid gazing directly at each other—that's a threat display—and are visibly spooked when humans look into their eyes. In many cultures, humans feel uncomfortable or even frightened if a person stares at them. We avoid eye contact with strangers in crowded places such as elevators and subway trains. Tests reveal that we usually know when someone is looking exactly into our eyes and when they are looking just a few degrees to one side or the other. If you think back a few years, you may recall the bothersome gaze of television news broadcasters when, prior to the perfection of the TelePrompTer, they looked slightly away from the camera. "He's *reading* it," we used to declare.

Recently, the highway code in Britain was revised to include tips on how to avoid verbal clashes that might provoke "road rage." One of the suggestions was to avoid eye contact. This is precisely what I was told by Marc Hauser, a professor of evolutionary biology at Harvard, before he took me on a tour of Cayo Santiago, an island off the coast of Puerto Rico that is home to hundreds of rhesus monkeys. This reaction to staring is a characteristic of all primate species, and it is very deeply embedded in our biological nature.

The eyes being so informative, it is only natural that people would want to see each other while talking. What better way to catch a liar? During the Watergate hearings, Herbert Kalmbach, one of President Nixon's lawyers, found himself in a very delicate situation. He had been told by John Dean to solicit funds and convey them to the so-called burglars, ostensibly to cover the costs of legal defense and family support. But he was troubled by the fact that this was to be done in absolute secrecy. According to his testimony before the U. S. Senate, when he had a chance to finally meet with John Ehrlichman, one of Nixon's right-hand men, Kalmbach said,

> I was beginning to have concern about this assignment . . . and I said, "John, I want you to tell me"—and you know, I can remember it very vividly because I looked at him, and I said, "John, I am looking right into your eyes. I know Jeanne and your family, you know Barbara and my family. You know that my family and my reputation mean everything to me, and it is just absolutely necessary, John, that you tell me, first, that John Dean has the authority to direct me in this assignment, that it is a proper assignment, and that I am to go forward with it."

"And did he look at you in the eyes?" Mr. Kalmbach was asked. "Yes," said Mr. Kalmbach, "he did." And when, caught by Ehrlichman's gaze, Kalmbach was told that the action was proper, "the effect," he told the Senate, "actually was that it washed out the concern that I had had." The face-to-faceness of the exchange, complete with interconnecting gaze, obviously made a real difference to Mr. Kalmbach. Unfortunately, as he was later to learn, John Ehrlichman lied, apparently with his eyes as well as his words.

In England a preelection television interview with Tony Blair was submitted to an unofficial ocular analysis. According to a media watcher for *The Sunday Times* of London, "Mr Blair's eyes conveyed fear. The smile was there to start with but the eyes told another story—of suspicion and anxiety." Four days later Mr. Blair's opponent, John Major, held a press conference in which, according to a different media analyst, "he kept his head immobile and facial muscles tight, smiling once in half an hour. His eyes were narrow. He blinked often but slowly." Later the reason became clear. Major was about to be buried by a massive Labour landslide, and knew it.

In Iraq, Saddam Hussein was said to have blinked 113 times per minute during a CNN interview with Peter Arnett. What this means is less clear than the fact that we think it must mean *something*. There is a different ocular behavior whose meaning is less ambiguous. Recently, the psychologist John Gottman reported the results of hundreds of interviews with husbands and wives. Remarkably, Gottman found that if a wife rolls her eyes while her husband is talking, the outlook for continuing marriage is decidedly dim.

Being There

With all this concern about the face and eyes, the question naturally arises as to how well we communicate without visual cues, without *being there*. When the telephone became commercially available, concern about this question was so great that the Bell Telephone Laboratories, the Australian Post Office, and the British Post Office all commissioned studies to explore public reactions to this impersonal instrument. The last found that "a considerable proportion of the population never use the telephone and, it is presumed, cannot."

Being there matters. In 1716, toward the end of a long career as a French diplomat, François de Callières, published *The Art of Negotiating with Sovereign Princes*. In this "bible" of diplomacy, Callières wrote that while negotiations are usually conducted either orally or in writing, "it is more advantageous for a skilful minister to negotiate by word of mouth, because he has more opportunities of discovering by this means the sentiments and designs of those with whom he treats; and of employing this dexterity to inspire them with sentiments conformable to his views, by his insinuations, and by the force of his reasons."

Woody Allen's maxim that "90 percent of life is showing up" has been taken seriously by business people. Traditionally they have set up special meetings rather than trust the mails or a telephone call when interaction is necessary. The massive hotels that ring major airports are physical evidence of this practice. Business people routinely converge on a city with no intention of sampling the nightlife, the museums, the street life, or the food. They are there for the meeting rooms at the airport hotel. They show up. They come to talk.

Sports agent Mark McCormack believes that it is often worth traveling six thousand miles to hold a five-minute face-to-face meeting. The reason, as the saying goes, is that "you can pretend to care, but you can't pretend to be there." Bill Raduchel, of Sun Microsystems, claims that "the necessary complement to the Net is the 747."

People willing to give up faces with only the greatest reluctance are people who enjoy the intimacy of human communication. They like "just the two of us" experiences. They care whether they're being spoken to or talked with, a distinction discussed in the next chapter.

TWO

Duty and Pleasure

The first duty of a man is to speak; that is his chief
business in this world; and talk, which is the harmoni-
ous speech of two or more, is by far the most accessible of
pleasures. Robert Louis Stevenson, "Talk and Talkers"

In the previous chapter we looked at the personal things that are
learned about us when we talk intimately. But what about the ways of
speaking that reveal our inner selves, that even unmask or undo us? To
pursue voice and speech on their own level, we need to consider two
related types of verbal behaviors: speaking and talking. These terms are
often used synonymously, but they are not identical, as Stevenson
pointed out above. As we will see shortly, speaking and talking are
unequally affected by social de-voicing.

Both talking and speaking require *sound-making*. From a physical
standpoint, sound-making involves the production of syllables in a repetitive and rhythmic fashion. This is done by moving the jaw up and
down while forcing expired air through the larynx. In parallel, various
other parts of the vocal tract—the tongue, lips, soft palate, and pharynx
—are used to squeeze or chop up the air stream at different anatomical
points, thus creating a range of different sounds.

Examples of pure sound-making include the babbling of human infants, the scat singing of jazz vocalists, and the glossolalia ("speaking in tongues") of adults participating in ceremonies of the Pentecostal religion. In all cases, speechlike sounds spill out in a steady stream, but the sounds are merely the public version of movements, the specific inspiration for which comes from somewhere within the sound-maker. Sound-making requires no listeners—talking to oneself is proof enough of that. Nor does one need knowledge of language. The infant lacks it, and the glossolalian suppresses it.

Speaking is sound-making activity directed to one or more listeners. It expresses linguistically encoded information that the speaker, in the typical case, thinks the listener does not know. Fluent speaking is coordinated primarily by mechanisms that are situated in the left cerebral hemisphere of the brain. The rhythmic and melodic aspects of sound-making, and many of the emotional components, involve the activity of mechanisms that are housed by the right hemisphere, the one that for most of us is "nonlinguistic." Since the speaker aims to say words that were learned by listening to others, speaking also accepts contributions from the diverse brain regions that contain information about the physical form of words and their meanings.

People speak to convey factual information. Some of it is embedded in the utterance that is produced. Other information is expressed by nonverbal behaviors that occur during the act of speaking. Although these other behaviors are produced by the speaker coincidentally, they are no less valued by the listener, who needs them to interpret the intended messages as well as the speaker and the social interaction itself.

Speaking is more formally structured than talking. It is also more factually communicative. No one would dispute the informational burden of these statements by an airline pilot and his ground controller, recorded just before the plane's takeoff:

KLM 4805: The KLM four eight zero five is now ready for
           takeoff, and we are waiting for our ATC
           clearance.

Tower: KLM eight seven zero five, you are cleared to
           the Papa Beacon, climb to and maintain flight
           level nine zero, right turn after takeoff, proceed

with heading four zero until intercepting the
three two five radial from Las Palmas VOR.

KLM 4805:   Ah—roger, sir, we are cleared to the Papa
Beacon, flight level nine zero until intercepting
the three two five. We are now at takeoff.

Tower: OK. . . . Stand by for takeoff, I will call you.

Exchanges like this one are all about information. That is why the
Royal Air Force Air Traffic Control requires that recruits "have the
ability to assimilate complicated information quickly." Any missed syllables can be fatal. In the transaction above, some syllables *were* missed or
misinterpreted. Several seconds after KLM 4805 was advised to stand
by for takeoff, it collided with another plane, killing 583 people, the
largest disaster in aviation history. But cases such as these only tell us
that precise communication of impersonal details is *one* of the functions
of sound-making. It tells us nothing about any of the *other* uses of words
and phrases.

Formal, fact-filled speaking provides us with limited information
about who the other person is. We learn something about his identity
as well as his biographical and physical characteristics, but there are
several important kinds of emotionality that are inexpressible when a
person speaks. These feelings do come through in social talking.

Nearly eighty years ago, the richer benefits of social talking became
evident to a young anthropologist, Bronislaw Malinowski, while doing
fieldwork on the Trobriand Islands of New Guinea. Later, Malinowski
reflected on the ways of the islanders in relation to members of more
progressive societies, writing that "we use language exactly as savages
do. . . . Our talk . . . serves to establish bonds of personal union between
people brought together by the mere need of companionship. . . . It is
only in certain very special uses among a civilized community and only
in its highest uses that language is employed to frame and express
thoughts."

Malinowski's claim was little noticed at the time and received scant
attention in the succeeding seventy-five years, but that is not because he
was wrong. Indeed, research in the last several decades confirms the
accuracy of his views about human communication. We are all intent
on saying something appropriate, on avoiding utterances that would be

wrong. But what we say is frequently less important than the fact that we are saying *something*, or *anything*, to some particular person. Regardless of verbal content, it can be dangerous to say anything at all to a stranger in some circumstances, and it may be extremely risky not to address one's boss or a person who has long considered himself a close friend.

The emotional and interpersonal functions of talking are no less important to us modern humans than they were ages ago to our more simply living ancestors. This was Malinowski's point, one that he dramatized when he referred to the social functions of talking as "phatic communion," an appellation intended to capture "a type of speech in which ties of union are created by a mere exchange of words." The meaning of the words, he said, was "almost completely irrelevant. Inquiries about health, comments on weather, affirmations of some supremely obvious state of things—all such are exchanged, not in order to inform, not in this case to connect people in action, certainly not in order to express any thought."

Words whose meaning is irrelevant? Sentences not intended to convey thoughts? This is hardly the view of language that we have come to know and recognize, the view that Noam Chomsky and fellow generative linguists have championed. They drew our attention to the abstractness of grammar and the capacity, through grammatical utterances, to convey complex thoughts. In *The Language Instinct*, Steven Pinker said this behavior was one of the great marvels of the biological world and perhaps the highest potential of our species.

By contrast, Malinowski might seem to be saying that language is some sort of tribal ritual, a behavior that parallels dancing or music. Perhaps you are thinking that he, a distinguished scientist and a founder of social anthropology, was overly exposed to "savages" or spent too much time in the Trobriand Islands sun. Surely we educated members of modern, information-oriented societies use speech only to say things that are worth saying, things our listeners need to know. Whose conception of language is closer to the truth, Noam Chomsky's or Bronislaw Malinowski's?

Neither is, because there are two broad sets of facts about language. One pertains to the form of language, and this has been the concern of modern linguists. Malinowski, on the other hand, was more interested in the functions of language, and the ones he observed in the Trobriands were perhaps less intimately linked to grammatical subtleties. Let us consider the speech of strictly oral cultures. These, after all, are what evolved.

Word of Mouth

Imagining a strictly oral culture is actually very hard to do. The reason is that our speech habits are not, in the strictest sense, completely natural, for we routinely see something no evolutionary ancestor ever did—words. On streets and highways, large colorful words stare down at us from shops and billboards. At the movies, small white words flash at us from subtitled foreign films. When retrieving the morning paper, black headlined words stare up at us from our doorstep. If we come across a novel word, we get out our dictionaries and read all about it.

Literacy training incidentally influenced the speaking habits of all of us, and it did so in a variety of ways. If taught to read phonically, we learned to identify the sounds that make up words. In composition classes we learned to write in full sentences, with verbs of proper agreement and tense, and pronouns and articles in all the right places. This training was not necessarily undertaken to alter our speech, but it did.

Conditioned by literacy as we are, about all we can do to appreciate the nature of unadulterated speech is consult the recorded observations of people who lack our bias. Nearly forty years ago psychiatrist J. C. Carothers offered his interpretations of the oral cultures of eastern Africa. He said that "great freedom is allowed for at the temperamental level, and a man is expected to live very much in the 'here and now,' to be highly extroverted, and to give very free expression to his feelings."

For many, speaking is a performance. This is underscored by Joel Sherzer's description of the verbal performances of the Kuna, a people living on the island of Sasartii-Mulatuppu, near the Panama-Colombia border. After a day of work and relaxation, the Kuna walk to the gathering house. The chiefs, their spokesmen, and other village dignitaries arrive first. Then women arrive, carrying small tables, lamps, and sewing baskets. The women sit near the chiefs, sewing their colorful appliqué blouses as they listen to the performances. It sounds like a summer concert in the park, and in some sense it is.

Often descriptions of oral societies emphasize the social and emotional interactions rather than "the message." Malinowski's field observations of the Trobriand islanders indicate that after their evening meal, the natives would rest and chew betel nuts and smoke while talking. Their conversation, said Malinowski, focuses on "famous exchanges . . . quarrels over Kula grievances, cases in which a man was killed by magic for his too successful dealings."

Among the Nharo people of Botswana—a small tribe of herders, gatherers, and hunters—the time spent talking, including arguing, absorbs most of a person's waking hours. A major pastime of the Limba people, rice farmers who live in the hilly savannah country of northern Sierra Leone, is storytelling. Each story told by the Limba, according to anthropologist Ruth Finnegan, is "a unique artistic creation in that the narrator himself enacts the tale, depicts the action with more, or less, characterization, mimicry, exaggeration, and effect through the use of tones, length, speed, singing, or onomatopoeia in order to make his narrative vivid, attractive, and amusing to his audience."

Among the !Kung, far to the south, the sounds of conversation are said to be continuous. Anthropologist Lorna Marshall likened them to "the sound of a brook, and as low and lapping, except for shrieks of laughter. People cluster together in little groups during the day, talking, perhaps making artifacts at the same time. At night families talk late by their fires, or visit at other family fires with their children between their knees or in their arms if the wind is cold. There always seems to be plenty to talk about."

Other characterizations indicate that !Kung talk frequently "verges on argument, often for its own sake and usually ad hominem. . . . Accusations of improper meat distribution, improper gift exchange . . . laziness, and stinginess are the most common topics of these disputes. . . . The most common kind of argument . . . is often punctuated by a joke that breaks the tension and leaves the participants rolling on the ground helpless with laughter."

It is fortunate that anthropologists recorded their observations about the !Kung forty and more years ago when they were so different from the rest of us. Today, hunting and foraging are down, roaming is reduced, and huts are built to last more than a few seasons. And nowadays !Kung tribesmen know a few things about life outside their villages. While poisoning an arrow, one elderly native asked a westerner recently whether he believed O. J. Simpson was guilty.

In oral cultures, everything that is said is completely *in context*. Their politicians cannot complain, as ours regularly do, that their statement "was taken out of context." In contrast, writers are removed in time and space from their audience. Their task is to do what the oralist never would. They *attempt* to decontextualize content so that readers in different places and times can fully understand the message.

I suspect that much of the talk in oral cultures is less grammatically creative than it is in literate ones. One reason is that oral cultures favor idioms and other frozen forms. These stereotyped utterances keep people from forgetting what cannot be preserved in writing. This includes laws, which in oral cultures are encoded in the form of proverbs. Set word patterns also reduce hesitations and facilitate two vocal attributes much cherished in oral cultures: fluency and rhythm. A researcher at the University of Canterbury in New Zealand, Koenraad Kuiper, found that auctioneers and sportscasters attain fluency and speed by manipulating the pat expressions associated with their professions.

What about the rest of us, the linguistically creative speakers, the *literati?* Are we more informative? Are we less inclined to laugh and exaggerate than people who cannot read and appear to live simply? Probably so, but it would be hard to prove it with this lighthearted exchange supplied by a newly married American couple on a summer holiday. (Jock is rowing Roz across a lake.)

Jock: Look how dark the water is down here.
Roz: You tip this boat over with me in it, and I'll be very
        upset. Uh, uh, huh, huh, huh.
Jock: I just felt the . . .
Roz: (laughs) Jock, I just made a joke. Have you no sense of
        humor?
Jock: Look how [inaudible]
Roz: Why are we going way out in the middle? I'll get
        sunburned.
Jock: (laughs) What's the difference whether you're in the
        middle or not?

Roz: You get more reflection in the middle.
Jock: (scoffs) Oh!
Roz: Jock, I know!
Jock: How do you know?
Roz: I can see! You put on your sun-specks before you get a
        headache, huh?
Jock: No.
Roz: No? Okay. Wanna take your shoes off?
Jock: No.
Roz: (taunting in a singing way) Ah, Jock's gonna be sore
        tomorrow because he insists on showing off.

I think we can agree that "Oh!" and "No" are not grammatically complex and that Roz's and Jock's utterances are playful and teasing but not chock-full of impersonal information. In fact, an analysis of nearly two thousand separate messages spoken by the couple revealed that fully three-fourths of Jock's utterances were comments that involved no transmission of facts or other concrete information.

If we could magically peel away the layers of formal education and breeding, eliminate the need to appear age appropriate and responsible, banish all worries about job, home, and children, I think we would discover an impish and playful, occasionally raucous or rowdy, inner core that rarely comes to the surface. But we have no more layers to peel than Roz and Jock when we are on summer holiday in a place far from home.

Linguistic scholars have concerned themselves with the highest and most rational of human behaviors. They have chosen to analyze the complete, fully grammatical statements that we make or can make when operating in our most logical and thoughtful mode. And this makes professional sense: the analytical challenge of complex grammatical problems, and the academic reward in "solving" them, is greater. But since linguists are famous for studying language, and formal speech is usually what they study, innocent bystanders may erroneously conclude that the behaviors *not studied*—casual conversations with incomplete sentences, supported by tones of voice and facial and bodily gestures— are *not language.*

For behaviors to be presumptively linguistic, the things that are said don't even have to mean anything. Several decades ago, Warren Fay a speech and language pathologist at the University of Oregon, conducted a very illuminating experiment. He tried out some nonsensical utterances on some English-learning three-year-olds. When he *stated* "El camino real," 24 percent responded in the affirmative. But when Fay *asked* "El camino real?" with the rising intonation associated with American English questions, the frequency of affirmative responses shot up to 62 percent. These children were not particularly bothered by the lack of lexical meaning. Indeed, some offered a counter-remark of their own, such as "Just Jerry" and "Because anyhow Mom said."

Content-free talk also ranks fairly high with some middle-class Jewish families in northeast Philadelphia who produce the ritual singsong of complaint called "kvetching." The kvetching mother, according to Raymond Birdwhistell at the eastern Pennsylvania Psychiatric Institute, says something like " 'Look how I've suffered, I worked very hard, I went down to the store and the guy was bad to me and I didn't get the stuff you wanted and the traffic was bad and I'm having trouble getting this on the table,' with that 'nyaah' sound over all of it. Suddenly another child comes in and the mother changes her voice and says, 'Oh, by the way, tell your father that the mail came.' "

You may have seen the relevant Gary Larson cartoon. It implies that spoken words sound like "blah, blah, blah" to a dog being scolded by his master. But for all the specific action that it leads to, a great many conversations might just as well sound that way to humans, too. A reviewer observed that Wallace Shawn's characters in *My Dinner with Andre* and similar works "don't talk to avoid action, they behave as if talk *were* action. It's as if they believed that just articulating their hidden thoughts were enough to make something happen, as if language were in itself magic."

If talk can *mean* so little, it may not be surprising to know that while many verbal behaviors originate with a thought that cries out to be expressed, intimate talking rarely does. Rather, talking usually begins with the impulse to congregate or engage in verbal behavior followed by a search for a topic to *justify* the talking that is already under way. If that level of discourse is insufficient, silence would ensue, and this is usually unacceptable. In the presence of strangers, silence may cause anxiety or stronger feelings of fear. In "Leave a Tender Moment Alone,"

Billy Joel sang that he feared saying "something so wrong just to have something to say," but we all utter things not quite right in our effort to avoid silence. And so we get into various predicaments, all the while unaware of the reasons for our fear of silence and, thus, the source of the troublesome impulse to talk.

Silence can be seriously threatening, whether it is maintained diplomatically by a country or by an unfamiliar person encountered late at night on an isolated street. A friendly greeting or even neutral comment can reduce the fear. It is interesting to note in this connection that *merhaba*, the Turkish word for "hello," used to mean "I have no weapons."

People Talk

With the possible exception of looking at one another, talk is the purest and most sublimated form of two-wayness. Georg Simmel, *The Sociology of Georg Simmel*

I have come to believe that the more deeply biologic function of talking was created to be, and remains, social and emotional; that talking reveals a disposition to connect with other members of our species, other members of our group. Commercial advertisers have no doubt about this. They regularly play to our "weakness" to commune with others. Not long ago an American telephone company attempted to induce television viewers to make long-distance calls with the ditty "Reach out and touch someone. Call up and just say 'hi.' "

We have seen, then, a few things that talking is not—intellectually complex, grammatically creative, factually informative; and a few other things that talking is—personal, intimate, and emotional. But what is talk about? The weather is a major topic, obviously, as well as the latest news and the events of our everyday lives. But one theme stands above all others.

Robin Dunbar, an evolutionary psychologist at the University of Liverpool, found that about 60 percent of the conversations of one group of Britons pertained to personal relationships and experiences. Now with this penchant for discussing people, one might suppose that Dunbar sampled some pretty ordinary folks with no particular education or breeding. But the supposition would be wrong. The data were not gathered in a working-class pub but in the refectory of a major university. The conversations were not recorded during a summer outing but in between intellectual endeavors at the talkers' place of work. The utterances had content, of course, but personal and social interests comprised more of it than events and ideas.

Dunbar's data included a slight but intriguing trend—the conversational bias toward personal relationships and experiences was stronger in women than men. Such sex differences in the function and content of talk can be fairly large, as several of the books by Deborah Tannen make clear. Something of their nature is evident in the conversational habits of people in Oroel, a small village in northeastern Spain, as described by Susan Harding. "In their talk and thought," said Harding, "village men are primarily occupied with the land and what pertains to it—crops, the weather, prices, wages, inheritance, work animals, and machinery. On the side, they may discuss hunting, play cards, quote facts and figures of all sorts, and argue about sports. In casual dialogue, a man is interested in what a person thinks and in what a person knows and does as a larger social and economic being in the public sphere."

By contrast, "the talk and thought of women are wrapped around people and their personal lives," according to Harding. "The first thing a woman wants to know when she meets someone is about her family. . . . In her daily life in the home and village, a woman is likewise more interested in how someone feels than in what someone thinks, in who a person is and what a person does in the private, rather than the public, sphere. . . . If a man's world of words revolves more around objects and his own concerns, a woman's revolves more around subjects, around persons and their concerns." It is a different kind of information.

There might seem to be exceptions to this preoccupation with people. For example, some years ago an investigator reported that 59 percent of all !Kung conversations were about food. This seems logical enough. After all, they *are* hunter-gatherers; surely they need to think about food and plan ways to get more of it. But a second glance revealed that most of the food conversations were actually about *social* aspects of the subject. Complaints about people who hoarded and failed to share meat and other foods were prominent.

Much the same is true of the black teenagers residing in south-central Los Angeles in the seventies. On first listening it appeared that much of their talk was about cars, and it was, at least superficially. They discussed how to get cars and how to fix them. But a great deal of their car talk, wrote Edith Folb in *Runnin' Down Some Lines*, "involved who did and didn't have one."

These studies and anecdotes force us to ask whether there is a necessary connection between the most natural form of language, which is speech, and the most natural topic, people. Dictionaries define language without reference to subject matter. Indeed, they imply that language can be used to discuss anything that can be put into words. Are they wrong?

Marshall McLuhan once said that it is the way a thing is used that defines what the thing really is. According to the usual sequence in techno-history, we first have the invention, then we look around for ways to use it. And when we discover these applications, they and they alone define the object. After World War II, the natives of Trinidad found fifty-five-gallon fuel drums near the U.S. Army Airforce base at Mucarapo. The Trinidadians discovered that when the drums were reshaped in certain ways, they could be tuned and used as instruments of melodic percussion. The drums still physically existed and were readily reusable as containers, but they had taken on a new function, a new "meaning." They were the instruments of all-steel bands. When asked his occupation, I assume the drum manufacturer said, "I make fuel drums," but he could have said, "I make musical instruments," for he did that, too.

Not Saying Anything

It's not . . . that you're saying something . . . the other person's contributing and it goes back and forth.
Elderly person quoted in H. Giles, N. Coupland, and J. Wiemann, *"Talk Is Cheap" but "My Word Is My Bond"*

Language *is* a tool, a neutral tool. Its "meaning" derives from the ways it is used. We therefore cannot define language without observing how and why people exercise their linguistic ability. When we do, we find that "language" is a set of behaviors comprising vocal displays. Since these displays frequently promote relationships, we are encouraged to conclude that an important function of language—perhaps even the primary one—is the creation of intimacy. But language is also used for other purposes, many of which may—for interesting reasons—be more conspicuous.

You may have already discovered your own need to "just talk" if you ever spent long periods in a country where the natives speak no language that you know. My own discovery of this happened years ago while on a protracted tour of Europe and northern Africa. Technically, I could communicate many of my needs with language. I could ask the usual *turista* types of questions about the locations and costs of things, but I wanted to open up more personal, small-talking conversations with people whom I encountered. I longed, in effect, to be recognized as a potential friend of the people I met, to be seen as a *person*.

When we do talk personally, what is our language like? In 1930, before telephone eavesdropping became seriously taboo, a team of researchers at Bell Laboratories did a study of the words used in telephone conversations. They tuned in to the talk of unsuspecting callers until they had recorded eighty thousand English words, which were said mainly during business-oriented telephone conversations in New York City. Much to the researchers' surprise, this massive corpus of words contained only 2,240 *different* words, and 819 of these words occurred just once! Even more surprisingly, a tiny core of just 155 words made up 80 percent of all the words used!

If no particular conversation requires more than several hundred words, everyday social language may not be as complex as the phenomena that linguistic grammarians write about. But the inhabitants of industrialized societies know many thousands of words—the average graduate of an American high school recognizes about sixty thousand. Why do we bother to learn so many words? Why carry so many around in our heads? Some words, we might speculate, facilitate understanding of complex, work-related tasks. If so, their chief function may be to support private intellectual activity—thinking, planning, problem-solving, and the like—rather than communication.

But a cognitive explanation cannot account for all our lexical entries. Blind children do not necessarily shy away from color names even though their literal meaning cannot be understood. Some children with a rare form of mental retardation called Williams syndrome use words whose meanings escape them. Clearly, there must be other things that determine the size and complexity of modern language besides thought and the drive to convey it. Literacy and academic training are undoubtedly among them, but I believe that much of our capacity for linguistic material is social, that ornate utterances comprise the better part of contest-winning social displays as impressive to our species as feathers to the peacock.

I will discuss this view more fully in the next chapter, but there are other distinctions between speaking and talking that we should consider here. One is that a person can speak to many listeners simultaneously but cannot talk with more than a few at a time—a numerical limitation on intimacy. Another is that where speaking ends with message transmission, the basis for terminating a talking episode is achievement of a feeling state that meets some internal standard. In most cases this standard will be met when the parties reach a desired feeling of closeness or recognize that their views have been heard or accepted. Physiologically, as we will see in the next chapter, the "standard" could be neurochemical.

There is a strong bond between eating or drinking and talking. It's as though ingestion of food and expulsion of sound somehow enjoy a natural association. When Sweden's rulers in the eighteenth century became convinced that malcontents were planning revolts against the government, they closed down the coffeehouses. They did this by forcing several medical researchers to report "scientific" evidence that coffee was harmful to health. And when coffee fell, it undoubtedly dragged down a lot of the revolting talk with it.

Openings and Closings

As intellectually light as talking can be, it is not a meandering stream with no banks or current. There is structure to talk; it begins with an opening or greeting phase. In much of the world, when acquaintances approach each other from a distance, they achieve mutual eye contact, smile, and then usually look away. They make slight movements of the hand or head to indicate to the other party that he has been noticed. The parties then assume a facial expression that is attentive or friendly and continue to move toward each other. As the greeters come into talking range, they resume smiling and eye contact. Finally, the participants begin to exchange information about their identities and social intentions. At this point it is likely that comments will be made about appearance or state of health, and information will be exchanged about the individuals themselves and their mutual friends. In the last stage of the opening phase, the interactants finally initiate their "business," if they have any, through a variety of postural and gaze shifts and transitional remarks.

Closings are just as important. They serve a holding function, setting the scene for any verbal exchanges to come without prejudging what those exchanges might involve. One needs time to achieve the right amount of closeness before breaking the contact. Telephone closings can sometimes be rather complicated, with the parties going back and forth repeatedly until they achieve mutual verbal climax, reaching exactly the desired feeling at exactly the right time. This seems to be exaggerated in the case of lovers, for whom the faintest hint of rejection could be fatal. Consider the following excerpt from a surreptitiously recorded conversation between a prominent English gentleman and his paramour:

> He: Night, darling . . . night.
> She: Love you.
> He: Don't want to say good-bye.
> She: Neither do I, but you must get some sleep. Bye.
> He: Bye, darling.
> She: Love you.
> He: Bye.
> She: Hopefully talk to you in the morning.
> He: Please.
> She: Bye, I do love you.
> He: Night.
> She: Night. Love you forever.
> He: Night.
> She: G'bye. Bye, my darling.

He:	Night.
She:	Night. Night.
He:	Night.
She:	Bye-bye.
He:	Going.
She:	Bye.
He:	Going.
She:	Gone.
He:	Night.

There were eight more back-and-forth exchanges before "He" hung up.

Recently, the Security Service of Her Majesty's Government (a.k.a. MI5) placed a newspaper advertisement for people who are unusually good at openings and closings. If you were the ideal applicant, said the ad, you would be "adept at talking your way into situations with the opportunity for gathering useful information, as well as the resourcefulness to extract yourself from less promising circumstances." At least twenty thousand Brits must be proud of their openings and closings; that's the number that applied for the fourteen spaces available.

Many linguistics books say very little about these things, nor do they comment on verbal seesaws like the one in the protracted closing above. Given their motives, linguistic grammarians are probably wise to ignore intimate talking. The utterances contained therein may not be complex enough to analyze. So if you want to study social talk, you won't need to rush out and get a Ph.D. in linguistics first. But that doesn't mean that talking is a trivial matter or is of no academic interest. Indeed, there is now an interdisciplinary field called "conversation analysis" and several journals that deal with verbal and nonverbal behavior. The research reported makes it clear that when familiar people talk, the combination of vocal, facial, and gestural cues that convey meaning, with and without the help of words, is every bit as complex as linguistic grammars. And every bit as important, for when UCLA linguist Susan Curtiss completed her studies of Genie, the girl who was socially isolated for most of her youth, she said that Genie "told us of her feelings. She shared her heart and mind. From that perspective, who cares about grammar?"

• • •

In the previous chapter I asked how personal information is conveyed by social talking. It should be evident by now that observant listeners learn things about a talker's character, personality, emotionality, and attitude toward his verbal partner that do not come through in fact- or business-oriented speaking. To talk is to be expressive in all these ways and therefore not merely to be verbally understandable but personally understood. To be privy to the vocal displays of other people is to have the information needed to live and work and do things in groups.

The True Size of Small Talk

I once attended an all Latin American cocktail party in Caracas which began at 7 and finished at 1 A.M. There were 300 people present, very little to eat, nobody stopped talking except to draw breath for six hours flat; I do not remember a single word that was said.

Richard Lewis, *When Cultures Collide*

It is fashionable to denigrate cocktail parties. They're superficial. You can't really *talk* to anyone. If there were a Richter scale of semantic significance, cocktail parties would scarcely jiggle the needle. Indeed, some children suffer from a condition, aptly termed the "cocktail party syndrome," in which they spew out social sounds as though speaking meaningfully but articulate few identifiable words. Children with hydrocephalus and Landau-Kleffner syndrome, a rare seizure disorder, are among those who display this lexically empty chatter.

Real cocktail parties can also be semantically arid. The veteran people-watcher Desmond Morris believes that the host may even go out of his way to keep them that way by repeatedly breaking up long conversations and rotating the chatterers. Talkers are thus limited to the greeting and leave-taking phases of verbal interactions, phases that feature relationships more than messages. This permits a triage process, enabling partygoers to decide which of the guests they might like to spend more time with in the future. If initial impressions prove reliable, then the cocktail party chatter that launched the successful new pairings was anything but insignificant.

The desire for intimacy, twinned with overflowing address books, explains our fondness for large banquets, conventions, and cocktail parties, which Staffan Linder called "a highly efficient way of exploiting the time allocated to social intercourse." From the guests' standpoint, the function of these gatherings may seem to be meeting new people. But the reason for having the party is more likely to be the host's need to service a fleet of existing relationships. Our sociable species thus has reasons to talk even when we have nothing to say. This automatically yields "small talk."

It is widely acknowledged that small talk needs no particular topic. V. H. Friedlaender said that "small talk was invented not for the sake of saying something, but for the sake of saying anything." "It is not what is said that matters," agreed linguist, Edward Sapir. But these perfectly true statements should not persuade us that to say something "small" is to commit a trivial act. It could be significant that a person happened to know the inconsequential thing that he said, or that he chose to say it to a particular listener. For example, merely referring to a third party by a family nickname may suggest that the speaker is on more intimate terms with that individual than the listener had assumed. Revelation of this familiarity may imply that the speaker is seeking to elevate his personal standing or to alter his relationship with the listener in other ways.

If you don't think much of small talk, try living without it for a while. One of the chief complaints of those in so-called commuter marriages is the inability to discuss the inane. One commuter wife observed that "you have a lot of immediate impressions and little jokes and observations that you can't save for a week. You can't reconstruct that kind of trivia in an effective way. I find the loss of that material really annoying." Another geographically displaced wife lamented lost opportunities "to share the everyday things like 'What did you have for lunch today?' "

There is an interesting paradox about small talk. It surfaced in a Harvard professor's recollection of the night he met a future president of the United States. In *The White House Years*, Henry Kissinger recalled that Richard Nixon arrived just as he was leaving a party. Nixon said that he had read Kissinger's first book, had learned from it, and had written Kissinger a note about it. "I replied stiffly," Kissinger said. "At that time I was still highly uncomfortable with small talk."

The paradox, of course, is this: if small talk is so natural, if it requires so little intelligence, how could it elude the grasp of a Harvard professor? Why the discomfort? But of course the problem was not just Kissinger's. Many of us can recall standing around at parties at which we knew nobody, wondering what we could possibly say to a stranger. That's why the self-help section of many American bookstores includes guides for the small-talker. One suggests that the tongue-tied ask, "If you could choose one icon to serve as the symbol for the world's kindness, what would it be?" Viewing this with understandable alarm, one British columnist exclaimed, "It's a constant amazement that Americans ever manage to breed at all."

The paradox resolves when we consider that as members of an informationally oriented society, we have to struggle to recover our primordial communicative ability, one that was altered by years of formal education that included literacy training, composition practice, and perhaps even elocution classes. We have been given to understand that we should not speak unless we have something to say. We have been told that "it is better to keep silent and appear stupid than open your mouth and remove all doubt." And so it is to be expected that something as fundamental to our species as small talk would be buried under layers of familial, pedagogical, and cultural training.

The irrelevance of information to the act of talking is revealed in many ways. Once upon a time, before cellular phones and e-mail burst on the scene, citizens band radio was emblematic of the desire for social connectivity. Although many of us associate these radios with trucking, twenty years ago one in every eleven American families had a CB radio, and about thirty million were in use in homes, vehicles, and pleasure boats. But here surely is an example of use preceding need. In an analysis of verbal content, Jon Powell and Donald Ary found "a seemingly endless series of exchanges revolving around such questions as 'Where are you going,' 'What are you going to do,' 'What did you do this morning' which repetitiously underscore the current routine state of affairs between the conversing CBers." In fact, these communications had so little real content that their primary purpose seemed to be achievement of a feeling of acceptance, as in a fraternal organization. The CB set owner, according to Powell and Ary, must demonstrate that he "is part of the club and prove membership by employing the code.... Belonging to the CB fraternity offers the advantages of a fraternal brotherhood ('good buddy' substitutes for the traditional 'brother') without much obligation.... A brotherhood exists, but without binding obligations and without anything more than a usual sense of commitment."

Vacuous Vocalizations

In purely sociable conversation, the topic is merely the indispensable medium through which the lively exchange of speech itself unfolds its attractions.

Georg Simmel, *The Sociology of Georg Simmel*

If one can converse with several hundred words, one might suppose that the grammatical structure of ordinary talking is not particularly complex. The supposition would be right. I got my first inkling of this as a fledgling language clinician assigned the task of helping stroke patients recover from the socially debilitating word-retrieval problems associated with aphasia. Watching these patients in conversation with hospital personnel, I was astonished to see that many chatted easily with a full range of gestures, expressions, and emotions. I initially concluded that the referring physicians were being overly cautious. But when the patients were asked to follow simple commands or answer specific questions, they responded inappropriately. Then I realized that the conversation that had seemed normal to me earlier had been achieved with empty phrases such as "sure, sometimes . . . well, you know . . . of course . . . I used to be . . . you gotta," and so forth, with the content of the conversation being supplied by the normal interlocutor. Here is an actual conversation between a therapist and an aphasic patient:

> Therapist: so this is where they adapt cars so that you can drive them
> Patient: right right right

Therapist: right right right
Patient: right right
Therapist: yes
Patient: right
Therapist: oh right
Patient: so maybe this time you know
Therapist: so you'll have a set of wheels and be a lot more mobile then t-t-to drive around
Patient: yes yes yes
Therapist: right
Patient: right right
Therapist: well I'll keep my fingers crossed for you
Patient: right
Therapist: so is that coming up fairly soon that you're going to
Patient: uh three weeks
Therapist: three weeks right right

In this exchange the therapist plays a leading role but at times is indistinguishable from the patient on the basis of utterances alone. Indeed, the reason aphasic patients such as the speaker above fail to stand out is that we *normal* individuals talk in similarly uncreative ways when chatting with others. We, like the aphasic patients, use semantically empty phrases. Anyone who doubts this might wish to inspect the Watergate transcripts in which H. R. Haldeman, serving in an advisory capacity, supplies much of the content, and President Nixon responds "That's right.... Right.... Um huh.... Yeah.... Yeah.... Well, I mean, ah ... All right. Fine.... All right, fine.... Um huh.... Uh huh.... Good. Good deal."

For all their problems in understanding spoken words, aphasic patients can be surprisingly good at picking up emotional nuances in the speech of others. Damage to the left hemisphere's language processing machinery may deny these patients access to good, clean, honest words, but there is no reason that they cannot still pick up "tone of voice" with the socially cognitive systems in their undamaged right hemisphere. In *The Man Who Mistook His Wife for a Hat*, Oliver Sacks described a televised address from President Ronald Reagan: "A roar of laughter

from the aphasia ward, just as the President's speech was coming on.
. . . The President was, as always, moving—but he was moving them,
apparently, mainly to laughter. What could they be thinking? Were they
failing to understand him? Or did they, perhaps, understand him all too
well?" Indeed, "to demonstrate their aphasia," according to Sacks, "one
had to go to extraordinary lengths . . . to speak and behave un-naturally,
to remove all the extraverbal cues—tone of voice, intonation, suggestive
emphasis or inflection, as well as all visual cues."

The aphasia evidence pointed me in the right direction, but it was
not until I began to study language development that I understood the
fundamentally nonlinguistic nature of talking. Infants begin to engage
in social sound-making long before they know any words. They look at
family members and babble out strings of da-da-da–like sounds, often
with normal sounding pitch patterns. They pause and allow others to
respond. They sometimes go on as though they were discoursing on a
subject of some concern to them. Since they are not using words, we
cannot strictly say that they are talking, but they are doing most of
the things that talking involves. As I watched babies, I wondered what
motivated this behavior.

When infants begin to use words, uninformativeness goes off the
charts. True, they point to objects and name them, but they do so for
the very people who taught them the labels in the first place. Moreover,
they do much of their talking when no one else is present. And if
someone else does happen to be nearby, the infants rarely check to see
if they're paying attention or getting the drift. Since the newly lexical
seem not to talk *in order* to convey information to others, I concluded
that the true motive must lie elsewhere, perhaps in a desire to converge
emotionally with family members, to become a fully fledged member of
a group that prattles.

I suspect such motives continue to guide us in adulthood. Social
talking is inherently intimate. Since it's not about an issue that requires
discussion, the talkers are forced to work together to come up with a
topic. The rules for doing so are simple. The speaker must mean something, which is inherently an approach behavior; to the Cambridge
philosopher Ludwig Wittgenstein, meaning something was "like going
up to someone." For his part, the listener must understand something;
to the Russian linguist Mikhail Bakhtin, comprehension was "inherently

responsive." Message-making thus requires that unfamiliar people jump in and begin to relate in a personal way before they might be emotionally ready to do so. It's a curious process. You wonder how it all got started and what it does for us.

THREE

Social Work

Towards the end of his life, John [Lennon] talked about his
cats and padding around doing the dishes in his robe and
making bread and playing with the baby. We just had
those great kind-of-nothing conversations which are so
precious. Paul McCartney, "The Word According to Paul"

When humans get up in the morning—after a night of talking in
their dreams, if not in their sleep—one thing is clear: no matter what
else they may do that day, they will look for opportunities to talk even
if they lack any information that needs to be communicated. Their use
of talk will seem casual and unplanned, but in talking they will obedi-
ently follow a set of biologically and culturally transmitted imperatives.
These will be revealed in tones of voice and movements of eyes and
hands. There will be at least one topic per conversation, which may
have to be negotiated after the conversation begins. At critical junctures
the ballistic "ha-ha-ha" pulses that characterize laughter may burst
forth. The exchange will provide talkers with lasting impressions of
their verbal partners that outlive many of the specific facts that may
have been conveyed in words.

All of this has been laid down in advance. The brain mechanisms that permit and control talking, the developmental processes that prepare the child for speech, the psychological and social benefits to our species —in effect, our own personal reasons for talking—were put in place by forces that operated long ago in evolutionary history.

Humans have an inherent drive to talk. This tendency is so strong that it survives a range of organic and environmental obstacles. Case studies give testimony to unimaginable horrors, as when infants are born with no tongue or with a gaping hole in the roof of the mouth or a damaged brain, or are raised by parents who don't speak. But these infants usually vocalize, babble, and talk, and many of them express themselves with a surprising degree of clarity. Even profound deafness fails to discourage vocalization in young infants. And when congenitally deaf mothers express affection to their infants, they tend to do so vocally even though they cannot hear their own displays and otherwise are disposed to sign. Emotion loves the voice, launching it on many occasions, plunging into it on others.

If asked why they talk, most people would probably say "to communicate." Intentional communication involves a transfer of information from one person (such as Ginger) to another (such as Fred). However, some of the information that is most important to Fred will not be *knowingly* conveyed by Ginger and would not be conveyed by her if she knew it was going on. For example, Ginger might be attempting to appear more knowledgeable, experienced, or innocent than she really is and would be aghast if Fred were aware of her deception. But Fred's only reason for listening to Ginger may be to evaluate her truthfulness!

The investigators who launched basic research in human communication had no scientific knowledge of emotion. They were mathematicians who approached speech from the standpoint of something called information theory. In doing so, they treated speech like written statements that occur nakedly, with no context, and measured the information embedded therein in "bits" (short for "binary digits"). This approach worked well on the emotionally parched statements that were devised for laboratory experiments, but it would have fallen flat on its face if used on a sample of real-life talk. The "yeah"s and "right"s and "hmm"s of talk; the eyebrow raisings, smiles, oral clicks and whistles; the displays of mock horror and snootiness; the manual gestures and gesticulations —all these, interpreted against an intimate knowledge of the communicating party, present circumstance, and recent events, are excluded by mathematical analyses of desocialized strings of printed words.

If people spoke only to convey factual information, ambiguity would be intolerable. But, in fact, talkers often go out of their way to create this ostensibly objectionable state. On paper a sentence that is unfinished will be hard to interpret, but stopping in the middle of any oral sentence may convey more information than fluently proceeding to the end. A shake of the head or roll of the eyes at a critical point in an utterance can express things that visually unsupported verbalizations do not. These extra-verbal strategies give talkers a way to leave an impression with their listeners without having to spell out, and thus become the quotable source for, the details. Those who use ambiguity skillfully are even considered verbally artistic.

Linguistic knowledge is a marvelous means of encoding thought, but the more important functions of talking are achieved through sound-making behaviors that promote feelings of harmony, feelings achieved less by a meeting of minds than a meeting of hearts. And these behaviors appear to have their own neural hardware. One reason for believing so is that Nature occasionally knocks out language but leaves talklike behaviors alone, or damages sound-making without harming linguistic knowledge. These dissociations of language and speech have long been known, but clinicians recently discovered a new, so-called semantic-pragmatic disorder that arises in childhood and requires no bump on the head to do so. Victims have a nearly normal grasp of language but are unable to use it effectively in social and emotional interactions, frequently misunderstanding what conversations are about or what the individual statements might signify. When asked, "Would you say that the boy looked ill?", one child with the disorder dutifully responded, "The boy looked ill." Another child when asked to "write the days of the week" in a series of seven adjacent boxes, wrote "the" "days" "of" "the" "week" in five of the seven. These children are the potentially overlooked middle class of miscommunicants; they have a fully serviceable voice hooked up to a reasonably competent linguistic mechanism, but they remain socially incapacitated.

Social communication and grammatical language are thus divisible in Nature as well as in theory. But there are trenchant connections between the two. When our species' capacity for linguistic grammar developed, it failed to drive out preexisting communicative behaviors. And this left us intellectually evolved and modern humans with some "primal" social dispositions—dispositions that continually force their way to the surface, reminding us that we, the furless and feather-free, are also fully fledged members of the animal kingdom.

Primal Acts of Sociality

Whatever advances have occurred in our cognitive and linguistic capabilities in the past hundred thousand years, our species retains many of its ancestral dispositions. Recently, the English archeologist Steven Mithen wrote that there is little difference between the meal-time behavior of Kalahari Bushmen and Cambridge dons at high table. He readily acknowledged that while the high table provided nutrition, "it was also used for sending social messages . . . to bond the group of Fellows together and to establish their prestige. The seating arrangements," he said, "were as much socially inspired as those of hunter-gatherers when they seat themselves around a fire: the Fellows' High Table literally on a podium, looking down to where the undergraduates would sit. The Master seated in the centre."

What does social sound-making do for us? Since we service our relationships vocally, it may be illuminating to look at the ways that other primates create and maintain social relationships, as well as the ways that they vocalize. After all, we human primates share as much as 98 percent of our genetic material with our closest ape cousins, the chimpanzees. It's bound to be instructive if we clear away the cultural underbrush and see how nonhuman primates conduct their interpersonal business.

One of the first things we see is that group living is critical to primates. Social structure arises very rapidly. This was dramatized some years ago when several hundred rhesus monkeys were transported from various parts of India to Cayo Santiago, the island off Puerto Rico. On the ocean voyage the monkeys were intentionally underfed to heighten their receptivity to the new diet that awaited them on the island. On shipboard they were also denied any sense of their usual territoriality. In consequence the monkeys became socially destructured and anarchical. But if monkeys can have dreams, their wildest ones came true when they disembarked on the island, a lush paradise with plenty of space, no natural predators, and a daily supply of man-supplied food. There were no common foes to team up against, no environmentally insoluble problems. Nevertheless, within a year the entire group had "divided itself into social groups, each holding and defending a permanent territory and living in permanent hostility with its neighbours." So much for a fresh start in the New World.

When unfamiliar humans are caught up in a natural disaster or other *Lord of the Flies* type of situation, they organize themselves as quickly as the monkeys on Cayo Santiago. Of course, every society also has alliances of the more enduring and stable kind. These are as obvious in today's youth gangs as they were in the extensive clan system in ancient China and parts of Africa, protecting individuals against prospective foes and ensuring adequate distribution of resources.

Apes and monkeys are vocal animals, and they command a small repertoire of calls, including those emitted in alarm. When vervet monkeys see an eagle, a snake, or a leopard, they use these alarm calls to warn other monkeys. To test the way alarm calls work, ethologists record the calls, taking note of which predator was present at the time, then play the calls back through a loudspeaker that has been hidden in the bushes. Notice is then taken of the animals' response. If they stand on their hind legs and look down to a snake call, and climb trees to a leopard call, ethologists assume that the calls must have been more than general alarm signals since they actually *told* animals about the source or nature of the caller's alarm, or instructed them on what to do.

Alarm calls are relatively easy to study and they do communicate, but there are good reasons to question their relevance to talking or human language. One reason is that monkeys don't play around with alarm calls. They rarely use them to fool or lie, things we do with language continually. In fact, we humans have been forced to enact laws to prevent the more capricious in our midst from yelling "Fire!" in a crowded theater.

If there are vocalizations more relevant to talking than alarm calls, they would be conversational in style, the product of contented animals interacting quietly among themselves in a family or small group situation. These sounds would be difficult to get on tape, and they would elicit no particular response if blasted over a disembodied loudspeaker hidden in the bushes. How much would be learned about our own gossip and small talk if casually interacting people clammed up, fled, or broke into an agitated type of vocalization when approached by strangers with recording equipment? What observable response would we make if someone played chitchat at 120 decibels?

But don't kid yourself. When primatologists trudge back to camp, the subjects of their earlier attentions don't necessarily call it a day. The "close calls" of wild African gorillas are usually made during feeding and resting, typically as part of an exchange with another animal. They also occur as threats or appeasements when conflict seems likely. But these signals are usually audible only to other members of the group and are frequently too weak to record. Dian Fossey heard them as a series of "grumbles, belches, croons, purrs, hums, moans, wails, and howls." When a day of foraging is over, the call of the wild gets up close and personal.

Of course, as closely as we resemble the other primates at more "primal" levels, there are massive differences closer to the top. Not having words, monkeys and apes convey personal facts directly, without dreaming up a lexical message that might seem to be saying something of an impersonal nature about politics, the weather, or fluctuations of the stock market. Their calls, like our talking, provide information about the individual's species, group affiliation, and social relationships as well as his sex, age, personal identity, internal state, and reactions to other individuals.

What if we conducted our social business in the same way as other primates? Imagine a woman walking up to a man, looking him in the face, and attempting to appear important, honorable, decisive, or sincere purely by animating her face like a silent screen actress. Envision a man approaching a woman and seeking to convey his desire to engage in sexual activity merely by making vocal sounds. People who try to convey information about themselves with facial expressions and vocal variations *while not talking* are likely to be considered unutterably odd, if not insane.

Here Comes the Groom

Monkeys and apes have a manual format for much of their small talk. A friendly encounter between two animals frequently begins with a bout of grooming. In grooming, one animal combs through the hairs of the other animal with both hands, dislodges parasites, and eats them. Since manual grooming has little to do with hygiene or diet, it is usually referred to as *social grooming*, a form of social relaxation after a long day of wariness and aggression.

Social grooming has an etiquette. Dominant animals tend to be groomed more often than subordinate ones. In a study of female baboons, over eight out of ten grooming episodes were directed to the three top-ranking females in the group. In another study, wild vervet monkeys groomed a female two or more ranks above them more often than they groomed a female just one rank higher. A third study showed that female rhesus macaques of intermediate rank were likely to prevent lower-ranking females from reaching over them, as it were, to groom dominant ones. Similar findings have been reported in chimpanzees, where dominant males tend to receive more grooming than subordinate ones. Using their hands, these animals chat *up* other animals in their group.

Grooming produces the alliances that scare off predators, raise the young, and defend shared territories. Alliances enhance each individual's competitive ability, thereby effectively raising that animal's own dominance rank and possibly that of his relatives. As animal behaviorist Andrew Whiten has pointed out, "simply *to be seen by others* grooming with high-ranking A, or chatting with high-status B, is worth something to the individual because of what this advertises with respect to future coalition."

With grooming the key to so many benefits, it should not be surprising that it is done *competitively.* If an animal wishes to keep a little support "in the bank," it needs to provide more or better services than competitors. This produces a pressure to groom and to do so well enough to be accepted as a most-favored groomer of higher-ranking individuals.

At some point in evolutionary history, hominid grooming "went vocal." What could have provoked such a switch? Leslie Aiello, a professor at University College London, has suggested that the process began with the transition to a fully terrestrial lifestyle. When our premodern ancestors moved into large open areas, they teamed up to protect themselves against attack. This would have increased the possibility of competition and aggression from *within* their own ranks. In nonhuman primates there are smaller subgroups that protect their constituents from harassment by members of the larger group. The effectiveness of these coalitions, as measured by the willingness of members to come to each other's aid, is directly related to the amount of time they devote to social grooming. Thus, we may assume that our own terrestrial ancestors had to engage in social grooming for their own protection.

While manual grooming works well on a very local basis, its strength as a bonding agent stems from a limitation: grooming with the hands is inherently one-on-one. But primates are busy guys. They have other things to do besides "sit around and groom." Their agenda includes nest building, feeding, sex, and infant care. Robin Dunbar has reported that no group could have spent more than about 20 percent of its time grooming without encroaching on these other functions.

Dunbar has evidence that total grooming time goes up with group size, but it is not because there are more animals to groom. Rather, each member of a larger group spends more time grooming the same small number of "best friends" or coalition partners. The reason is that the felt need for alliances rises in proportion to the number of perceived competitors and aggressors, and grooming—the means of strengthening those alliances—also increases. Thus, as larger groups became commonplace, this practice, which could be compared to tutoring, would have had to be replaced by a one-to-many form of grooming, analogous to lecturing. Enter the voice.

But what voice? Surely they wouldn't have appropriated alarm calls to convey the desire to be friendly. Dunbar suggested that the class of vocalization that would have been enlisted for vocal grooming was contact calls. These calls meet certain requirements of social sound-making in that they are produced during affiliative behaviors, can be produced loudly, and may assume various forms. But contact calls cannot be the source. Although some of them, like speech, are issued repetitively, the source is laryngeal or respiratory rather than articulatory. That is, contact calls are not characterized by regular raisings and lowerings of the jaw while closing the lips or elevating the tongue. Affiliative calls therefore bear little resemblance to the sound-making that occurs when people talk. Where did the sounds of speech come from?

Vocal Support

I think the seeds of an answer are to be found in two different sound-making patterns, each unsatisfactory when considered by itself. One is the oral smacking sounds that frequently precede or accompany grooming. Baboons produce tongue smacks by pressing the moistened tip of their tongue against the upper incisors and anterior portion of the hard palate. Contact is repeatedly broken and reestablished by rapidly retracting and protruding the tongue, at a rate of about six to eight smacks per second. The human conversational speaking rate is about five to six syllables per second. As the tongue is retracted, the jaw is lowered slightly. The sound is made when the tongue is forcefully withdrawn from the roof of the mouth. Tongue smacking thus shares some temporal and mechanical properties of human speech.

Tongue smacking may have signaled interest in a parasite feast, the smacks acting not so very differently from the "yum-yum" issued by humans before sitting down to a bountiful meal. But smacking arises in many different social circumstances, including manual grooming, greeting, confronting, and copulating, and it is frequently offered as a gesture of pacification, affiliation, or appeasement. One might speculate that because manual grooming is a cooperative, nonaggressive activity, the associated smacking sounds convey the message "I come in peace."

Tongue smacking seems to be used in much the same way as the greeting phase of talking. Like that phase, smacking tends to occur when the individual is seeking to decrease the physical or social distance between another individual and himself. At the physical level, however, a theoretical problem remains. Smacking involves jaw, tongue, and lip movements, but it has no vocal support. Without the decibels produced by the larynx and lungs, these movements would have been useless for public address. The smackers could groom several others at a time and anyone at a short distance, but they couldn't reach a crowd.

There is a type of close call that appears to have some of the phonatory properties of speech. It is the *girney*. In vervet and rhesus macaque monkeys, girneys seem to be produced behind closed lips and, perhaps for that reason, tend to sound nasal. They resemble the subdued murmur of conversational speech and even seem to be used in a conversationlike way. Although girneys are emitted just after birth, they are most frequently produced by mothers who are interacting with other mothers or juvenile females. Males rarely girney, although young males entering a new social group may girney to high-ranking males. Girneys may be intermixed with tongue smacks. If our hominid ancestors were able to combine the laryngeal activity of girneys with the articulatory activity of lip and tongue smacking, they could have achieved a rather humanoid variety of social sound-making.

With phonatory support, it would thus have become possible to *broadcast* peaceable intentions and affiliative desires by mouth. Strangers would be able to tell instantly from a distance that a particular individual was peaceable and wished to socialize. Going vocal would thus have been a step toward mass communication, the benefits of which are now taken for granted. For as one rhetorician observed, "Political hierarchies in an age of mass media are established and reaffirmed largely through discourse. Politicians can nonverbally press only so much flesh."

Vocal grooming would have carried with it some additional benefits, for hominids would have learned more about each other from the new set of cues than from the old ones. The voice contains far more information about individuals and their feelings than the hands. But this new medium that was so useful with larger groups could still be reduced to a whisper for the benefit of special individuals. Hominids would have continued to vocally groom each other in pairs, much as speaker and listener enjoy the intimacy of one-on-one conversations today. And, of course, the vocal grooming of us moderns is frequently accompanied by the historical artifacts of manual grooming—gesticulated movements of the hands.

If our prelinguistic ancestors were able to engage in social and emotional sound-making before they invented words, what was this sound-making like? For clues we can examine systematic variations in the vocal forms of monkeys and human infants. A study by Steven Green, a professor at the University of Miami, documented as many as ten acoustically distinct variants of the coo calls of Japanese macaques, vocal variants that corresponded to the circumstances in which the monkey found itself. Similarly, a professor at the City University of New York, John Dore, reported that human infants are capable of a number of "primitive speech acts" that allow them vocally to label, request, answer, repeat, and greet long before they use sentences.

Thus we may suppose that our hominid ancestors varied their pitch contours to convey emotionality, but to achieve more than a "mouthful" of distinctive sound patterns—the words of the future—our ancestors would have needed to differentiate their vocal displays in other ways. In the animal kingdom, display repertoires are of modest size; most mammals, birds, and fish have no more than thirty-five. This may be all they can use and interpret. If so, our hominid ancestors—not so very different from their ape cousins—would have been pressured by group life to come up with additional displays.

If intimate talking is a display, so are arguing, scolding, teasing, praising, warning, joking, and other forms of verbal engagement. But if we kept adding to this list, it wouldn't have satisfied all our ancestors' expressive needs. The alternative was to subdivide their displays, and this is what our predecessors did: they varied the sound of individual vocalizations by moving their lips and tongue in audibly different ways. This endowed us moderns with the capacity to say very specific things —in words made of individual phonemes—*while* scolding, teasing, or praising, things our ancestors did long before phonemes.

Intimate talking is a social sound-making display that brings individuals close together. And this is a favorable circumstance in and of itself. If you are seen talking with Pope John Paul II or John F. Kennedy, Jr., that will give your social standing a boost regardless of what gets said. But proximity was a critical condition in linguistic evolution, for it enabled finer (consonant- and vowel-like) variations of sound and meaning that would have been too subtle for the old yelling and screaming distances.

That talking served as and continues to fulfill a display function is suggested by a host of nonverbal displays that co-occur with intimate talking. These include changes in vocal affect as well as blushes, eyebrow raises, smiles, frowns, grimaces, and a host of other displays, such as an interesting behavior called "tongue showing." In tongue showing, the tip of the tongue is protruded through the lips, usually when a social interaction becomes aversive. Why we do this, nobody knows.

Lingering Fingers

During the coronation of Queen Elizabeth in June of 1953, most eyes were trained on the royal proceedings. But some people saw the Queen's sister, Princess Margaret, flicking some "fluff" from the coat of Group Captain Peter Townsend. When word of this got out the next day, the ordinary newspaper-reading public suddenly knew something with absolute certainty—the relationship between Margaret and Captain Townsend was *intimate*.

How could people be so sure of this? What are the social, emotional, perhaps even sexual implications of manual grooming in our own species? Although vocal grooming evolved from its manual predecessor, the social use of hands and fingers persisted. Consider the interviews conducted by Jacques Fournier, a bishop at the turn of the fourteenth century, with the residents of Montaillou, a small village in the French Pyrenees. His detailed notes in the Inquisition register provide a fascinating account of social life over seven hundred years ago. In the village, delousing activities were commonplace, and they strictly obeyed social constraints. For example, only women deloused, and they reserved this activity for men with whom they shared a romantic or familial relationship and—here we go again—women of higher status.

Manual grooming occurred in the early part of the present century as a preliminary to sexual intercourse in the Trobriand Islands of New Guinea. According to Malinowski's account, lovers "inspect each other's hair for lice and eat them—a practice disgusting to us and ill associated with love-making, but to the natives a natural and pleasant occupation between two who are fond of each other, and a favorite pastime with children."

Manual grooming was documented in the 1980s by a Japanese researcher, Kazuyoshi Sugawara, in the central Kalahari area of Botswana. Among the people there, grooming consisted of one person manually removing lice from the scalp hair of the other (less commonly the loincloth or the skin covered by it). Sugawara's analysis revealed that in about 80 percent of the adult grooming episodes, the groomer was a female, as in fourteenth-century France. Males participated in fewer than 15 percent of the episodes, and they never groomed females, though females occasionally groomed their husbands or unrelated adolescent males.

Taken with findings examined earlier, these observations reveal interesting sex pattern similarities in the manual grooming of humans and other primates, and the vocally equivalent behavior in humans. For intimate social talking also predominates among female pairs. Moreover, where the humans in grooming incidents were genetically unrelated, the groomer was the younger of the two parties in 70 percent of the cases. This finding reveals another parallel: both groups tended to groom higher-ranking individuals.

We also share with the other primates some manual laterality patterns. In our own species, right-handed adults make more self-grooming and touching movements with the *left* hand, at least while speaking. The right hand is more often used in gesturing. In apes, face-touching movements also reveal a marked laterality: the left hand is used more than twice as often as the right hand, usually to touch the mouth. These handedness patterns reflect the way the primate brain is organized. The right cerebral hemisphere takes much of the responsibility for the emotion that is displayed by both human and nonhuman primates. It is also responsible for the frozen phrases and idioms that occur so commonly in small talk. These include greetings (such as hi, how are you, you're looking good, what's happening, long time no see) as well as the leave-taking expressions (bye-bye, nice seeing you, take care, see you later). Thus it is probably safe to assume that manual grooming makes disproportionate use of the right cerebral hemisphere and that vocal grooming makes greater use of that hemisphere than does informationally oriented speaking.

Another manual activity that may have been "handed down" from our manually grooming ancestors is gesticulation, an activity that punctuates speech but, unlike gestures, carries no literal meaning. Gesticulation may be a residual behavior that was left behind when the switch was made from manual to vocal grooming. Monkeys sometimes vocalize to "request" a shift in manual grooming roles, and humans talk and gesticulate simultaneously. There is a synonymous interchangeability here, for even our metaphors imply functional equivalence between intimate vocalization and touching. The telephone companies remind us of our need to "reach out and touch someone" and to "stay in touch."

In a large study of actual touching behavior in humans, Stanley Jones and A. Elaine Yarbrough counted twelve separate categories of touch. Some were displayed only when two people were greeting, some when departing or showing affection. Additional analyses indicated that females did more same-sex touching than males, and mothers touched their children more than fathers did. These findings parallel sex and parental patterns observed in nonhuman primates.

Similar research by Judith Hall indicates that real physical touching, as with grooming, serves several different social functions in humans. From surreptitious observations at academic conferences, Hall determined that higher-status individuals tend to touch the arm or shoulder of lower-ranking individuals, probably as a form of affection or nurturance. By contrast, lower-ranking individuals tend to touch by formally shaking hands with higher-ranking members of the academy, apparently in an attempt to express respect and elevate their own status. These social applications of the hands join with other findings to suggest that our species retained the disposition to service relationships manually. It's not surprising that we would use our voices this way, too.

The early survival functions of sound-making are still with us today in the acoustics of speech and the preferred word shapes of languages. Following Darwin's lead, Eugene Morton, a researcher at the Smithsonian Institution in Washington, D.C., reported some years ago that small animals tend to vocalize with a higher pitch and that animals of various sizes appease prospective foes by raising their pitch. One might expect similar patterns in grooming talk, and the evidence is that the act of smiling perceptibly raises vocal pitch. This is why listeners can tell whether a person is smiling when conversing on the telephone.

An experimental phonetician at the University of California at Berkeley, John Ohala, has observed that in humans, like other mammals, a high-pitched voice indicates that the sender is or may be small, infantile, uncertain, frightened, submissive, or all of the above. He reported finding that as a speaker's average pitch was electronically lowered, estimates of his perceived dominance and self-confidence went up. Ohala was therefore not surprised that in a variety of cultures the intonation contour associated with question asking—an expression of uncertainty—involves rising frequency in utterance toward the end of the statement, precisely where pitch lowering is physiologically more natural. He also noted a connection between high pitch and politeness or subordination.

We pitch our voices higher when addressing small individuals, such as infants and kittens, and when pleading our case—to a ticketing traffic policeman, for instance—or when wishing to appear innocent or help-less. There are specific sounds like the "ee" vowel that also serve these functions. High frequency components of "ee" cause it to sound higher than the other vowels, and when adults talk to children, they often use "ee" to highlight the diminutive or innocent nature of things, hence birdie, fishy, doggie, and so on. This connection between high and small also explains why the diminutive in Spanish is formed by adding "ito" to a word and why little dogs are more likely to be called "Fifi" than big dogs. It also explains why Israel's prime minister Benjamin Netanyahu seems too large, physically and politically, for his nickname—"Bibi."

Synchronizing Our Selves

Social relationships benefit each of us directly. They also produce groups and thereby enable socially cooperative individuals to enjoy ad-ditional benefits. Cooperation is inherently satisfying, even when it ac-complishes nothing in particular. The basis of it is synchronic action. Behavioral synchronies can arise quite spontaneously. For example, when basketball players shoot but completely miss the hoop and back-board, crowds often begin to chant, "Air ball, air ball, air ball . . ." An English professor with a passion for college basketball noticed that no matter where the game was played or which teams were on the court, the crowd invariably chanted in perfectly coordinated time and pitch— the two words falling on the keys of F above middle C and D, hence F-D, F-D, and so on. What struck the professor most was the contrast with choir directors, who usually need a piano or pitch pipe to ensure that everyone begins on the proper note.

There are also highly practiced situations in which people strive for days and weeks to achieve perfect coordination. In America these activi-ties include barbershop quartets, choirs, figure skating, college marching bands, military drill teams, and if you watched the Jackie Gleason show in the 1950s and 1960s, the June Taylor Dancers. What is the basis for our attraction to synchrony? Why does an act that signifies nothing by itself take on special significance when it is per-formed simultaneously by several people? This question occurred to a young army recruit while marching day after day around a dusty military base in Texas in 1940. Over fifty years later, as a professor emeritus of the University of Chicago, he wrote that "keeping in step so as to make the next move correctly and in time somehow felt good. Words are inadequate to describe the emotion aroused by the prolonged movement in unison that drilling involved. A sense of pervasive well-being is what I recall; more specifically, a strange sense of personal enlargement; a sort of swelling out, becoming bigger than life, thanks to participation in collective ritual." The professor concluded, after a half-century of reflection, that "something visceral was at work."

Physical synchrony is usually achieved by vocalization in the form of speech or song, whether it has any content or not. One thinks of workers driving a railroad spike or relocating a heavy object to a rhythmic chant or song. This even spawned the "yo heave ho" theory, which holds that language evolved to coordinate joint effort. But the coordinative effects can be more vocal than linguistic. Edward Hall described workmen who "were talking to be talking."

> If the conversation lagged, the work lagged. Two or three men could work in a very small area without ever seeming to interfere with each other, and they worked very close together. Whether adobe bricks were being laid, plaster was being applied to the walls, or cement was being smoothed, the whole operation was like a ballet, with the rhythm of the conversation providing the unconscious score that strengthened the group bond and kept them from interfering with each other.

Synchronic action can also be achieved through judicious use of appropriate words. Seventy-five years ago Malinowski wrote that in the Trobriand Islands the bush was "alive with men who call out encouragements to one another, issue commands, and coordinate their movements by verbal action at a distance." He noticed that on fishing expeditions the movement of small fleets of canoes was frequently halted by a fish-discovery call, then coordinated by other verbalizations so that nets could be properly cast and the fish driven into them.

An intimate conversation involves a certain amount of "verbal fishing." Laughter, expressions of sympathy, head nodding, and levels of animatedness coincide in a "good" talk, as do bodily orientation, mood, degree of openness, and many other aspects of conversational behavior. These behaviors seem to satisfy some sort of drive, apart from whatever satisfaction arises from successful linguistic communication. Does our species have an "appetite" for the verbal-vocal behaviors we consider intimate?

Talk: The (True) Opiate of the Masses?

The initial frisson of uncertainty in an untested relationship, the gradual surrender to another's avid fingers flickering expertly across bare skin, the light pinching and picking and nibbling of flesh as hands of discovery move in surprise from one freckle to another newly discovered mole. The momentarily disconcerting pain of pinched skin gives way imperceptibly to a soothing sense of pleasure, creeping warmly outwards from the center of attention.

A scene from *Peyton Place? Lady Chatterley's Lover?* Neither. It's from a rather different source—Robin Dunbar's book *Grooming, Gossip and the Evolution of Language.* And the experience about which he wrote was his own pleasure while being groomed by a monkey.

When humans are groomed, they enter some sort of hedonic state. Sugawara noted "the joyful enthusiasm" shown by the groomer and "the intoxicate facial expression of the groomed" who, "with closed eyes and a rapt expression, emit[s] sharp fricative sounds made by the tongue and teeth, similar to the dental click, just as the groomer flattens lice." Likewise, when rhesus monkeys groom each other, the recipient "often assumes a very relaxed posture: the limbs go limp and the groomer can manipulate them without resistance."

Does vocal grooming, like the manual kind, simulate the action of a drug? Suzanne Langer seemed to suggest as much when she said that talking is "an irresistible desire. As soon as this avenue of action opens, a whole stream of symbolic process is set free in the jumbled outpouring of words—often repeated, disconnected, random words—that we observe in the 'chattering' state of early childhood. . . . There must be immediate satisfaction in this strange exercise, as there is in running and kicking. The effect of words on other people is only a secondary consideration."

Certainly there is plenty of evidence that talk is, as Robert Louis Stevenson said, "the most accessible of pleasures." In suburban America, adolescent girls spend sixteen hours a week "just talking." And as parents might guess, the lion's share of this—80 percent, to be exact—takes place on the telephone! In a normal day, adults use as many as forty thousand words, an amount equaling about four to six hours of continuous speech. In an hour of relaxed conversation, the typical American pumps out about twenty-four thousand individual speech sounds. "We may like to think of humankind as distinctively tool-using," said Corinne Nydegger and Linda Mitteness, "but we spend most of our time talking."

The Tzeltal culture of Tenehapa, Mexico, recognizes over four hundred different kinds of talk. Speakers of Tzeltal have terms for talk that occurs at night, in a grassy area, or that promises things that are never delivered. With a one-word modifier, Tzeltal speakers can specifically refer to the speech of a person now dead that occurred while he was still living, and distinguish this form of speech from that of a mean person who deceives his listeners by speaking nicely.

By my calculations the typical member of progressive societies will say about seven hundred million words by the age of eighty. If you doubt this, recall times when you have observed people spilling into a vestibule during the intermission of a concert or play. Unless they used sign language or had taken a vow of silence, the people chattered as noisily as birds in an aviary—as if they needed to make up for a whole hour of *not talking*.

People even talk to houseplants and pets. Over 98 percent of dog owners in one study confessed that they talked to their pet; more than 80 percent said they addressed their canine "as a person" and not "as an animal." Little wonder—many of them believed their dogs understand large numbers of words. One owner, a professor of laboratory chemistry, claimed that her dachshund had a recognition vocabulary of five thousand words. Twenty-eight percent of the respondents in the survey said they *confided* in their dog. In another survey, 90 percent of the respondents indicated their pet knew how they "felt about things." While out dog walking, elderly people usually talk to their dog as well as human passersby, with a similar length of utterance in the two situations.

For one fairly important woman in the American government, dog talking became the focus of an international brouhaha. The U.S. ambassador to Guatemala, Marilyn McAfee, was surreptitiously recorded in her office by the Guatemalan army. The tape, turned over to the CIA, contained cooing and crooning, "smoking gun" evidence of a lesbian relationship by any measure. Only later did the supersleuths that handle American "intelligence" operations realize that the object of the ambassador's vocal affections was a dog (sex unreported) rather than a human of any persuasion.

Intimate talking seems to alter our mood. It's not unusual to feel contented or mellow after a good talk. Is talk addictive? Possibly so. The research of Jaak Panksepp and his colleagues at Bowling Green State University suggests that "social affect and social bonding are in some fundamental neurochemical sense opioid addictions." Barry Keverne and his fellow animal researchers at the University of Cambridge have found that when monkeys groom, it boosts levels of endorphins—brain opiates—in the cerebrospinal fluid of recipients. They also have discovered that opioid agonists (naltrexone and naloxone) foster grooming and grooming invitations while leaving aggressive behavior, self-grooming, scratching, and general locomotor activity alone. Thus the positive feeling arising from social bonding appears to be mediated by cerebral systems containing endorphins.

It is interesting that drug-induced increases in grooming behavior are not accompanied by any changes in *self*-grooming. The grooming enhancement effect of opiate receptor blockades are specific to *social* attachment. When endogenous opiates are reduced by naloxone or naltrexone, monkeys seek support and comfort by grooming other animals. When a monkey is being groomed the beta-endorphins in its cerebrospinal fluid go up. In experiments with primates, opioid receptor blockades tend to increase the need for social attachment, while opioid agonists usually reduce solicitations for grooming.

There is a heavy concentration of opioid receptors in the limbic system, particularly in the amygdala, a small structure situated bilaterally at the base of the brain. Studies of electrical activity in the amygdala show higher levels when animals are presented with socially relevant vocal signals, and lower levels when animals are engaged in behaviors that reduce social tensions such as grooming and huddling. In nonhuman primates, lesions of the amygdala decrease social interaction, grooming, and proximity. Indirectly, they cause a fall in social rank. In one human, removal of both amygdalas destroyed interpretation of vocal anger and fear.

If vocal and manual grooming have a similar effect on the human brain, it is understandable on neurochemical grounds that we humans might use talk to soothe, comfort, and reassure people who are fearful. Does the sound of talking elevate opiate levels? If confirmed by appropriate research, this might explain the feeling of well-being, relaxation, the "warm glow" that comes from a quiet, deep conversation with good friends.

It might also explain certain findings on the cyclicity of talking. Fifteen years ago an unemployed young couple was persuaded to spend one month in a laboratory apartment where they would have no clocks or other time cues and no communication with the outside world (except notes to the researchers). Audio recordings taken continuously during this period revealed that talking occurred in episodes that were spaced about ninety minutes apart. This rhythmicity has never been explained, but if replicated, would seem to be eligible for a physiological explanation.

Vocal soothing also occurs when babies are induced to sleep with lullabies or a book, in effect a massage of the emotion mechanisms of the brain. These effects may also be achieved by the infant's own crib talk. After the lights go out at bedtime, many infants continue to talk, doing so freely, perhaps even more freely than when their parents were present. The effect is not limited to infants and young children. When thousands of Brits go to bed at night, this American transplant included, they listen to Radio 4's "Book at Bedtime."

These real-life experiences remind one of the sensory deprivation experiments that were in vogue many years ago. The volunteers were nothing if not courageous, for they had to lie still in a tank of room-temperature water in the pitch blackness of a soundproof room. One thing learned in those experiments was that perfectly normal, healthy individuals talk or sing when denied the usual amount and range of environmental stimulation. The sound of human vocalization is soothing. Although Marshall McLuhan is famous for his statement that "the medium is the message," he also said, appropriate to the present point, "The medium is the *massage*."

The First Word in Evolution

Our ancestors may have had lots of reasons to engage in social sound-making, especially if it gave them an opiate high! But when did this behavior evolve into articulate language? Robin Dunbar has suggested that social sound-making emerged several hundred millennia ago, during a time when the skull's volume (hence the size of the brain) was expanding. Others have said that a simplistic level of language entered our species' capabilities in the last hundred thousand years. How can one date such behaviors? Talking, after all, evaporates without a trace. No acoustic residue is left behind. And there are no cave paintings that show socializing people with balloons over their heads filled with the printed form of the words they were saying.

But there might be physical remains. Perhaps someone dug up a skeleton somewhere in eastern Africa and found evidence of the same bony structures that are used for talking. Perhaps they estimated the age of the bones through carbon-dating procedures and were then able to write "onset of talking" in the right place on the evolutionary linguistic calendar.

It makes a nice story, but these things never happened. In two notable cases, investigators did try something paleontological, but with no clear result. In one attempt the physical evidence was the hyoid bone, a horseshoe-shaped structure from which the larynx passively hangs in the throat. Investigators digging around in an Israeli cave found a sixty-thousand-year-old hyoid that looks very much like a modern one. Unfortunately, as critics were quick to point out, mere physical similarity of this bone, without information about its position in the vocal tract, says little about the phonatory abilities of the Neanderthal owner. In related research, an attempt was made to date the appearance of the pharynx, the vertical chamber between the back of the tongue and the larynx. But a pharynx would have expanded only slightly the vocal repertoire of its bearers, the Cro-Magnons, who could have achieved a modern-sized vocabulary without one.

Since our species has no other bones that are dedicated to speech, it is unlikely that anyone is going to pinpoint the year that our ancestors began to speak a language. Some scholars speculate that language began at some time in the last hundred thousand years due to a dramatic rise in creativity—as revealed in art, complex technology, and the relics of religion—that occurred in that interval. Of course this argument, correct as it may be, tells us nothing about the preferred form or modality of language. But such hikes in creativity could, as alleged, reflect enhanced capacity for symbolic behavior, as would presumably have preceded or co-occurred with language.

Evolution can be cumulative, of course. When our hunting and gathering ancestors learned how to farm and make tools, they didn't lose the ability to hunt and gather. When our emotionally expressive progenitors developed the ability to convey complex information of an impersonal type, they continued to entertain, amuse, impress, and persuade. Anyone who thinks that the "pant hoot" is the exclusive province of the chimpanzee has never watched British MPs "discuss" parliamentary business.

Our species has acquired the ability to speak and think, and perhaps because of these advancements we consider ourselves "rational," but our behavior is still controlled by primordial dispositions. Grooming, as we have seen, is alive and well in contemporary humans. Emotional displays abound, with influence. Like monkeys and apes, we humans have alarming components in our vocalizations, signals that are apparently processed differently from other types of sound-making. The uniquely human rationality of which classical philosophers and psychologists were so proud is not our only way of being. To be sure, our behavior is sometimes guided by the "linear" thinking that underlies formal logic, but then we do things emotionally and impulsively and without conscious knowledge of our own motivation. It's interesting how much of this primordiality finds its way into our speech.

Thought for Food

If language has been with us for a relatively short time, our ability to learn multiple languages hasn't suffered for the lack of preparation.

Monolingual English speakers may be surprised to hear it, but most of the world's inhabitants speak more than one language or dialect, often three or four. Adults who know a half-dozen languages are not particularly rare and may not be unusually talented. When bilinguals work as interpreters, they monitor and mentally translate one language while uttering the sounds of the other. No wonder Steven Pinker referred to our species' capacity for language as an "instinct."

How did we get so good at language? I have suggested that we came by social sound-making and talking honestly, on the sweat of our ancestors' brows. It is a suggestion that requires no stretching or bending of accepted evolutionary principles, for these vocal behaviors could have been launched with little more than an increase in the motor control enjoyed by apes, with preserved sociality. But the oft-cited force behind linguistic evolution—group cooperation in hunting and defense—wouldn't seem to require more than several hundred words, and modern humans have rich vocabularies and complicated grammatical systems. Could social factors just as easily have heightened these more complex linguistic capabilities, too?

Some theorists have suggested that language, and therefore vocabulary, evolved to enable users to inform each other, that is, to pool their knowledge and discuss possible courses of action, enabling them to plan and thus cooperate more effectively. But the activities better done cooperatively by hominids—hunting, fishing, and self-defense—could have been accomplished with no more than several hundred words and a handful of impromptu gestures. And what about all the syntax? "Would it be a great advantage," asked David Premack, psychologist at the University of Pennsylvania, "for one of our ancestors squatting alongside the embers to be able to remark: 'Beware of the short beast whose front hoof Bob cracked when, having forgotten his own spear back at camp, he got in a glancing blow with the dull spear he borrowed from Jack'?"

If food procurement requires no more than the simplest of utterances, it is still conceivable that language somehow enhanced the survival of our ancestors individually. University of Hawaii's linguist Derek Bickerton has claimed that words and syntax made it easier to think about the things and actions that language represents and thus enabled those with a little knowledge of language to somehow out-think their less linguistically sophisticated competitors. I think it is theoretically less adventurous to suppose that language, as speech, enabled social work—allowed people to persuade others to do things—and that this increased fitness.

Even if thought were dependent on language—a dubious claim at best—our ancestors would have needed less language to sniff out and find food than to discuss all the people who comprise their complicated food-sharing networks, which means not just discussing who is stingy or generous but who is becoming self-important or jealous or unapproachable. This is doubly true of another critical area of daily living—the avoidance and resolution of conflict.

The voluminous word stores of contemporary speakers would thus seem to be no more a reflection of relatively modern needs to think and inform than ancient desires to impress and control, for our ancestors would have shared with us moderns a disposition to gravitate toward individuals displaying an elaborated, artful, almost magical use of verbal behavior.

Show Time

Don't hafta make whole buncha sense, long sounds pretty.   Teenage Afro-American girl quoted in Edith Folb, *Runnin' Down Some Lines*

Let's see how speech might actually have increased the fitness of our ancestors. Earlier we saw that members of oral cultures in Africa talk into the wee hours of the morning, telling stories, laughing, daring, putting down, arguing, and scolding. In the inner cities of America, young blacks freely exercise these same activities. Their repertoire of verbal styles includes rapping, shucking and jiving, copping a plea, gripping, and sounding (formerly known as "playing the dozens"). Each of these registers has its own distinctive form and function.

Rapping is probably the best known in the larger culture, largely because of a commercial musicalization of the raw verbal form that occurs on the street. Real rapping is a spoken narrative used to create a favorable impression at the beginning stages of a new relationship, in-

cluding a courtship. A black teenage boy from Los Angeles explained
that "yo' rap is your thing . . . like your personality. Like you kin style
on some dude by rappin' better 'n he do. Show 'im up. Outdo him
conversation-wise. Or you can rap to a young lady, you tryin' to impress
her, catch her action—you know—get wid her sex-wise." It must work.
A black teenage girl from the same part of Los Angeles said, "I likes to
hear a brother who knows how to talk. Don' hafta blow heavy, can sweet
talk you too. Don' hafta make whole buncha sense, long sounds pretty."

Shucking and jiving refer to a combination of talk and gesture that
"puts someone on" by giving a false impression. The others in the group
often know the true facts, however, so shucking and jiving are likely to
be regarded only as verbal play, with appreciation showed for the quality
of the act. Copping a plea and gripping are used to regain one's social
integrity following a loss of face.

Sounding is a stylized expression of aggression, occurring only in
crowds of boys or young men. It begins when one insults a member of
another's family, often his mother. Members of the "audience" make
sounds of disapproval, causing the insulted party to feel he must reply
with a similar slur on the protagonist's family. If the victim is able to
defend his honor, the attacker, verbally wounded, is under pressure to
articulate additional insults. This ritual continues until everyone is
bored or distracted, or the victim loses his temper and physically attacks
the tormentor. If this happens, the original tormentor wins in the eyes
of observers, both because of his artful verbal provocation and because
he became the unfortunate victim of an attack. The physically combative subject loses face both because he was unable to respond with the
same quality of verbal behavior and because he failed to restrict his
attacks to the verbal level.

When verbal performing is honed sufficiently, it becomes a talent and
an art. It is "Good Talking," as Roger Abrahams called it, a register
characterized by "ornamental diction and elaborated grammar and syntax." Over a half-century ago W. J. Cash wrote of the black speaker's
"remarkable tendency to seize on lovely words, to roll them in his
throat, to heap them in redundant profusion one upon another until
meaning vanishes, until there is nothing left but the sweet, canorous
drunkenness of sound, nothing but the play of primitive rhythm upon
the secret springs of emotion."

Good Talking is a *performance*. The audience's attention is held by the way the talker moves and sounds. Verbal skills allow black teenagers to "front off," that is, display their appearance, talents, and possessions. "The concept," said Edith Folb, "is very much like the dramaturgical notion of the persona—it is a mask, the personality you wear for the world to see and to react to; it is . . . closely aligned with the performancelike quality of the theater."

When we talk, all of us are "on" to some extent, and physiological measures reflect this. Perfectly normal people experience a significant rise in heart rate and blood pressure just by speaking or reading to a stranger on a subject relating to everyday life. Doing so incessantly can be hazardous to one's health. Men who monopolize and dominate conversations are at greater risk for premature death than their softly spoken equivalents, even when no more hostile.

What causes a bout of sound-making to be received as a performance? From where does the entertainment value and ultimately the social advantage of speech arise?

Verbal Plumage

In oral cultures, rank is earned by dazzling the assembled listeners and by attracting more. Good Talkers do this not with a thoughtful command of everyday language but with verbal *plumage*—mastery of a broad range of words and phrases, many of them outside the more limited repertoire of their audience. According to Joel Sherzer, the chant of Kuna leaders "is in an esoteric language, phonologically, morphologically, syntactically, and semantically different from ordinary Kuna. It is characterized by the use of metaphorical and allusive language." It is different enough that the chants must be translated by a spokesman, who puts them into more colloquial Kuna. Similarly, it has been estimated that three-fifths of the words used in the oral epics of people in northeastern Russia do not appear in everyday speech. The novelty is taken in stride. Indeed, it seems that lexical novelty may be part of the attraction.

And so it was in ancient China where the intellectual fringe met to debate current events, philosophy, and religion in a register called "Pure Talk." To succeed, Pure Talkers had to speak with wit and eloquence in a way that was "euphonious, elevated, and elegant." If defeated, the Pure Talkers had to restrain their tempers and act gracious, just as inner-city teens are supposed to if they lose at sounding.

None of this magical power of orality detracts from the role of language as a complex code for the transmission of thought. But language must be physically enacted, and in this sense it is, at its roots, a personally expressive way to fraternize and resolve conflicts. It is language that, as speech, performs social work, not with semantic precision but with fluency and timing and, in some circumstances, grandiosity.

What accounts for oral society's preoccupation with verbal skills? Why devote so much time to speech competitions of one kind or another? For insight let's consider the nature of daily life in the inner city. "Who you are (and very often how well you survive) depends . . . heavily on how well you talk," according to Folb. "Words," she said, "are tools for power and gain. . . . A good rap can save your life. It can also get you a woman (or man), money or other material things, and recognition and stature. All these 'commodities' are potentially purchasable through the power of words. Among teenagers who have limited access to capitalism and its payoffs, words buy you important things—and no one can take them away from you."

Plumage produces rank. Good Talkers tend to be group or community leaders. Geneva Smitherman noted that except for athletes and entertainers, "only those blacks who can perform stunning feats of oral gymnastics become culture heroes and leaders in the community." Likewise, in the telling of Limba tales, "the ability to 'speak' well is continually given as an essential quality of anyone with authority, especially a chief; without a chief, it is often said, there would be fighting and quarreling everywhere; and, in practice, chiefs do seem to spend a great deal of their time in formal speaking with and between their people." Much the same has been said of the Kuna, whose community leaders are verbal artists; the two—eloquence and leadership—are one and the same.

How does Good Talking lift one's rank? The deeper biological links have yet to be uncovered, but research indicates that people who are verbally dominant—either because they speak in long, multi-word sentences or hold the floor for long periods of time—tend to be perceived by their conversational partners as more powerful than those who produce shorter utterances. And this is no trivial connection, for having rank increases people's access to many of the things they might want.

I assume that verbal competition for status contributed to the expansion of lexical capacity, abetted by the parceling routines that produced individual speech sounds (phonemes), but how did ancestral eloquence with structurally simpler systems lead to modern-day levels of syntax? It seems likely that in evolutionary history, as in modern times, verbal facility enabled tribal leaders to persuade and entertain, and to achieve positions of leadership through those skills. But utterances could not proliferate beyond some modest limit without the services of a regulatory system. Such a system would dictate the proper form of words and the sequences in which they can occur. It would allow for creativity, in conformity with structural rules, and rapid decoding of the utterances of others. The system would permit these mental operations to occur effortlessly and automatically. It would be a grammatical system.

Effortless management of elaborate speech patterns would have required neural support, but no living being can manufacture new anatomical parts. Individuals can't even generate new neurons. So we must suppose that in the initial stirrings of linguistic life, some speakers were more verbally ornate and fluent than their peers, a superiority owing to more efficient appropriation of existing nonlinguistic mechanisms. Countless generations of selective mating in societies that increasingly valued orality as well as relationships and rank produced mechanisms that were increasingly specialized for language.

Even in the literate societies of today, community and business leaders are orally inclined. Successful businessmen spend much of their time orally presenting diverse types of information to groups, a disposition that surely helped them climb the organizational ladder in the first place, whether by verbally performing or vocally "pressing the flesh." To this day the chief executive officers of Japanese companies continue to eschew the e-mail systems used by subordinates.

In many governments, politicians who achieve exceptionally high office typically are men who look and sound good, regardless of what they believe or advocate. Indeed, in politics, eloquence and leadership are merging into one. W. J. Cash called rhetoric "the *sine qua non* of leadership" in the pre–Civil War American South. And there are obvious parallels here between the street corners of black Philadelphia neighborhoods and the House of Parliament, where British MPs debate but also tease, hoot, taunt, and put down their opponents before a crowd of jeering and cheering peers. Those who do well at this find themselves in line for even higher positions in government.

In American politics, according to Roderick Hart, rhetoric has overtaken action, has become synonymous with it. In his *Sound of Leadership*, Hart pointed out that "even if leaders know not which direction to take, they can still speak in public, thereby certifying an ability to at least search for leadership." The real reason Richard Nixon left office, according to Hart, is that rhetoric left him. "Even the impending impeachment proceedings," he suggested, "could have been 'toughed out' by Richard Nixon for months, if not for years, *if he could have found an argument* that would have satisfied *him* that he could have satisfied others. The public record shows that he never found such an argument. And so he stopped presiding soon after he stopped speaking."

The power of words was well known to Malinowski, who wrote that Trobriand islanders regarded verbal acts as a kind of magic capable of unleashing powerful forces that could ease a host of real-life dietary and social problems. At no more than a moment's reflection this may seem extremely odd, but are we progressive moderns so different? After World War II, Japan refused to apologize for its hostile actions against other nations and individuals. Although wave after wave of government officials expressed their "remorse," "regret," and need of "reflection," these words were considered insufficient, and demands for a stronger apology continued for half a century. Finally, on the fiftieth anniversary of the war's end, Japanese Prime Minister Tomiichi Murayama went on national television to offer his own "heartfelt apology." This more explicit or intense expression was immediately pronounced an improvement over previous declarations, thus presumably clearing the way to more harmonious relations between Japan and other nations. But many observers felt the apology should have come from the Japanese people as a whole (not just the prime minister) and should not have required a half-century wait. According to an article in the *Boston Globe*, "Fifty years of reluctant throat-clearing have left the depth of Japan's self-examination perhaps permanently in doubt."

The largely rhetorical nature of political life is revealed in many disparate cultures, from the Pure Talkers of ancient China to the "chattering classes" of modern England—those who are said to know about *caffe latte* and pine kernels. The speeches of the Maoris of New Zealand, according to Anne Salmond, convey little or no information, their purpose being "to keep an orator in the game without venturing his reputation, and to provide a frame for more adventurous attempts." If a Tshidi politician from the border of South Africa and Botswana were asked to describe his political career, observed John Comaroff, he "would usually do little more than recall a series of public speeches."

To the English, verbal jousting is jolly good sport. In the waning days of the most recent Tory government, the minister of agriculture, a gentleman with the unlikely name of Douglas Hogg, was the butt of numerous verbal assaults. Indeed, the "weekly Hogg-fight" was compared to a Spanish bullfight in which "Hogg is dragged to the chamber, where he snorts and stamps his feet." Then, "frontbench matadors and backbench picadors infuriate the beast by waving brightly coloured distractions and spearing him with spikey inquiries. . . . The Hogg maintains an air of jaunty and bellicose confidence, charging around the ring, bellowing and butting people. . . . After more than an hour of this sport the irrepressible Hogg, much fought but alive and kicking, departs."

Whether they know it or not, British MPs are only able to carry on so demonstratively for one reason: benefits accrued to the loquacious hominids who walked this earth scores of millennia earlier, vocally and verbally impressing, agitating, entertaining, persuading, and importuning. Natural selection acted on these verbal abilities, which now contribute to status, leadership, and diplomacy. Those who talked the best line were more likely to thrive and pass on whatever social genes, and ultimately linguistic ones, enabled us to confront verbally "the short beast whose front hoof Bob cracked."

A Way with Words

Some people have a way with words, and others not have way. Steve Martin

For verbal eloquence to have increased fitness, individuals would have had to vary in their verbal performance ability. They still do, but we members of information-oriented societies are probably less aware of differences in verbal ability than those living in exclusively oral cultures. When Ruth Finnegan listened to Limba storytellers, it was immediately obvious that some individuals were more skilled than others. The Limba people themselves commented on the differences "by referring to someone's intelligence or ability . . . in storytelling in such approving phrases as 'he knows how to utter stories' . . . or 'so-and-so knows how to speak.' " Marjorie Shostak commented that some !Kung story tellers are "more proficient" than others. The same is true of the Tikopia, who, according to Raymond Firth, "are very conscious of great individual differences in speaking quality." In some of the black cultures of America there are names for people who lack this aptitude. One of them is "lames," a word that also, not surprisingly, refers to those who are outside the in group.

Anthropological studies indicate that most Good Talkers have predominantly been young men, whether located in Sierra Leone, Madagascar, Philadelphia, or San Blas. In the Maori culture of New Zealand, women are allowed to introduce public speaking by calling and wailing, and to sing ancient songs as a "warm-up act" for the real (male) orators, but the women themselves are not permitted to speak. This is also true in the western highlands of Papua New Guinea, where women can decorate and dance but "are specifically debarred from engaging in the most prestigious forms of public decision-making and oratory." It is unknown whether men are actually better at this kind of speaking or just louder, but when Edith Folb tested black Los Angeles teenagers, she found the males superior in the recognition and use of vernacular vocabulary.

The reason for this sex bias may stem from the fact that men are more likely to physically hurt each other and therefore need ways to prevent physical combat. But this would not be the whole reason, for it is also rare for the women of oral cultures to engage in storytelling. Instead of taking the floor, Limba women "sit and listen, clap to show their respect and appreciation, or join in the chorus of the songs."

For decades, evidence has converged on a persistent verbal variation in our species—a developmentally swifter and ultimately greater linguistic facility in females. Of course, some qualitative verbal differences are also linked to sex. For example, in Anne Machung's study of women who operate office computers, it was found that talk centered less on the job than "on food, sex, and weekend plans, the conventional topics of office gossip. Unlike managers and supervisors, operators' talk is not embedded in language about routines and procedures, decision algorithms, and microprocessor capabilities, but rather in talk about each other—whom they get along with, whom they are friends with, whom they find difficult to interact with."

Deborah Tannen's writings have drawn attention to sex differences in intimate talking, as have nonscientific books such as John Gray's *Men Are from Mars, Women Are from Venus*. These differences have been affirmed in research. They have also long been evident to ordinary people, such as the married woman who said, "I'm not sure what I want. I keep talking to him about communication, and he says, 'Okay, so we're talking; now what do you want?' And I don't know what to say then, but I know it's not what I mean."

Just over twenty years ago Lillian Rubin wrote that when a woman talks to a man, "she relies on the only tools she has, the mode with which she is most familiar; she becomes progressively more emotional and expressive." The man, on the other hand, "falls back on the only tools he has; he gets progressively more rational—determinedly reasonable. She cries for him to attend to her feelings, her pain. He tells her it's silly to feel that way; she's just being emotional."

Sex differences do not stop with speaking styles, intentions, and topics. Analyses of nonverbal behaviors indicate that women tend to smile longer and more often than men. They also laugh more often, both during and in between speaking turns, and as we saw earlier, touch more often. In conversation women also spend more time gazing at their partner than males do, regardless of whether they're speaking or listening at the time.

Do females also talk more in general? Certainly this is the folk wisdom. I can recall from my youth television programs in which some harried or self-important husband is called at the office by his wife. Presumably she has phoned to complain about some domestic matter. Rather than direct his attention to the call, the man holds the telephone away from his ear while continuing to do his office work. In the background his wife is heard continuously squawking through the receiver. Periodically the man says "Yes, dear" into the mouthpiece and again removes the phone from his ear.

There are cultural factors that contribute to an impression of female verbosity. Many men seem to feel that the primary function of speech is to convey impersonal information. They rarely get together with other men in order to discuss their feelings. Men are likely to believe, therefore, that women are "not really saying anything" when they talk about theirs.

In Valloire, a small village in the French Alps, both men and women engage in social talking, but their behaviors are regarded rather differently. Men's talk, called *bavarder*, is "a friendly, sociable, lighthearted, good-natured, altruistic exchange of news, information, and opinion." Women's talk, called *mauvaise langue*, is "gossip, malice, 'character assassination.' " I suspect attitudinal differences such as these produce the impression that when women gather together with their female friends, they generate more words per legitimate thought than men do. If so, this would add to the impression that women are usually "wordy" or "gabby."

Putting cultural biases aside, what does research show regarding volubility? Certainly no evidence for the latter possibility is to be found in studies of mixed-sex conversations, for these reveal that men frequently interrupt more and hold the floor longer than their female partners. Some other studies seem to show that even in same sex conversations there is no greater female talkativeness or even a greater volubility on the part of males. But on closer inspection it becomes evident that these studies were usually highly contrived, with the topic, conversation partners, setting, and talking time prescribed by the investigator. When females are free to choose the listener and the subject, they usually engage in a more intimate brand of talking than their male counterparts, and it is in this vocal register that females usually take the lead.

And they do so across their life span. Young girls talk more than young boys. The sixteen hours each week that teenage girls in the United States spend just chatting with friends is precisely double the male chat time. Among adults there is also evidence of greater female volubility in face-to-face interactions with other females.

What accounts for the human female's greater preference for intimate talking? It has been suggested that whereas men historically had positions in the community and were able to earn what they needed, women lacked such positions and were therefore dependent on men. Women needed relationships in order to develop as individuals. They satisfied their own needs for wealth and position through their relationships with men, and achieved emotional support through relationships with other women. According to Penelope Eckert, influence without power requires moral authority, and this requires *symbolic* capital.

I think Sally Quinn, veteran observer and writer on the capital scene, would agree. She wrote recently that when Washington was forming there were just three ways that women could exert an influence. If a woman were married to a politician rich enough to have household servants, she could be a so-called political wife. Alternatively, she could run a boarding house or work as a prostitute. "There are elements of all three," said Quinn, "in what eventually evolved into the phenomenon of the Washington hostess, and for many decades to be a hostess was virtually the only way a woman could acquire power" in the city that Henry James called "the city of conversation."

Women have thus become "good" at the behaviors that earn and preserve social relationships, especially social and emotional talking. One recent study indicates that females, especially those who have experienced misfortune, derive greater emotional benefit from conversations with other females than males receive from talk with other males.

Such a culturally based explanation seems reasonable enough, but my own disposition has been to dig deeper. Among male primates rank is more closely associated with physical size than with family blood lines. But this is not true of the females. For them, rank is inherited from the mother. The daughters' own ranks are thus not evident on visual inspection and must therefore be broadcast by grooming and other social practices. Although alliances determine the outcome of rank-related interactions in both sexes, when females fight, the outcome rarely depends on the intrinsic strength of the contestants.

Just before I left Boston, I discussed these differences with my colleague at Harvard, Marc Hauser. We wondered if there were any parallels to these female volubility findings in nonhuman primates. If there were, we reasoned, culturally based explanations might be wrong, unless of course they converge with speculations generated by a model of "primate culture." It was easy for Marc to check, for he had done his doctoral research on vervet monkeys in Africa and in his thoroughness had recorded the rate of contact calls among female and male infants of three different ranks. Interestingly, Marc's data showed significantly higher rates of calling for females and a great many more calls for higher than for mid- and lower ranking animals.

Since monkeys are not known for their cultural learning, one is naturally suspicious that volubility differences between the sexes in our own species may be attributable to intrinsic variations in brain structure or chemistry. If so, it would not be surprising to find that language mechanisms in the human brain are larger or better developed in females. Some recent neuropathological research seems to support this. The researchers interpreted their results as the cause of a documented linguistic superiority in women, but of course this needs to be confirmed.

Mandibular Diplomacy

As we have seen, human language is broadly dualistic. It is a marvelous tool for the transmission of thought but no less valuable when it enables us to create and maintain social relationships and organize ourselves into productive groups. Peaceful groups. Recently Richard Wrangham and Dale Peterson documented the naturally homicidal nature of our closest primate cousin, the chimpanzee. It is clear that if we human primates began murdering each other at the same rate as wild-living chimps, we would never again know a moment's peace. Talking is among the human activities that prevent and defuse conflict.

We could debate whether the greatest benefit of language is the knowledge-sharing activities that have so conspicuously advanced our species—the inventions, the literature, the improvements in our ways of living—or the prevention of millions of daily conflicts in an extremely populous and competitive world. After all, our first "responsibility" as biological creatures is to keep existing, and this requires some measure of harmony and social stability. We do nothing to keep our biological commitments by building skyscrapers and supercomputers, and actually threaten our viability with the massive environmental changes produced by human progress—holes in the ozone layer, pollution, nuclear power —not to mention war on a massive scale.

Much of the world's talk is prophylactic, helping us keep from eradicating our species. In *Theatre of Power*, Raymond Cohen pointed out that the content of talk between nations may even be less important than the fact that they are talking at all. He gives as an example President Nixon's trip to China in 1972. Since the festivities were televised, the whole world got to see the leaders of the two nations talking, even though the viewers had no clue as to what they were talking about. In diplomacy, according to Cohen, "the contents of a message are sometimes less significant than the fact of its delivery."

In some societies several different talking practices have been worked out specifically to disentangle individuals from their disputes. As long as two nations are "talking" or "engaged in talks" the rest of us worry less that they are about to do each other in. Who could disagree with Winston Churchill's assessment that "jaw, jaw, jaw is better than war, war, war"?

If mandibular diplomacy is a recognized alternative to warfare, it follows that casual forms of talking such as chatting are unlikely to co-occur with acts of aggression. We would not expect a monkey to approach and begin to groom another animal and then, when in a strategic position, bite or swat the object of its manual affections. Likewise, we would not expect humans, *except as an act of deception*, to initiate talks at precisely the same moment that they launch an attack. This explains the outrage felt on December 7, 1941, when Japanese ambassadors arranged to meet with U.S. Secretary of State Cordell Hull while war planes were on their way to bomb Pearl Harbor. The two acts, talking and attacking, are simply inconsistent. The following day Mr. Hull specifically referred to this incongruity, the attack having come "at the very moment when representatives of the Japanese Government were discussing with representatives of this Government, at the request of the former, principles and courses of peace . . ."

In the next chapter I will show how intimate talking helps us kindle and fan the flames of personal relationships, fosters greater human endeavors, and does both of these things while facilitating the development of our selves.

FOUR

Lip Service

The organs of talking . . . are at least two normally associ-
ated human beings. John Rupert Firth, *The Tongues of Men*

Grooming, whether by the hands of an ape or the voice of a human, promotes personal relationships. With these may come a measure of predictability and trust, conditions favoring cooperation. As Harvard professor Robert Putnam observed, "Members of Florentine choral societies participate because they like to sing, not because their participation strengthens the Tuscan social fabric. But it does."

This is a lot of responsibility, even nobility, for behaviors as modest as delousing and gossip. And yet there is every reason to believe that their underlying motivation is frequently hedonic—the superficial enjoyment that comes from enacting relationships.

As do the other primates, we socially groom for pleasure. We chat to occupy ourselves, to pass the time of day. But in doing so we nonetheless contribute to a fund of goodwill that can be tapped later if and when the need arises. Of course, one piece of gossip won't turn the spigot of personal assistance. According to Cambridge ethologist, Patrick Bateson, members of a group must have been together for some time if mutual aid is to occur. "As familiarity grows," he said, "individuals come to sense the reliability of each other." When the requisite level of familiarity has been reached, support can be sought. And since each individual will usually enjoy multiple relationships, each may have networks of reciprocal associations that can be pooled and consolidated into coalitions. The two parties continue to exist as individuals, of course—each has his own rank and hard-earned reputation—but they are also linked to a network of socially related people. The links are maintained by nothing more complicated than self-disclosure and everyday gossip.

Talkin' 'bout People

People are talkin', talkin' 'bout people. I hear them whisper "You won't believe it."   "Something to Talk About," Shirley Elkhard

One thing that is importantly related to a person's character is his reputation. But clues to reputation are unlikely either to be "given off" or "given," to use terms favored by sociologist Erving Goffman. This informational shortfall—the blame for which must be shared equally by the face and voice—may be among the reasons for our almost irrepressible disposition to gossip, thus to supply facts that personal observation cannot.

No one is in the dark about what gossip is. When people do it, they pick apart the lives of other people. This seems naughty to those who were instructed in their youth never to say anything about others that they wouldn't like to hear others say about them. But there is a ready self-defense against the naughtiness charge. It was supplied by W. H Auden sixty years ago in a comment to a BBC radio audience. Avoiding gossip, Auden said, "is ridiculous and impossible."

The reason gossip is enjoyable—actually, the reason it's *possible*—is that all the participants know the individuals whose actions and reputations are under review. If Penelope Eckert is correct, people may even need to belong to a group just "to know how to gossip in it and to be allowed to." And although group members gossip for the pleasure, in doing so they negotiate community norms and identify themselves with those norms.

People gossip to achieve a feeling of intimacy, and at the same time they incidentally share information. But the activity can be beneficial even when the factoids are frivolous, misleading, or false. The veracity of the information may even be irrelevant, at least to the social benefit of gossip, which is more closely bound to process than content. In some cases of gossip, no information is exchanged about the topic whatsoever. Consider two Americans discussing Paula Jones's reasons for bringing suit against President Clinton. Whatever is known to one of the gossips is likely to be known by the other, since neither is acquainted with anyone that is familiar with Paula Jones, and both read the same tabloids. All they can do, then, is trade their opinions about the matter. If there is any information at all, it radiates from these personal views.

Where the gossips do know the "victim," playing it fast and loose with personal data can be dangerous business. In our species, reputation is linked to rank. A good one is difficult to create and easy to destroy. That is why it is illegal in the United States "to induce an evil opinion of one in the minds of right-thinking persons, and to deprive one of their confidence and friendly intercourse in society." And that is why in England it is against the law to say or write anything that "tends to lower another in the estimation of right-thinking members of society."

Recently an English physician, aided by five pints of Guinness on an empty stomach, blurted out in a pub that the youngest child of the manager's wife had been produced by artificial insemination, causing instant distress to her teenage daughter, who overheard the remark, as well as the husband and other children. The family's embarrassment was so acute that they abandoned their work at the pub to make a fresh start in a different business in another town. For his part, the doctor was banned from treating patients for up to three years.

Gossip can even be physically dangerous. One English woman was evidently driven to suicide by the vicious gossip of neighbors who ruined her reputation. The coroner's jury brought in the verdict "killed by idle gossip."

Its poor public image notwithstanding, gossip can helpfully inform participants if it conveys needed information about other people's bad and good reputations, thereby saving one from making socially or financially disastrous mistakes. How else are we to know that a particular mechanic charges too much for the work he does or that a dentist can be particularly rough or that a person to whom we are romantically attracted has an infectious disease? Without gossip, how can our youth know what kinds of behaviors their community considers extreme or inappropriate? How is the nongossiping person to avoid falling into a pattern of conduct that could lead to his own downfall?

There is an interesting reciprocity to gossip. When you tell a friend a piece of "juicy" gossip, the friend owes you a piece. I have known gossips to express irritation when they conveyed "secrets" to recipients who failed to lob equally "hot" information back to them. Gossip can be regarded as a gift, an intimate gift. It says, in effect, I know and like you well enough to share privileged information with you. When I tell you a secret that is known to few other people, I am expressing a willingness for our relationship to be intimate. But intimacy is a two-way street.

Full Disclosure

The same is true of self-disclosure, a form of gossip about one's self. When a friend tells you something about himself that, if revealed or mishandled, could hurt him, he has exposed his soft underbelly to you. He has shown that he trusts you, for if you cannot be trusted, why would he be handing you the very weapons that could bring him down? But trust is also reciprocal. If he chooses to disclose embarrassing or shameful facts about himself, it is implicit that you should share with him some equally intimate things. In doing so, a protective pact is achieved: if you tell his secrets and he finds out about it, he can tell yours.

One needs to know how and when to self-disclose. If a personal fact is revealed too near the beginning of a conversation, it will be difficult to interpret, possibly off-putting. A truly personal fact is something that "comes out" during an increasingly intimate conversation that inches its way in the direction of the fact, not something that is blurted out without an appropriate introduction.

Self-disclosure has a directionality that is biologically predictable. In a large, hierarchically organized group, people tend to disclose *upwardly*. In corporate life an employee is far more likely to divulge personal facts about himself to an immediate superior than the superior is to reveal intimacies to his subordinates. Children disclose more to parents, college freshmen more to seniors, and seniors more to professors than the other direction. The main exceptions occur when the two parties either don't care about or can't change their status. Self-disclosure is thus like grooming, where a lower-ranking animal grooms a higher-ranking one. It acts like deference, but insofar as it creates indebtedness and reciprocity, self-disclosure also resembles gossip.

These facts indicate that while we may not go up to the boss and pick lice off his body, when we do make our approach, we are careful to make the right buzzing noises with our mouths. We also do this when speaking French, Spanish, or any number of other languages that use one set of pronouns for people who are unfamiliar, older, or otherwise deserving of our respect, and a different set when addressing a family member or close friend.

Mode of address also reflects recognition of rank differences among members of the human tribe. Thirty years ago members of a large insurance corporation in San Francisco were surveyed to see which ones were called by first names and which ones were addressed by title and surname. It was found that all members of the corporation called their fellow workers and subordinates by first names. But in just over one-fourth of the cases, the boss was addressed by title and surname, an incidence that escalated to over 80 percent for the boss's boss. Titles were preferentially extended to those with superior status.

Laughable Relationships

When it comes to rank, people tend to use humor in much the same way as they greet and disclose. Years ago Rose Coser, a sociologist at Harvard Medical School, recorded all the intentionally humorous remarks made during staff meetings at a psychiatric hospital near Boston.

Coser's most salient finding was that humor tends to be expressed down-wardly. Senior psychiatrists directed humorous remarks at the junior staff more than anyone else. Less commonly, they poked fun at the patients and themselves. When junior psychiatrists took a stab at humor, they directed it at patients predominantly and much less often at other junior staff (or themselves) and senior staff. Predictably, on neither of the occasions that junior staff made witty remarks about senior staff were those potentates actually present.

Laughing is an inherently social behavior. It is rarely done in solitude, except in muted form, perhaps while reading or recalling an earlier experience. Whether the result of intended humor or not, laughter often works like gossip. It decreases distance between individuals and acts as an invitation to respond reciprocally. The humorous "material" derives its laugh-producing potential from personal or situational facts that are shared by the participants. The speech that provokes laughter is *not necessarily funny*, at least when excerpted from the situation in which it occurred. Neuroscientist Robert Provine commented that "most pre-laugh dialogue is like that of an interminable television situa-tion comedy scripted by an extremely ungifted writer."

Not only does the conversation not have to be amusing per se, but there need not be a conversation or even a "situation" for there to be laughter. It occurs contagiously—the mere sound of laughter can induce people to laugh. I once had dinner with Provine and two other neurosci-entists. At one point Bob pulled out a "laugh box" and put it on the table. The rest of us looked skeptically at the box. Bob activated it. And when the tinny, not even natural human sound of laughter arose from the box, one of us began to giggle and another snorted. And in a snigger I understood why television sitcoms used laugh tracks for so many years.

Once a whole village got the giggles. The year was 1962, the place was Tanganyika, now Tanzania. The event—a bout of contagious laugh-ter—lasted six months. It was set in motion not by a laugh-box but by real, live teenage girls, their laughter rapidly spreading throughout the village as well as adjacent communities.

Another type of bonding talk, at least among the male members of some social classes, is the feigned insult. When two old friends meet each other, one may call the other "an old son of a bitch" or similar term of endearment, perhaps while giving him a playful cuff on the jaw. This pseudo-aggressive display sends a message—that the insulting individual believes and is seeking to remind the other individual that they share a personal relationship so close that offense is not expected to be taken. Sixty years ago the Tallensi, a group of people living on Africa's Gold Coast, used insults to keep the boundaries between clans in good repair. When a man from one clan happened upon a woman of a different clan, according to Meyer Fortes, the observing anthropologist, "they abuse[d] each other with impunity, in such terms as 'you ugly thing' . . . or 'you good for nothing' . . . or some similar objurgation. Spoken in anger, these are deadly insults. Between joking partners, who shout them out with mock seriousness, they arouse only a roar of laughter."

In Talk We Trust

When I was growing up in South Dakota . . . I was the only kid in town who didn't plan to stay there and farm. . . . I had the silly notion that I wanted to learn more about farming so I went on to the university. I became the town scholar. The local political party chairman even helped me get a scholarship. Later on, when I got into a protest thing at the college, I was able to help get the thing settled because I knew a lot of the politicians personally. Some of them were my cousins. . . . But now I am a big professor working for social issues in the state of New York. I don't know the people I have to work with. It is hard to find someone to trust. When someone agrees with me, I don't know why. I don't know who is loyal and who isn't. Sometimes I think it was easier when people knew me better than they knew the problem. Anonymous American professor, quoted in G. M. Phillips and N. J. Metzger, *Intimate Communication*

Decisions about what to do and when and with whom to do it require reliable information. When we are thinking about buying a used car and the owner tells us the vehicle runs perfectly or that he drove it only at low speeds, we scan for evidence of truthfulness. When a physician approaches us after running diagnostic tests, we look at his face to see if there is any news we would rather not hear. When a person with whom we are romantically involved tells us that we alone matter, we listen and look for vocal and facial confirmation. We are ever scanning the emotional landscape for cues that tell us it's okay to trust.

Trust is like the air we breathe—it's basic to all human activities, so basic that the distinguished Harvard legal scholar Charles Fried declared that "in the end we pursue it for its own sake." A feeling of trust enables individuals to do things on their own—accept a date, buy a car, hire a house painter—or act in concert with others, whether as members of a small ad hoc working group or a stable community.

A community is no trivial thing. A well functioning one is alive with acts of kindness and helpfulness, some palpably real and others latent potentials waiting to be activated. This reserve of goodwill makes possible the things that civic communities do: clean up neighborhoods, pave streets, upgrade water systems, build shelters for the homeless, provide scholarships to promising young students.

What are the primal bases of trust and cooperation? In the other primates, competition for limited resources and protection from predators are facilitated by alliances. Maintaining these relationships requires that they convene on a regular basis. But the immediate or proximal reason for socializing is not because it will further the relationships; they come together because doing so is pleasurable.

This is not to say that our primate cousins never socialize strategically. Recently, Ronald Noë and Redouan Bshary reported that two different species of Ivory Coast monkey, the red colobus and the diana, are more likely to congregate during the hunting season of their natural predator, the chimpanzee, than the other three seasons of the year. But they don't just drift toward each other. The red colobus, which for some reason is the more frequently attacked of the two, usually seeks the company of the dianas. In an experimental phase of the study, tape recordings of chimpanzee "loud calls" caused loitering members of the two monkey species to assemble; if already together, they remained so more often than when there was silence or inanimate sounds.

Like monkeys, we humans also have reasons for socializing and even have a distinct need to do so for its own pleasurable and spiritual merits, quite apart from our need to avoid getting into trouble. We "chew the fat" without ulterior motivation. This was what Robert Putnam was saying when he suggested that Italians who play in musical groups incidentally find themselves in a position of familiarity and trust, with an unintended potential for other types of cooperative action should the need arise.

A great deal of social capital is created intentionally. We create familiarity or indebtedness knowing that doing so may produce the possibility of cooperation or assistance in the future. We know the rules—"I scratch your back, you scratch mine"—according to which, wrote James Coleman, a good deed creates "an expectation in A and an obligation on the part of B. This obligation can be conceived as a credit slip held by A for performance by B. . . . These credit slips constitute a large body of credit that A can call in if necessary."

If we are nursing along an old Volvo, we take particular note when we learn that the man moving in next door works at the Volvo dealer's service department. A gift or an act of kindness, perhaps an invitation to dinner, may be extended in the hope that a feeling of indebtedness will ensue. Scratch a social relationship between normally strategic human beings, and you may find an "exchange relationship" underneath. In such a relationship, "friends make gifts," according to Marshall Sahlins in *Stone Age Economics*, and "gifts make friends. . . . Material flow underwrites or initiates social relations."

Networking

Consider the food sharing of !Kung hunter-gatherers. In 1968 when food was plentiful in Botswana and Namibia, no more than 45 percent of their social calls were to people residing more than thirty kilometers away. In 1974 when there was a severe food shortage, the !Kung suddenly became very interested in family members who lived beyond their immediate area; 85 percent of their visits involved treks from thirty to two hundred kilometers from home.

Those walks paid off. The reason is that the !Kung have an efficient mechanism for distributing risk. That mechanism is a highly developed

social network (called a "hxaro") based on mutual reciprocity. To join
or create a hxaro, a person gives something of value to an older relative.
After some reflection, the recipient may respond by providing the donor
with a similar gift. This and other such exchanges produce a tight
relationship. When either party is lacking or needs something, that
party can go to the other. In time, today's "haves" become tomorrow's
"have nots," and the process reverses.

To the naive observer, the !Kung might seem lazy. After all, they only
spend about twelve to fifteen hours per week actually procuring and
preparing food, and much of the remaining time is dominated by discussions of "who had what and did or did not give it to whom." One is thus
tempted to conclude that the !Kung are "gossipy," but if such discussions are gossip, they represent a strikingly non-idle brand of it. One
can think of few important uses to which the !Kung could put their
knowledge of language. By verbally maintaning hxaros, the !Kung keep
food in the bank, to be withdrawn when there is little to hunt and
gather.

Like the other primates, we humans are also aware—though perhaps
at a higher level of consciousness—of the need to avoid certain kinds of
difficulties and the need to secure for ourselves certain kinds of help.
We know we lack the personal autonomy to go around thumbing our
noses at people who could help us if assistance were needed. At work
we cannot be too difficult to get along with if we value our job, and
most of us cannot afford to live without a steady flow of remuneration.

Individuals who are aware that they live in an imperfect world, a
world of inherent dangers and stresses, see reasons why assistance might
occasionally be needed. To assure that option, they engage in social
behaviors that promote familiarity and, with it, trust and reciprocity
that can be activated in the future.

Consider those who live remotely in severe climates. My parents
reside in Marquette, Michigan, a city of about thirty thousand that is
located on the shores of Lake Superior. Although there are several
smaller towns a dozen miles away, Marquette is extremely isolated from
the population centers that lie hundreds of miles "downstate." Conse-
quently most of the people who live in Marquette also work there. Once
a thriving mining center, the area has long been economically depressed.
The winters are extremely long, bitterly cold, and snowy—over twenty
feet of snow has fallen in the last few winters.

Under circumstances such as these it would not be surprising if Marquette residents thought they were "all in this together," and, indeed, they do give this impression. There is a fair amount of local pride, and there are many social networks that stand ready to assist those in need. There are civic groups and churches that are prepared, even eager, to play a part should a person or family fall on hard times. And as we Lockes have learned from hardships within our own family, many of the individual residents of Marquette are also ready to do so. Some of this helpfulness is undoubtedly attributable to a pace of living that invites unhurried socialization, but when I visit, I also pick up an underlying perception that alliances are necessary.

Marquette and many other small towns in America are not rich. Wages run a bit lower than elsewhere. Homes appraise less expensively. Paradoxically, the people of Marquette are loaded with capital—social capital. Unlike physical capital, which you keep in your wallet, and human capital, which resides in the skills and knowledge of individuals, social capital is less tangible still, for as Coleman said, "It exists in the *relations* among persons."

An economic term like "capital" is not a misnomer. We can pay strangers to do things for us, or we can ask friends to do things for us. But the latter is an option only if we have friends who can be, or perhaps even expect to be, asked. If we have done enough for them, they may even be relieved that we are requesting their help or offended if we fail to do so. The likelihood of their being helpful may even exceed that of the hired strangers who fail to show up because our job was considered too small, too difficult, or too untimely.

There is, of course, a sense in which the conjunction of the terms "social" and "capital" may make us feel uncomfortable. Many of us work for money, so we certainly would be justified in thinking that our employer owes us our salaries and wages. But do our friends *owe* us favors? On one level we may think they do, at least if we have done favors for them. But if it is a warm, personal friendship, a favor is not something that we would *demand* like an overdue payment from our employer.

Still, social capital is real. Intimate talking promotes the development of social support systems and thus the buildup of social capital. When people discuss everyday life situations, they find out about their friends' views, values, and personal characteristics. This knowledge permits them to gauge the likelihood that friends will panic in a crisis or, alternatively, be there for them in time of need.

In today's economic climate, there is stiff competition for scarce resources. Adaptive business people do just what their evolutionary ancestors did: they band together. This competitiveness has produced a series of alliances or "governance structures" in which individual firms are held together by an incomplete contract. Recent years have seen dramatic increases in alliances in several different fields of business, especially information technology.

As popular as alliances have become, businesses are not quick to give up their independent status. According to Benjamin Gomes-Casseres, a firm will use an alliance only when it must, "when a weakness in its internal capabilities makes collaboration attractive, or when it is forced by governments or powerful rivals. Either way, the firm seeks help because it cannot go it alone." But of course, this is the one sure path to survival, as over six hundred firms in the United States have discovered.

Stocks and Stones

The trust that is required by business is no less dependent on familiarity than personal trust. Personal relationships and trust have played a prominent role in several industries, ranging from construction to book publishing, architecture, and filmmaking, but they have been indispensable to the wholesale diamond markets. When negotiating the sale of diamonds, merchants frequently entrust each other with bags of stones to examine in private, with no assurance that inferior versions will not be returned in place of the originals. The stones may be worth hundreds of thousands of dollars, but without this free exchange, the market would operate much less efficiently. Now, you ask, what keeps diamond merchants from cheating? Fear of going to jail? Enormous fines? Threat of bodily harm? The correct answer is none of the above. Cheating is prevented by invisible social mechanisms that were put in place thousands of years before the transaction. For if a diamond merchant ever substituted cheaper stones or stole diamonds that were in his temporary possession, he would destroy himself and his family, and religious and community ties would dissolve.

Dealing with fairly small or stable networks of business people makes good economic sense. "The widespread preference for transacting with individuals of known reputation," said Mark Granovetter, "implies that few are actually content to rely on either generalized morality *or* institutional arrangements to guard against trouble." They have the security of knowing that cheating will incur a cost they could never repay—irreparable damage to their reputation. Often, this offers greater security than a contract. Indeed, as Pierre Bourdieu pointed out, "It would be insulting to presume to authenticate a transaction based on trust between trustworthy people."

One might suppose that the more personable ways of doing business are abandoned when the cost of a mistake is measured in millions of dollars. On Wall Street, for example, one would think that trading relies heavily on computers, or people using computers, so that buy and sell decisions are reached on only the most dispassionate financial grounds and the most equitable personal ones. These commonsense suppositions would be wrong. Electronic trading is becoming more frequent, but buying and selling still utilize traditional methods of floor trading. In London the "open outcry" is considered the most efficient method of buying and selling stocks available. And although the cost of stocks and bonds is influenced by supply and demand, prices also reflect the relationships and the social behaviors of the buyers and sellers.

If you have visited a stock exchange, you know why. In an atmosphere reminiscent of a Mexican cockfight, the traders, who maneuver themselves in a pit, engage in face-to-face, shout-to-shout "combat" as they scream out their orders. It resembles an auction being held by dozens of auctioneers instead of one. Screams are often accompanied by hand signals and other types of body language. But it gets even more interpersonal than that. It gets conspiratorial.

Just ask newly enfranchised stock traders. One veteran broker said, "We call them the carp, the boat people. The old-timers have the rights, or so they feel; it's a kind of territoriality." And they exercise their rights with the "first" rule. According to this rule, the first person to yell out his response to an offer is entitled to the entire volume that has been offered, at the offering price. Although competitors may want the stocks, they cannot, by the first rule, preempt the person who responds first. But this is one place where prejudice against newcomers is revealed. For even though a newcomer may be the first to respond, the stocks may go to a slower but older member of the club. It can be a great way to reciprocate for past favors.

Obviously, personal relationships are helpful in ordinary types of sales as well. Salesmen pass along gossip about competitors, shortages, and price increases to their favorite purchasing agents, said University of Wisconsin law professor Stewart Macaulay, and if they fail to satisfy their customers, they become the subject of gossip themselves. Similar relationships occur in business and government. Corporate foreign language teacher Richard Lewis has said that the corridors of economic and political power in Brussels "reverberate with gossip." European countries that lack access to this privileged information are severely disadvantaged.

The need for trust is one reason that success in business is so often the result of socialization; employees ride into managerial positions on the backs of associations and friendships—what are pejoratively called "connections." It isn't really "who you know" so much as who trusts you.

It has long been said that you have to spend money to make money, and it costs something to set up trusting relationships. Business managers join more than their share of clubs and societies. But as Edward Lorenz said, "While trust is costly, lack of trust is more costly still." George Mason University professor Francis Fukuyama agrees. You cannot have an "arm's-length relationship with either customers or suppliers," he said. "You've got to have an intimate relationship that grows over years."

In London, the spoken word has weighed in heavily, even on the stock exchange. "The visitor in the City is impressed by the absolute confidence placed in the spoken word," wrote Joseph Wechsberg in *The Merchant Bankers* in 1966, "A lot of work is done with very little paperwork." In Japan personal relationships greatly influence business, and agreements may bypass language altogether. Many "contracts" are not written and are essentially nonverbal. The reason, according to Masao Kunihiro, is the "almost abnormal concern about how what one says will affect the other person, whose feelings one tries to surmise without being told." The contracts based on oral agreements usually consist of a few understandings, some exceptions to those understandings, and an escape clause that says something like "All other problems will be settled through consultation." Perhaps these cultural differences are the reason that there supposedly are fewer lawyers in all of Japan than there are in Washington, D.C.

This avoidance of written contracts is linked to the fact that Japan is occupied by a single ethnic group that has spoken the same language throughout its history. In other words, the people of Japan are remarkably alike, with a common lifestyle and a high level of mutual understanding. There is less need of memoranda because communication is technically impossible if both parties already know the same things and have the same beliefs. In traditional Japan, a contract needed to say little more than "Disagreements will be handled in the usual way."

Such a "contract" would seem pretty odd in relation to the morass of fine print now necessitated by diminishing familiarity in the United States, Britain, and many other diversely populated nations. Americans and Britons are no longer insulted by voluminous contracts. In fact, it is getting harder to insult us at all. Defamation suits are down from colonial American days when slander litigation could be triggered merely by verbally lowering one's reputation. Nowadays, many people don't even *have* a reputation.

Unfortunately, things are getting worse. The reason is that we are losing our personal voices.

FIVE

De-Voicing

> People are becoming an endangered species. Just try to find
> one on most switchboards, where recorded voices take callers
> through a mine field of "operations," usually ending in an
> answering machine or, worse, back to the beginning. Try
> to find a human at the gas pump or in the elevator or a
> hundred other places where they used to roam free. Things
> have gotten so bad that some consumers go inside their
> banks and cash checks just to have a conversation.
>
> The Boston Globe, May 1, 1995

Free speech is cherished in America, but citizens are now having to
settle for a more expensive brand. In June 1995, teller rationing was
begun by the First National Bank of Chicago. This practice effectively
limits interactions with a live employee of the bank. Now anyone who
attempts to talk to a teller is charged $3.00. In the flapper era early in
the century, they used to call out "ten cents a dance." As the century
ends, the analogous call seems to be "three bucks a chat."

In our modern, complex societies we are suffering from a social form
of progressive aphonia. That is, we are losing our personal voices. During a period in which feelings of isolation and loneliness are on the rise,
too many of us are becoming emotionally and socially mute. Just when
we need to reverse rising levels of distrust by achieving greater familiarity, we are becoming increasingly still. Both statistics and personal testimony disclose the extent of this problem.

The disposition to express one's self vocally is incredibly powerful—so powerful that it even occurs, as we saw earlier, in the congenitally deaf—so we may suspect immediately that if the voice is slipping, there must be a phalanx of powerful forces working against it.

Urbanization

The world's longest acting vocal suppressant has undoubtedly been urbanization. About eight thousand years ago, small bands of humans began to expand into "impersonal super-tribes," according to Desmond Morris. With this expansion, he said, "compassion, kindness, mutual assistance, a fundamental urge to cooperate within the tribe . . . came under pressure and began to break down."

Before urbanization, our ancestors lived in small groups. Each person knew all other persons. What this was like many urbanites can only guess, but I do have a guess. I spent much of my youth in a heavily forested area of northern Wisconsin, several miles from a town of about one thousand residents. When I went to town, I often had the experience of recognizing everyone I saw. I knew their names. We waved at each other and smiled or stopped to speak. When I went away to college, none of the people from my hometown came with me, and yet I found myself habitually scanning faces of passersby as I walked down the street, expecting to recognize someone. Several years of urban life did little to discourage this deep-seated expectation.

Like us moderns, our tribal ancestors' capacity to store and process faces would have been sufficient to recognize everyone they encountered ten times over. As our species grew, people began to live in small communities that brought or held people together because of a commitment they shared. Each resident of these communities had a well defined identity, a niche. Every person had continuous confirmation of his "self."

In these communities people didn't need to issue a lot of formal news-laden statements. Their associates usually knew many of the same things. It was like that on the Trobriand Islands as recently as 1914. When two islanders meet, observed Malinowski, "they know infinitely more, and more precisely, all about what they are going to do, what the other one feels, thinks, etc., than when two Europeans meet."

Our ancestors had as much in common as the Trobriand islanders. They would have known, or could have assumed, a great deal about each other. Their conversations would have dealt less often with novel facts than personal emotions. But the groups got larger, and the members grew less familiar. "It was this change," according to Morris, "the shift from the personal to the impersonal, that was going to cause the human animal its greatest agonies in the millennia ahead. As a species we were not biologically equipped to cope with a mass of strangers masquerading as members of our tribe." William Wordsworth reacted to this at the turn of the nineteenth century, shortly after visiting London for the first time. "Above all," he said, "one thought baffled my understanding, how men lived even next-door neighbours, as we say, yet still strangers, and knowing not each other's names."

Literacy

A second foe of vocal intimacy was the printing press. Literacy made it possible to exchange massive amounts of information without ever seeing other human beings. Our ancestors could not experience another person without that person being around. By releasing modern humans from those constraints, literacy did a great deal to still our voices. Much of the business that is now carried out, even social business, is conducted in print. Yesterday's interlocutor is missing.

Printed language is, of course, an extraordinarily efficient medium. Its benefits include almost every significant thing our species has ever studied, invented, built, explored, taught, created, or shared with others. Without literacy we would still be lurching along in a massively disorganized collection of overgrown ancestral villages. Literacy works so well that we can go for long periods of time without speaking. As a professor I spend a lot of time writing messages on my computer and electronically propelling them to colleagues—some of them across the street, others across the world. Although I lecture and supervise research, I spend more time reading and writing than listening and talking.

America is a world leader in many areas, for better or for worse, and de-voicing is no exception. At the turn of the nineteenth century, America was a rural society. New York City had a population of sixty thousand. In New England the larger villages had fewer than fifteen hundred inhabitants. Most people lived in or near small groups and knew many of their fellow citizens. Very few individuals could read or spent much time doing it. Most of what they wanted to know could be communicated orally. They already knew how to farm. They made their own clothes, provided their own food, and were able to fabricate a wide variety of objects.

Throughout the nineteenth century, literacy spread. But for all the mind-expanding discoveries that followed, there were also concerns, because when people began to express themselves in writing, it was quickly recognized that the Who System had never trained on, and didn't naturally work for, arbitrary movements of the fingers. And these concerns gave rise to graphology, a serious program of study intended to enhance one's ability to "read" the personality of cursive writers. During the 1870s a Frenchman named Abbé Michon published two "how-to" books on the subject, founded the Société de la Graphologie, and edited the journal *Graphologie*. A decade later American handwriting expert Daniel T. Ames warned that the would-be deceiver could no more conceal his unique and unconscious writing habits from graphologists than he could disguise his personal identity "by drawing up his nose, squinting his eyes, or walking with a limp."

Thanks to the supremacy of print, the typical member of progressive societies now reads thousands of words every day, all of them "carefully edited in advance," according to Alvin Toffler. Many thoughts that would once have been spontaneously uttered are now expressed in formal writing, undoubtedly in a somewhat different form. One can scarcely imagine a more significant factor in the stilling of our social calls.

The seeds of this graphic primacy were planted just over a thousand years ago. The ancient oracles were honored for their command of oral language, but new respect was shown for those who could express themselves in writing, and in printed language itself. The bias continues today. When we engage in business, we are told by consumer protection agencies to "get it in writing." In the courtroom the most valued observers are *eye*witnesses, the least favored form of evidence is "hearsay."

Atomization: The Rise of the Individual

Throughout the nineteenth century the literacy rate of America kept climbing as the country continued to populate. Between 1800 and 1830 the population of New York City grew from sixty thousand to two hundred thousand. Immigration and relocation in the present century has further increased diversity and unfamiliarity. After World War II, ownership of homes increased, suburbs formed, commuting intensified, and people began to isolate themselves in homes with television sets and other private amusements.

The pace of life picked up. Business interactions became more efficient and less chatty. My father was born in a small village just after the turn of the century. Through most of his adult life he has evinced, to his son's occasional embarrassment, a disposition to engage waitresses, clerks, and other unfamiliar service personnel in casual conversation. One would think he is either lonely or gregarious. Only the latter is true, but I think that in "his day" an interaction with another person, unfamiliar or not, was inherently sociable. Business was not separate from sociality; the two flowed together.

Even those who use toll-free numbers ostensibly to order goods from mail-order catalogues "often want more than a new shirt or sweater," according to Susan Dilworth, a telephone order-taker for L. L. Bean in Maine. She said that "a lot of people call and say, 'I'm coming to New England for the first time. How should I dress?' Other callers order merchandise but then begin talking about their personal lives. I think they're lonely."

If our species has had the capacity to speak for one hundred thousand years, we are beginning to do something different as the hundred and first linguistic millennium draws to a close—as we commence living in the "Information Society." Something has changed about the ways we use language in our personal lives. Within the oral language domain, intimate talking has been edged out by news bulletins. Our sentences are increasingly swollen with facts. Spontaneity has taken a plunge. The emotional warmth has gone out of speech.

My father grew up before the precipitous rise of the scripted world, before the "coded messages," as Toffler called them, "that have been artfully fashioned by communications experts." In Dad's youth, people believed what they were told by government officials and trusted what they read in the papers. He turned thirty-three just a month before a defining event. It was Halloween, 1938, and thousands of American innocents were truly panicked by a gripping radio report of an "invasion from Mars." Listeners prayed, fled in their cars, warned neighbors, and clogged telephone lines. Many were treated for shock. The next morning they learned that the previous evening's "news" was completely made up, the product of H. G. Wells's imagination via the voice of Orson Welles. Apologies were offered by the network for abuse of the medium. Studies conducted afterward indicated that no one, regardless of his social and educational class, was immune to panic reactions, including two geology professors at Princeton University who went out looking for a Martian meteor that was reported to have landed nearby.

Viewed from a contemporary standpoint, this level of gullibility verges on the clinical, but these perfectly normal people were our parents and grandparents, living in a different time. Now, several generations later, it is the behavior of us moderns that requires explanation. It is we who have been exposed to decades of biologically unnatural experience. Live radio and television dramas are at most a distant memory, replaced long ago by carefully edited and painstakingly rehearsed programming and a host of staged "pseudo-events." As "Candid Camera" informed us, we now think gullibility is amusing. As "TV Bloopers" reveals, we are intrigued by the perfectly normal slips of the tongue that occur when media stars tape their weekly sitcoms. "Real life" has become a condition. The digerati even have a special code name, "IRL," for things that occur "in real life."

An America that was already heavily fractionated decades ago is steadily breaking into still smaller pieces. The United States is atomizing— citizens are drifting away from each other—and we cannot expect that watching the same network television programs, eating at the same chain restaurants, and staying overnight at the same coast-to-coast motels will do anything about it. Much the same thing is occurring in Britain and other European nations, and symptoms are appearing in Asia.

The signs of atomization abound. They appear in unlikely places, such as the bumper-stickers of Prince George's County, Maryland, on the northeast rim of Washington, D.C. In a study of these stickers (mentioned earlier), it was found that economic and racial groups differed sharply, almost categorically, in the ways they present themselves. Rather than finding that social mobility had blurred class differences, the authors were forced to interpret their data as evidence of "social fragmentation and isolation."

Businesses have a commercial stake in atomization. As Joseph Turow demonstrates in *Breaking Up America*, there's big money in social fragmentation. By recognizing and amplifying our natural divisions—media-generated "image tribes"—businesses are able to target advertising to specific groups, a far more effective practice than beaming commercials vaguely to the purchasing populace at large.

There's plenty for paid atomizers to work with. In the mid-seventies, a data-crunching entrepreneur named Jonathan Robbin fed zip codes, census data, and consumer surveys into a computer. The machine spit out forty "lifestyle clusters," each having a set of moral values, purchasing habits, and political beliefs that was almost as distinct as the boundaries of the corresponding zip codes. A decade later, Michael Weiss described these minicultures in his book, *The Clustering of America*. Weiss pointed out, for example, that while "the wealthiest blue-collar suburbs" comprise the largest cluster, the Blue-Chip Blues, "upscale urban high-rise districts" comprise the smallest one, the Urban Gold Coast. Remarkably, each of America's 36,000 zip codes corresponds to one of these clusters, occasioning the observation that we are where we live.

Between clusters there is as much variation in the television we watch as the food we eat, cars we buy, books we read, and candidates we vote for. Kmart couldn't be more popular with the Shotguns & Pickups ("crossroads villages serving the nation's lumber and breadbasket needs") but it is disdained by the Young Influentials ("yuppie, fringe-city condo and apartment developments"). Similar differences are found among those who eat croissants, watch public television, bowl, and book passage on cruise ships. We are the brand names of America, outwardly defined by the things we buy and consume.

When we peer inside the clusters, of course, the diversity narrows, at least superficially. Here, finally, we find that co-members "tend to lead similar lives," said Weiss, many "driving the same kinds of cars to the same kinds of jobs, discussing similar interests at similar social events—cocktail parties here, backyard barbecues there, stoop-sitting elsewhere." Homogeneity is to be found in America—or perhaps, more accurately, in the forty brands of America. And this is reinforced and targeted, as Turow demonstrated, by the marketeers.

As much as these similarities group us, they don't reflect group membership. Much of the "membership" we enjoy within our zip codes is primarily on paper, a statistical artifact of economic factors such as housing prices and proximity to places of employment. Many cluster members would be at least a little surprised to know that they share values and behaviors with their neighbors. That one might belong to a coherent social entity, might experience a feeling of belonging, is no longer high on our list of expectations. Except for our desire to get along with the people at work, what matters to most of us moderns is who we are. This necessitates some interest in others, of course, but mainly because self-appraisal is inherently relational.

Our present individualism got off to a roaring start in colonial America. Before that, according to Alexis de Tocqueville, the Europeans "did not have the word 'individualism,' which we have coined for our own use, because in their time there was indeed no individual who did not belong to a group and who could be considered as absolutely alone." And yet fifty years earlier a feeling of personal uniqueness was described by one of the more distinguished of de Tocqueville's countrymen, Jean-Jacques Rousseau; he wrote that "I am made unlike anyone I have ever met; I will even venture to say that I am like no one in the whole world. I may be no better, but at least I am different."

More than a century later, Americans "marched to their own drummer" and "did their own thing," emboldened by books called *Pulling Your Own Strings, Looking Out for Number One,* and *How to Be Your Own Best Friend.* "I gotta be me," people said. In *Individualism Reconsidered,* sociologist David Riesman argued that individuals should be encouraged "to develop their private selves—to escape from groupism." He needn't have bothered; Americans require no words of encouragement.

America is now brimming with individualists. Our "ideology of individualism," wrote Richard Goodwin back in the early seventies, "is so powerful that we still look on bonds as restraints; on values as opinions or prejudices; on customs as impositions. The remaining structures of shared existence—the times that make it possible for people to live with and through, and not merely alongside, one another—are assaulted as

unjust obstacles in the way of liberty, as impediments to the free asser-
tion of the self."

Ironically, Americans are afraid of the very conditions that their atomizing behaviors appear to promulgate. According to pollster Daniel Yankelovich, there are two fears felt most acutely by Americans. One is
anarchy, and the other is the "dissolution of the bonds that keep a
society together." Americans cannot easily describe or name this second
fear, according to Yankelovich, but "concern about societal breakdown
is surprisingly widespread."

When atomization breeds individualism, it lays the groundwork for
autonomy. Thirty years ago the late Sir Isaiah Berlin, then an Oxford
don, provided his version of personal autonomy in *Four Essays on Liberty:*

> I wish my life and decisions to depend on myself, not on
> external forces of whatever kind. I wish to be the instrument
> of my own, not of other men's acts of will. I wish to be a
> subject, not an object; to be moved by reasons, by conscious
> purposes, which are my own, not by causes which affect me,
> as it were, from outside. I wish to be somebody, not nobody; a
> doer—deciding, not being decided for, self-directed and not
> acted upon by external nature or by other men as if I were a
> thing, or an animal, or a slave incapable of playing a human
> role, that is, of conceiving goals and policies of my own and
> realizing them.

Is autonomy inching us toward anarchy, the other of the top two
American fears? In the next chapter we will see that some cyberwonks
foresee as many governing bodies in the future as there are individual
citizens.

Solo Sapiens

Following Reisman's advice, Americans have begun to crave social insu-
lation, to court the very condition that threatens our ability to function
socially and cooperatively. A British newspaper article about travel in

Greece pointed out that "unlike the Americans, who often like to stay in heavily guarded and isolated 'resorts,' British tourists prefer to become part of the local community." In their promotional material, American motels tend to emphasize the things from which lodgers are insulated—risk, noise, danger, even spontaneity—rather than what they provide.

Which is not to say that the English crave diversity under their own roofs. A recent survey uncovered a heretofore unrecognized creature, the Sinmoo—"Single Income Never Married Owner-Occupier"—typically a well-educated and well-paid male in his thirties with a fairly new car and a modest mortgage. Although the Sinmoo may not be particularly domestic, he owns a three-bedroom house and has all the accoutrements of domestic life except a wife and children.

According to a study by Britain's Office for National Statistics, Sinmoos have tripled in the last twenty years. The number under forty-five has increased sixfold during the same period. One Sinmoo, a twenty-seven-year-old woman, said that the main reason she chose to buy her own place was financial—the rents in London being out of reach—but her reasons for living alone were different. "Nobody comes in and finishes off the milk and doesn't replace it," she said. "Now I have my own space and privacy." A man of the same age, for whom Sinmoovian life remains a goal, said, "I desperately want to get my own place. I think everybody does. Nobody really likes living with other people."

In the United States, Madison Avenue has successfully traded on the social disconnectedness of Sinmoo-like men. The successful television commercials for Dockers pants "proved that you could sell fashion to men," according to an article in *The New Yorker*, "by training a camera on a man's butt and having him talk in yuppie gibberish." The advertising firm didn't just get lucky, however. The ads were based on market research showing "baby-boomer men felt that the chief thing missing from their lives was male friendship."

Sinmoos and their ilk aren't the only people who find themselves feeling or living alone. Wishing to minimize risk and danger, residents of Miami's suburbs now hide behind eight-foot-high walls. When returning home to these so-called gated communities, residents must first hoist a gate with a plastic card. This, says Albert Reker who lives in a gated development just south of Miami, "gives you a very good sense of security." In older neighborhoods where walls and gates aren't possible, street barricades are being used.

Florida is not the only state to accommodate such enclaves. In fact, it's become a national trend. Press reports indicate that up to two-thirds of newly constructed residences in California are situated in gated communities. In about 30 percent of the new homes in San Antonio, Texas, the protective walls are already in place before the house is built. Similar figures are available for Washington, D. C., and Phoenix, Arizona. In 1994 it was estimated that four million Americans already lived behind walls (voluntarily).

But there's a hitch. Some residents say these security systems are destroying community life. Maria Velez of Coral Gables, Florida, is among them. In recent years many of Velez's neighbors have fought traffic and crime with street barricades and gates, but, says Velez, they're creating "a kind of fiefdom." Robert McCarter, dean of the University of Florida College of Architecture, agrees. Barriers are causing the "disintegration of the city," he says, as "one group protects itself against the other."

Distant Encounters of the Third Kind

A friend in east Texas tells me her community has a zoning law that makes it illegal for the "windowed" side of one residence to face the windowed side of an adjacent one. Since many of the homes in her area have attached garages with remotely controlled doors, when coming home modern Texans now steer their armored cars directly into their walled fortresses without an accidental sighting of or by the neighbors. Fully shielded from view, they can only detect "the presence of animated creatures"—the hallmark in UFO parlance of a Close Encounter of the Third Kind—from a safe distance.

Before long we won't have to hear the neighbors, either. In the next five to ten years one may be able to neutralize next door noisiness with an "active sound control" system. These systems require that a chair, bed or other quietness zone be outfitted with a microphone and a loudspeaker. The microphone picks up the noise, sends it to a mechanism that performs an acoustic analysis, then programs the speaker to send out a neutralizing signal that renders the neighbor inaudible.

Progressive societies are breeding an isolated being who is distinguished by his avoidance of entangling social relationships. Nearly thirty years ago Philip Slater wrote in *The Pursuit of Loneliness* that Americans "seek a private house, a private means of transportation, a private garden, a private laundry, self-service stores, and do-it-yourself skills of every kind. An enormous technology seems to have set itself the task of making it unnecessary for one human being ever to ask anything of another in the course of going about his daily business." Moreover, according to Slater, even within families there is the feeling that "each member should have a separate room, and even a separate telephone, television, and car when economically possible. We seek more and more privacy," he said, "and feel more and more alienated and lonely when we get it."

Nowadays it seems to take a calamity such as a hurricane, fire, or other disaster to teach us the lasting personal benefits of natural coalitions. In previous centuries when there was less personal security and relationships were essential to survival, the ancients never lacked knowledge of the things that we moderns have had to learn. Then, the typical social unit, outside of the family at least, was probably the dyad or triad, our predecessors interacting with one or two other individuals at a time. But all too commonly now the member of progressive societies is relationally on his own. Much of his time is still spent in the vicinity of other people, but monadically. He relates, but he relates mainly to himself. He converses, even debates, but he does so silently, and he alone responds.

Relocation

The societal fractures that produce Monadic Man were formed by urbanization and accelerated by a behavior now so deeply ingrained in everyday American life that it occasions little notice—relocation. When relocation first began, people were documentably unhappy about the constant restructuring of their neighborhoods. The reason is that they expected to know everyone but no longer could. Relocation has broken up patterns of socialization and created new levels of unrelatedness. One older resident of an American town lamented:

> They come and go. Back when the company first settled here in town most of us were interested in the people, and we made every possible effort to meet them. But . . . just when you get to know them well, they move on. I don't know how they feel about moving on. . . . It doesn't seem to bother them. Maybe they are trained for it. But my wife and I are not trained to lose friends every other week, particularly not after we had to work real hard to make them. So we stopped bothering. Now they keep to themselves, and we get about the business of the town.

This man's problem was caused by corporate relocation, but for a half-century now Americans have also been leaving cities—where they knew the people in the next apartment or the adjacent house—for suburban plots of ground. There they live near, but don't necessarily know, other refugees with similar histories. Their interest in the city is nil because the things that they want—movies, shops, and restaurants—have moved with them, like camp followers, usually to a nearby mall.

Need to Know

Monadic living is also encouraged by the fast rate of societal change and the pressure that rapid change places on us merely to remain well oriented. The more complicated life becomes, the more events that escape our personal attention. To keep abreast of the world, to avoid the anxiety that comes from not knowing what is going on, we must take in more and more information. There are all-news television channels, and many of us watch several news broadcasts; we channel-surf; we may read several news magazines. If we commute, we may also listen to radio news to and from work, perhaps tuning in to an all-news station or a talk show on which the principal issues of the day are being picked apart.

By equipping the world with high-speed communication systems, we further multiply the things that each of us *can* know about, and therefore believe (rightly or wrongly) that we need to know about. When trading and investment are initiated with other countries, it begins to matter to us what is going on in those places as well as our own country and state and city. The result of this globalization, according to Toffler, is that "the entire system begins to pulse with higher and higher flows of data." When author Umberto Eco took note of the sheer volume of books in print, he declared, "Books are menaced by books. Any excess of information produces silence." No wonder there is now a book called *Data Smog*.

Ironically, although information has the power to play havoc with things that we need—rest, reflection, peace of mind—only a fraction actually does much for us. To those of us who are over-booked or self-absorbed, a great deal of ambient stimulation is destined to remain precisely that, ambient. It will never become a part of us. This is why a writer for *Wired* magazine, Evan Schwartz, commented that America could be on the way to becoming "the first *society* with Attention Deficit Disorder . . . the official brain syndrome for the information age.

From a physical standpoint, a community is a collection of individuals, but the residents of a true community act like members of something that is larger than themselves. What does monadic living do for our neighborhoods?

There Goes the Neighborhood

In the rural mid-South of America, the people used to do something called "sitting till bedtime," according to author Wendell Berry. "After supper," he said, "when they weren't too tired, neighbors would walk across the fields to visit each other. They popped corn . . . ate apples and talked. They told each other stories . . . that they all had heard before. Sometimes they told stories about each other, about themselves, living again in their own memories and thus keeping their memories alive." Unfortunately, according to Berry, "most of the descendants of those people have now moved away . . . and most of them no longer sit in the evenings and talk to anyone." Visitation is in decline.

In their arid way, polls confirm it. Each year in a large and respected poll, the General Social Survey, Americans from a range of demographic groups are asked how often they spend an evening socializing with a neighbor. In 1974 nearly one in four Americans visited with a neighbor several times a week. By 1994, that figure had declined to 16 percent. But in 1994 there was a shocking increase in the number of people who had *never* spent an evening with a neighbor—from one in five to nearly one in three—a 41 percent increase since the same question was asked twenty years earlier.

This social deficit is noticed. Wendell Berry lamented that "most of us no longer talk with each other, much less tell each other stories. We tell our stories now mostly to doctors or lawyers or psychiatrists or insurance adjusters or the police, not to our neighbors for their (and our) entertainment."

Less and less time is being devoted to socialization. In *Time for Life*, John Robinson and Geoffrey Godbey report the results of an activities survey taken at ten-year intervals from 1965 to 1985. At the beginning of the study, Americans spent an average of 6.8 hours per week in social activities. Ten years later that figure had dropped to 6.2 hours, with a further fall to 5.7 hours by the end of the study.

A transplanted Luxemburger, accustomed to an evening stroll to the cafe, said that after four years in the United States he still felt "more of a foreigner than in any other place in the world I have been. People here are proud to live in a 'good' area, but to us these so-called desirable areas are like prisons. There is no contact between the various households; we rarely see the neighbors and certainly do not know any of them."

Reduced socialization explains some statements on the evening news. When a person commits suicide or goes on a shooting rampage, television reporters interview the neighbors. What was the person like, they ask. "He was a loner," say the neighbors. "He pretty much kept to himself." I submit that many of us less newsworthy moderns are also alone more than we might like.

Several years ago an article in the *Boston Globe* showed us just how alone a person can be:

> It can never be said that Adele Gaboury's neighbors were
> less than responsible. When her front lawn grew hip-high,

they had a local boy mow it down. When her pipes froze and burst, they had the water turned off. When the mail spilled out the front door, they called the police. The only thing they didn't do was check to see if she was alive.

She wasn't.

On Monday, police climbed her crumbling brick stoop, broke in the side door of her little blue house, and found what they believe to be the seventy-three-year-old woman's skeletal remains sunk in a five-foot-high pile of trash where they had apparently lain, perhaps for as long as four years.

"It's not really a very friendly neighborhood," said Eileen Dugan, seventy, once a close friend of Gaboury's, whose house sits less than twenty feet from the dead woman's home. "I'm as much to blame as anyone. She was alone and needed someone to talk to, but I was working two jobs and I was sick of her coming over at all hours. Eventually I stopped answering the door."

In the end, Adele Gaboury gave up on socialization, just as many of the rest of us have. Nowadays we all "pretty much keep to ourselves."

More than thirty years ago an entire neighborhood in New York City kept to itself in what might be billed today as the first *literal* "neighborhood watch." While Kitty Genovese was being murdered on the street, thirty-eight of her neighbors flew to their windows and *watched* as she cried out in terror, but none came to her assistance during the half-hour homicide. One professor commented that the incident "goes to the heart of whether this is a community or a jungle."

Such unneighborly passivity continues right up to the present. In December 1996, a thirty-six-year-old English lady was badly beaten while walking along a busy street in Chislehurst, a "close" neighborhood of southeast London in which each street has its own Neighborhood Watch. Police believe that at least 150 motorists watched as the man first repeatedly punched the lady and then dragged her, screaming, into the bushes where he proceeded to rape her. The last thing she recalled seeing before leaving the roadside was the sight of dozens of gaping motorists. It is thought that if anyone had interceded, the rape could have been prevented. "Detectives were reluctant to condemn those who drove past," according to a news report, "saying the public were increasingly afraid to intervene for fear of being attacked or knifed themselves, or finding they face legal action."

At one time people would have helped. Several years ago an article about seventy-two-year-old Stanley Galczynski appeared in the *Boston Globe* merely to report the favors he offered the residents of his neighborhood. According to the article, Galczynski "walks up and down the street several times a day, stopping to visit with neighbors. He might fix a gutter or a fence, or give a resident a ride to the store. 'I watch out for my neighbors, all of them,' he says. 'I know what it means to help each other out. I bring encyclopedias to a neighbor. They are maybe old, but they are good and the neighbors are happy. They help me, too. They shovel my walk.' "

I quote this vignette not for its nostalgic but for its educational value. The article struck two psychiatrists in the area "as a sign of the times that a major metropolitan newspaper would find such a story newsworthy. It was not so long ago that this kind of neighborliness was the norm. Now it is news."

The Great Good Place

To Hang Out is a special thing. There is no specific way to define the experience, but everyone who has ever done it knows what it is all about. It means, first, that you have friends. . . . But aside from friends, there must also be a Place . . . the Great Good Place that every man carries in his heart, the place of safety, the place where the harshness of the real world is fended off. Pete Hamill, "A Hangout 'Is a Place . . .' "

A cause of de-voicing, but more clearly an effect, is the loss of places where people can assemble for the purpose of talking. The benefits of a Great Good Place are not restricted to socialization and the good feelings that flow from it. The people who go there may also offer specific forms of assistance to each other by lending tools, helping out on personal projects, or pooling knowledge of places to get a car fixed cheaply.

In the Caribbean, according to anthropologist Peter Wilson, talking places include bars, rum shops, cotton or palm trees, and street corners. "They play dominoes, cards, or checkers," said Wilson, "they drink in a ritual fashion, they argue, they sing, they boast, brag, and fight." Among the !Kung, according to Patricia Draper, "village space is small, circular, open, and highly intimate. Everyone in the camp can see (and often hear) everyone else virtually all of the time. . . . Even at nightfall people remain in the visually open space, sleeping singly or with other family members around the fires located outside the family huts." New Zealand's Maoris hold public discussions on a "marae," a speaking ground surrounded by buildings imbued with the history of the tribe.

A talking place can be just about anywhere. In Ibieca, a small village in northeastern Spain, the village well was a natural place to talk. Just what it did for the villagers was learned the hard way. When water was piped into the homes of residents, families bought washing machines. This saved scrubbing laundry by hand, but when the villagers no longer made daily trips to the village well, they also lost opportunities to commune and gossip. Susan Harding tells a similar story about Oroel, Spain. "When the village bakery opened twenty years ago," she said, "it ended their breadbaking circles, and ready-made clothes and more money to buy them has curtailed the sewing circles. The circles had, and the washbasin has, a reputation for gossip, slander, and attack."

Traditionally, all the great civilizations have had their own types of informal gathering places—the sidewalk cafes of Paris, the Forum of Rome, the pubs of London, the *piazzas* of Florence, the grocery store–pubs of Ireland, the *bier gartens* of Germany, the teahouses of Japan. The street can even be a Great Good Place. In 1967 it was estimated that Paris had fourteen thousand sidewalk cafes. In that year over one-third of the residents of greater Paris visited a cafe at least once a day.

Across the Channel, the equivalent in Great Good British Places several centuries ago was the coffeehouse. Then, according to Richard Sennett, "anyone sitting in the coffeehouse had a right to talk to anyone else, to enter into any conversation, whether he knew the other people or not, whether he was bidden to speak or not. It was bad form even to touch on the social origins of other persons when talking to them in the coffeehouse, because the free flow of talk might then be impeded."

Nowadays the English talking place is no longer a coffeehouse but a pub. England has several hundred thousand. The English pub, according to a study done some years ago, "is the only kind of public building used by large numbers of ordinary people where their thoughts and actions are *not* being in some way arranged for them; in the other kinds of public buildings they are the audiences, watchers of political, religious, dramatic, cinematic, instructional, or athletic spectacles."

These kinds of oases "have disappeared one by one," wrote Philip Slater in 1970, "leaving the individual more and more in a situation in which he must try to satisfy his affiliative and invidious need in the same place." Just as the cinema has lost ground to video and TV watching, many Brits now prefer an evening at home to a night at the pub. With additional concern for drinking and driving problems, domestic consumption of beer has more than doubled in recent years.

Standing in for yesterday's watering hole is a whole new generation of bars, but at these more upscale places the main attraction is TV sports contests projected on oversized screens. Now, rather than repair to the neighborhood tavern for a dose of the latest gossip or to shoot pool and laugh with one's cronies, people go there in an apparent effort to complete social isolation. The customers sit widely spaced from one another, hunched over their drinks. "They peel labels off beer bottles," said anthropologist Ray Oldenburg. "They study advertising messages on matchbooks. They watch afternoon television as though it were of compelling interest."

The Subvocal Suburbs

The suburbs are largely devoid of meeting places. Automobile suburbs, as Richard Goodwin called them, grew rapidly following World War II. "Life in the subdivision," Goodwin said, "rarely offered the sense of place and belonging that had existed for the returning GI's parents and grandparents." Little wonder, since the very rationale for suburbia, according to James Howard Kunstler, author of *The Geography of Nowhere*, "has been the exaltation of privacy and the elimination of the public realm."

In the late sixties I lived in one of the newer suburbs of a large city in the American Midwest. It didn't have any sidewalks. I was told that so few people walked that it didn't pay to build them. So I walked in the suburban streets and rarely encountered other pedestrians. Although I was new to the area and hungry for someone to talk to, everyone was sealed off in apartment buildings and homes that stood at a safe distance from the street.

The suburbs' lack of places to hang out becomes immediately apparent when a teenager is dragged along by his parents for a visit to friends. This hapless soul soon begins to act "like an animal in a cage," wrote Ray Oldenburg. "He or she paces, looks unhappy and uncomfortable, and by the second day is putting heavy pressure on the parents to leave. There is no place to which they can escape and join their own kind." What they miss is the mall.

In some ways teenagers have been tricked by malls. Malls are places to shop, of course, but they also like to present themselves as towns that include post offices, libraries, dentists, doctors, churches, even public schools. So what is a mall, really—a town or a shopping center? The answer was recently forced to the surface by some disorderly behavior at the Mall of America in Bloomington, Minnesota, in the heart of the upper Midwest. Some two thousand to three thousand teenagers regularly congregate at the mall on weekend nights. But recently they became unruly, and a 6:00 P.M. curfew was imposed. The reason can be discerned from the rationale supplied by the associate general manager. "Most kids just hang out," she said, *few shop.*"

The destruction of the American town and village has gone so far that builders are now attempting to create anew that which strip malls, gas stations, and fast-food chains have wiped out. Their goal is to build communities with proper sidewalks and places that people can go on foot. But "a community is not something you can *have*, like a pizza," according to Kunstler. "It is a local organism based on a web of interdependencies."

A Great Good Place can be a workplace, of course, but these, too, are under threat. Office workers used to talk to one another. They encountered each other at the water cooler or the copy machine. They caught up with each other in the hall. Now workers are ensconced in their offices or cubicles, or work out of their homes. The copy machine is no longer needed for memos, to be distributed by secretaries at a traditional gathering place, the employee mailboxes. Communications are conducted by e-mail even when the sender and recipient are physically close enough to see and touch each other.

Fading social calls threaten our *joie de vivre*. "The most stopped-up, intellectually constipated, and unhappy men I know," wrote Pete Hamill thirty years ago, "are men who work all day and go straight home to eat, watch TV, and sleep. There is no outlet, no special period of the day reserved for the company of other men, no private experience outside of work and marriage. They have jobs and they have homes, but they don't have a place to Hang Out." I can guess what Hamill must think of the burgeoning arsenal of electronic tongue depressors that now awaits us when we come home.

Tongue Depressors

A recorded message from one of those have-a-nice-day female voices invites you to enter numbers using a touch tone phone — requiring you either to know [the] extension, or listen to a numbingly-prolonged list of departments. Even if you get through eventually, chances are you find yourself consigned to Voicemail Hell. . . . For an industry which likes to tell us that it's good to talk, telephony is making it inordinately difficult in the business environment to locate anyone to talk to. *The Daily Telegraph*, London, November 7, 1996

Our social voices are slipping away, leaving people in social isolation. How many times have you left the house in the morning, feeling happy and full of yourself, and found that there was no one to share this with? You boarded a train, bus, or subway but discovered that your fellow commuters were reading the paper or listening to something on a hand-held radio or tape player. You walked along the street to your place of work and noticed that passersby were talking on cellular phones. You approached the concierge of your office building but saw that he was watching a portable television set. You wanted to share your good feelings with another person—merely by saying in a cheery voice "Good morning!" or "Lovely morning, isn't it?"—but in the end you were forced to wait until the feeling passed.

There are more and more people you cannot plausibly talk to nowadays and fewer opportunities to be sociable. Who's going to strike up a conversation with a person who is listening to a portable tape player with "boom-boppa-boom" audibly leaking out of the earphones? Who is going to address a person that is jogging past or running in place at a stoplight? Who will offer a passing comment to a person streaming by on roller blades?

Mobile Phones

If you don't mind the literal loss of face, you can try chatting on a mobile phone yourself. We have all seen cellular telephonists chatting while they walked down the street, sat on a park bench, or rode their bicycles through town. And their numbers are soaring. In America the number of new subscribers in 1995 exceeded the birth rate. The situation is so out of hand that the Israeli army was forced recently to order soldiers not to carry mobile phones when they went into action. The injunction was evidently issued when an elite unit phoned for pizza from a location that was supposed to be secret.

Mobile phones are very big in Scandinavia. Nearly one-third of the Finns own one, as do one-fourth of the Norwegians, Swedes, and Danes. A Finnish university student explained, "We've never been much good at talking to each other face-to-face. . . . All that's happened is we've found our ideal way of communicating—at arm's length." "We can be quite talkative," said another Scandinavian, a Swede, "and perhaps we prefer to talk on the phone than meet up at the pub." The Norwegians even take their slim-line phones skiing, using them to locate cellular friends on other slopes.

Cellular phones are popular in Japan, too; one in five Japanese owns one. Some companies give away mobile phones to entice new subscribers, and vending machines dispense cheap mobile phones that can be used for local calls. But a backlash is developing. Mobile phones are now banned on most commuter trains around Tokyo and in many restaurants. One firm now prohibits personnel from taking mobile phones into meetings. "It was getting ridiculous," said one executive. "Five managers would be in a meeting, each with a phone, and half the time one of them would be on the line. We weren't getting anything done."

Israelis have an affinity for cellular phones, owning nearly a million and using them for an average of five hundred minutes per month—three times as much as in other countries. When a phone rings in a public place, customers pat pockets and paw through purses to see if their personal phone is the culprit. Recently a city councilman in Tel Aviv, Yair Halevi, announced his intention to create no-phone zones. In a newspaper interview he said that his plan took seed when he heard a phone ring in the middle of a funeral. Businesses and public institutions were given printed placards depicting a mobile phone with the familiar red prohibition line across it and the admonition: "No talking on cellular phones here." Ironically, during his interview Mr. Halevi had to interrupt himself to take a call on his own mobile phone. "At least I'm not in a concert hall," he said.

Technology is producing some puzzling social behaviors, a fact driven home to me on a rainy November day in a seaplane office in Vancouver, British Columbia. While waiting for a taxi into the city, I noticed a woman talking while looking out at the harbor. Her remarks were intended for no one in the room, nor was there a telephone anywhere in sight. Was she psychotic? The riddle was solved when I made out the earpiece in one ear and the thin cord running into her jacket pocket below, though I never did see a microphone. If the cord had been invisible or if the woman had pointedly glanced my way while talking, it would have been a very eerie experience indeed. It was an uncomfortable one as it was.

Cash Machines

Other technologies provide us with mixed reactions. The automatic cash transfer machine is a dream come true. Walk through the commercial section of a city at any time, day or night, and your money is waiting for you in some kiosk or hole in the wall. No more must we wait until nine o'clock the next morning to stand in a queue and present a teller with a withdrawal slip. But some people want a little conversation with their money. What they get is conversation *for* their money.

The prospects of more or even the same amount of conversation in the future are nil. At present, banks increasingly are encouraging customers to conduct all routine banking by telephone and computer.

Shopping at Home

It used to save money when one "skipped the middle man." Now one is encouraged to skip all people. Most suburbanites used to get in their car, drive to a mall, park, find the relevant goods, line up at the checkout counter, locate their car in a sea of parked vehicles, and drive back home. Now many shoppers are "orderers"—they order their goods remotely from a glossy catalogue, television, or commercial online service from their home. Israelis can order a refrigerator, washing machine, or TV on the Internet. It is forecast that Americans will soon be able to order a car on the Internet. You choose the car, apply for a loan, and if your credit is good, get instant approval when the computer automatically accesses a database of financial data.

In some locations it is already possible to shop for groceries on the Internet. From a computer in their homes, shoppers cruise "virtual shelves" stocked with accurately priced food items and order shipment with credit cards. The orderers need not be home when the food arrives. A deliveryman admits himself to the customer's locked garage by entering a code in a keypad lock and leaves perishables in a "chill container." No one ever need meet.

Computer shopping offers a lot of benefits to our society. It works efficiently, saves time and money, keeps cars off the highway, conserves fuel, and reduces auto pollution. These are important benefits, and I am not about to advocate that we stop it. But we will never happen upon old friends or make new ones while phoning or computing in the comfort of our homes, nor does our living room resemble the marketplace of old —lively with the voices of our fellow man and woman.

Nor can we get these experiences by patronizing Super Roboshop 24 in Tokyo. Opened in April 1997, it is the first of an intended chain of fully automatic convenience stores with no employees behind the counter. In fact, there is no counter at all but a series of electronic buckets that circulate in vending-machine style around an island of aftershave lotion, milk, and fresh sushi. "This is everybody's dream," gushed the owner, Tsuneo Kanetsuka, as he announced plans to open a similar Roboshop on Fifth Avenue in New York.

Closer to home, a fellow professor at my own university, Sheffield, has helped invent a talking computer that can be programmed to converse. People "would rather deal with a companionable machine than a clerk behind a desk," he said. Is he right? Is silicon preferable to carbon and deoxyribonucleic acid? Certainly the order takers in fast-food restaurants are machinelike themselves, typically speaking in incomprehensible bulletlike pulses. And a computer could easily be more companionable: most of the teenage food dispensers evince neither the time nor the inclination or even the real-life experience to talk to customers. If fast food is what you want, you can even skip the visible person altogether by remaining in your car and yelling out your order to a circular pattern of holes in a metal plate.

Less Walking — Less Talking

In some locations the daily news is now available over the Internet when we want it, not when a broadcast comes on the radio or television. With this advance, as one observer commented, "We may even avoid being seen retrieving the morning paper in our pajamas." But of course the neighbors can still see and greet us when we go out for a walk. Out for a walk? In the last twenty years, the average distance that was walked dropped one-fifth in England. According to the Pedestrians Policy Group, few people do more nowadays than move "from front door to car." Indications are that the problem is even worse in the United States. According to one commentator, "About the only need that suburbanites can satisfy by means of an easy walk is that which impels them toward their bathroom."

Many people have traded in real walking for a virtual brand, ambulating on motorized treadmills while watching television or listening to their favorite tunes, neither reaching physical destinations nor satisfying social appetites, but "pretty much keeping to themselves." When domestic activity is insulated from view in these ways, serendipitous social opportunities are prevented, and this retards the expansion of one's network of friends.

People even experience difficulties under their own roof. Beyond the obvious chill imposed by television and computer games, older married couples tell me that they resent their automatic dishwasher for replacing the intimate after-dinner chats they used to have while doing the dishes. Daughters say the same about conversations with their mother. But they own a dishwasher and feel they must use it.

Technomania

Social interaction is also being kept down by some bizarre applications of technology. In Japan I recently saw a man talking on his car phone while driving into Tokyo. By itself this could be construed as an unusually social experience since the man was otherwise alone in the car, but he was also watching a dashboard-mounted television as he talked.

In New York City where the taxi drivers can be impolite if not boorish, electronic speech has been installed in cabs by order of the mayor. Now a canned voice tells alighting passengers: "Excuse me. Please remember to take your property and don't forget to ask for a receipt." But after using several different speakers and New York City dialects, residents are in a quandary as to which kind of voice should be used. Few seem to mind the use of an electronic voice, but some think the message should be heard in a standard dialect. Have we given up on the possibility of teaching the drivers to speak?

Some of the most effective "tongue depressors" are the electronic media. Radio and television absorb the majority of our evening hours—prime time, as it were, for social and emotional talking. Having little in the way of a civic life, home entertainment has become a major preoccupation of the middle class. The American home, now a technocopia, is overflowing with electronic gadgetry, from computers, answering machines, microphones, and cameras to sound and video play-back systems, VCRs, cable connections, and what has been called "that current version of heaven on earth for the socially exiled—the satellite dish."

Academics Anonymous

This goes in spades for university residence halls, which are rapidly being converted into a series of one-man electronic arcades. The main machines include a computer with high-speed Internet connection and e-mail account, stereo system with CD player and cassette deck, and voice mail. Optional items include cordless phone, TV, VCR, and a surround-sound audio system with four speakers. Extras include projection TV, laser-disc player, paper fax machine, pager, and cellular telephone. When the modern student goes out for an evening, his destination is often a commercial video arcade that is crammed with row upon row of flashing, buzzing computer games just like home.

When students apply to American colleges and universities, one of the things they check out, along with the library and the swim team, is the "wired rating" of each campus. The reason is that they want to know how e-mail-accessible their friends will be. And with good reason: a recent survey indicates that more than half of all residential campuses have network connections in the dormitory rooms.

Dartmouth College is wired to the hilt. All its residence halls are fully networked. Moreover, students who wish to send messages during the day, when away from the dorm, can do so by lining up at public terminals that are scattered around the campus. Each day they send a quarter of a million electronic messages—more than thirty messages for each of the eight thousand students, faculty, and staff. No wonder Dartmouth's system is called Blitzmail.

On other campuses academic atomization is proceeding apace as dormitory lounges are being transformed into computer areas and the uniting function of student unions is on the wane. Dorm rooms are becoming "high-tech caves," according to one news writer, and residential colleges are finding less and less to say about the once-touted benefits of cultural integration.

Much of the cyberaction revolves around dating. A young lady at Vassar, who had the self-assigned code name of Snow White, said, "I've . . . known people who sat home Friday and Saturday nights, broadcasting back and forth to people they know only by nicknames, while the rest of the world was going by. . . . Every broadcast conversation with someone new is the same for the first twenty messages, finding out who they are. It's easier to just meet someone. You learn how much of a difference it makes to see someone in person and actually talk to them."

Answering Machines

There is another inhibitor of chat and the intimacy that goes with it—the telephone answering machine. Not in its originally intended use as a message-taking device but as a public address system. Now when the machine kicks in, we can do something that previously would have been unthinkable as well as socially suicidal: decide whether to respond to the voice of our closest friends. And we can even decline the experience without threatening a valued relationship. We can also intentionally call friends when they're known to be elsewhere, taking the cowardly way out, telling embarrassing or unpleasant things to a machine that cannot question or judge us.

In England, answering machines are said to have replaced conversation. "In Britain," according to a recent article, "we have never liked talking to each other, anyway. And the intimacy without risk that the answerphone offers is irresistible. It is the only way we can bring ourselves to chastise tradesmen, end relationships, call in sick, ask for an overdraft, or apologise."

Although answering systems were originally offered as a way to intercept messages when the called party was absent or unable to come to the phone, in practice these systems often replace whole conversations. When Annie leaves a message for Rosemary, and Rosemary's call-back activates the answering machine of Annie, the two taped messages may actually achieve a successful exchange of information. Lost is the personal interaction, which may have gone on for an hour or more even when the "news" that prompted the call could have been conveyed in less than a minute.

Voice mail is not uniformly well received around the world. In Britain many consider it "robotic." British businessmen recently voted voice mail the "most useless communications technology." Some Americans feel the same way. I took a trip to northeastern Iowa just as voice mail was becoming more common in that part of America's Midwest. But they were having difficulty adjusting. An assistant professor at a nearby university said, "Sometimes it's frustrating that I can't actually talk something over with a receptionist." To prevent such frustrations, one of the new users, a local bank, put a real person at its main number. The president said, "It's vitally important that you have a human being as *an opt out.*" How reassuring that our species is considered sufficiently reliable that ordinary humans can be counted on when talking and listening machines don't do the job.

Actor Daniel Day-Lewis likes to use indirect communication systems as opt outs. Last year he contacted Isabelle Adjani, the mother of his child and pregnant with their second, to tell her some devastating news —their relationship had come to an end. It is reported that he did this by fax. Then he contacted Adjani to tell her he had gotten married. He left this message on her answering machine, but he neglected to give the name of his new bride. Adjani reasoned that she was the woman with whom he had been living, Deya Pichardo. When she placed a congratulatory phone call, she found that Pichardo knew nothing of the marriage. It developed that the new bride was an actress named Rebecca Miller. Finally, according to *The Times*, Day-Lewis "decided to come clean and admitted everything, that he had gotten married and had been thoughtless and was terribly sorry," and he said all this to Isabelle Adjani's answering machine.

Totally Tubular

Many people have been in a house that had no oil paintings or sculpture, but few have visited a home that lacked a TV set, now as much a part of a living room as the lamps and chairs. I realized this in the late seventies after returning home from a brief vacation. While I was gone, a handyman discovered that a basement window had been opened. He called the police, who crawled through a window and searched the entire house. Later, the investigating officer wrote up the incident. The official report said, in effect, that nothing appeared to have been taken "except the TV." The amusing thing was that I didn't own a TV.

Ninety-eight percent of American homes have at least one television set. That's 4 percent more than have a telephone and 7 percent more than have an automatic water heater. Television is cropping up in some unlikely public places, too. In the New York Hilton, for example, there are TV sets in the bathrooms of every suite and—reducing the ocular confrontation of small places—the elevators. TVs are also going into golf driving ranges, bowling alleys, and shopping mall food courts. "Everybody talks about freedom of speech," said a media studies professor at the University of Wisconsin, "but what about the freedom of my ears and eyes not to be bombarded every place I go?"

America seems to have misunderstood the advice of the 1960s drug guru Timothy Leary to "turn on, tune in, and drop out." The average American actively watches about four hours of television per day and has the set on for seven hours and forty-eight minutes. In Britain those in the age group forty-five to fifty-nine watched over seventeen hours of television per week and attended no public meetings in 1996. In Japan the average person over seven watches television for three hours and forty-seven minutes per day.

Television is affecting social talking in several different ways, and none of these is beneficial. For one thing, it reduces the sheer *amount* of talk. Time study data reported by John Robinson and Geoffrey Godbey indicate that TV owners spend 25 percent less time conversing than nonowners. These data also indicate that TV owners spend 34 percent less time than nonowners socializing outside the home. This is consistent with the claim of some media watchers that television inhibits participation in community affairs (an allegation that I will examine later). A study of the routine activities of Chicago area young people revealed that ten-year-olds spent more than four times as many hours watching television as they did talking.

Television doesn't just limit social interactions, it also robs us of some of our spontaneity, some of our spirit. Evidence of this has emerged from some unlikely places. One is ancient Ladakh, a trans-Himalayan region of Kashmir. Anthropologist Helena Norberg-Hodge was studying these people when radio and television came to their villages. Before radio, she said, "there was lots of dancing, singing, and theatre. People of all ages joined in. In a group sitting around the fire, even toddlers would dance, with the help of older siblings or friends. Everyone knew how to sing, to act, to play music."

Norberg-Hodge observed that when the media arrived, people became less inclined to sing their own songs and tell their own stories.

Instead, they sat and listened to the far *better* singers and storytellers in the little box. Norberg-Hodge commented that "the incredible vitality and joy that [she] had experienced in the villages was almost certainly connected to the fact that the excitement in life was here and now, with you and *in* you. People did not feel that they were on the periphery; the center was where they were." Norberg-Hodge concluded that the idealized stars that we now see on TV "make people feel inferior and passive, and the here and now pales in comparison with the colorful excitement of faraway places."

Radio and television have made talking a spectator sport. As one observer put it, "Rather than confide in close friends, we watch Oprah discuss astonishingly intimate matters with total strangers on TV." I believe that one of the reasons we tune in with such frequency is that we still have a biological appetite for *en face* interactions but no longer experience as many as we once did.

And the media moguls are ready for us. In his book *Hot Air,* Howard Kurtz tells us that America's media are "awash in talk. Loud talk, angry talk, conspiratorial talk. Raunchy talk, smug talk, self-serving talk, funny talk, rumor-mongering talk. A cacophony of chat fills the airwaves from coast to coast, from dawn to dusk and beyond, all talk all the time." Talk shows, Kurtz said, "revel in their one-sided pugnacity, spreading wild theories, delicious gossip, and angry denunciations with gleeful abandon. Anyone can say anything at any time with little fear of contradiction. It is raw, it is real, and it is immensely popular."

There's money in talk, and competition to have the most engaging forms of it. CNBC proclaims that it, among all television networks, is "first in talk." In America, about ten thousand radio stations have some type of talk or call-in shows, and they attract very large audiences. Proponents say that these shows bring people together, but London School of Economics and Political Science professor Stephen Coleman says a more appropriate reaction is embarrassment at the sound of "regular callers whose eccentricity would be manifested mainly by their belief in the reality of the phone-in as a real community, the presenter as a friend, their few seconds of weekly public exposure as real communication, and the silent listeners as their neighbours."

Much of the time spent listening to all this media talk is compensatory, making up for emotionally satisfying conversations that we have missed in real life and masking pangs of loneliness created by desociali-zation. Once the late-evening news is over, television gives us the tubu-lar version of a campfire and all the lighthearted chat, teasing, laughter, and self-confession we can stay awake for. But there's a difference. In the flickering lights of our TV screens we cannot make out the faces of dear friends. Instead we see talk show hosts and their guests. And they never laugh at our jokes, only their own.

There is another reason for the popularity of media talk shows. When talking is broadcast, we can sample it at our convenience. We can turn it on when we slip below our minimum adult requirement, turn it off when our daily dialysis is done. And when we've had enough profes-sional-grade talk, we don't have to worry that there's still some vocally ordinary person sitting in our living rooms or hanging on to our tele-phone line, craving more social vocalization. We can just hit the "off" button.

Although one occasionally encounters criticisms of adult viewing practices, it is more common for people to rail against the TV habits of children. The reason is obvious. American children from two to eleven years of age sit in front of the TV set for an average of 21.5 hours a week. Nearly half of the seven- and eight-year-old British children have a TV in their bedroom. So much for childhood, at least as their grand-parents knew that potentially glorious period of human development.

Currently in Britain there is a battle over a children's program called "Teletubbies." Critics claim that the animated characters' speech is too infantile or deviant, possibly (they suppose) harming their children's language or cognitive development. The odd thing is that the parents are delegating linguistic stimulation, normally the purview of the par-ents themselves, to television sets. That they should be angry when their electronic nanny performs less appropriately than they, the parents, merely affirms the obvious. A television set is a machine! If it doesn't meet parental standards, why don't they forbid the children to watch it and play with the kids themselves?

There is a statistic that might at first blush seem to be encouraging: American children are now watching five hours' *less* television a week than they did in the 1980s. Unfortunately, we find at second blush that much of the difference is due to children's increased use of computers and VCRs. A recent poll indicates that 90 percent of nine- to thirteen-year-old children average 1.4 hours of video games a day. In actuality, children's total screen time is up.

Hoisted by their own petard, television broadcasters have expressed alarm that as the generations they conditioned to watch small domestic screens increasingly turn on their computers, they will drift away from TV, taking revenues with them. Recently, it was announced that at the end of July 1997, over three million people were connected to the Internet in Britain. By 2000, it was projected that 40 percent of the population would be connected. In the United States, it was reported, Internet users were spending 12.8 hours a week staring at their computer screens—and these, to the television moguls, are the wrong screens! "If we don't understand where fourteen-year-olds are getting their media from in 20 years' time," said one BBC executive, "we won't have the BBC and once it is de-invented it will never be invented again."

Obviously, the battle of the screens is unlikely to wind down anytime soon. A recent market survey has projected that by the year 2000, computer games will be played in as many as ten million American homes, either on so-called stand-alone systems or through Web site hookups. Before computer games came along, early adolescent children in America spent *less than 1 percent* of their time talking with their parents. It will be interesting to see in a few years if they talk at all.

As computer time goes up, we cannot expect screen time to remain constant. Computers do not merely steal from television. Robinson and Godbey's time study indicates that on one particular day, adults who spent more than three hours on their home computers watched 20 percent *more* television than those with no computer time. They literally screened out normal social life.

Too Busy to Talk . . . or Help

Recent surveys indicate that television is devouring the time liberated by the household conveniences acquired in the past several decades. Feeling increasingly rushed, people have cut back on the time they usually spend with others to help improve their communities. One major American newspaper has decried "declining attendance locally, whether it be a PTA meeting, an election, or even a gathering of friends over a pitcher of beer." According to the article, Americans are no longer "volunteering, joining, getting-to-know-each-other, community-building citizens who once typified this nation to the rest of the world."

Significant drops have been documented in church attendance, union membership, participation in parent-teacher organizations, and membership in traditional groups such as the National Federation of Women's Clubs and the League of Women Voters. Similar reductions have occurred in the numbers of volunteers for traditional civic organizations such as the Boy Scouts and the Red Cross. Donations of blood are down both in America and England.

Recently, a team of reporters for the *Chicago Tribune* took a look at how a particular neighborhood in that city responded to the needs of Saint Alphonsus, a local church. What they found is that "the voluntarism that has supplied the manpower to run all the ancillary activities that made St. Al's a pervasive presence in the neighborhood is dying out with an older generation of parishioners. . . . Now parents [say,] 'I don't have the time. Just tack it onto my tuition bill.' That kind of checkbook voluntarism can keep an institution financially afloat. But without face-to-face participation, the networks that are the glue of community are bound to vanish."

This passivity is confirmed by a recent survey of citizen participation. It revealed that of those who had taken some part in political campaigns, more than twice as many limited their involvement to check-writing as those who gave time or time and money. Those who donated their time also reported more personal satisfaction than the financial underwriters.

Memberships in fraternal organizations such as the Lions Club, Elks, Shriners, Jaycees, and Masons have also declined. Robert Putnam uses bowling as a metaphor for desocialization. He points out that although more Americans are bowling than ever, "bowling in organized leagues has plummeted in the last decade or so. Between 1980 and 1993, the total number of bowlers in the United States increased by 10 percent, while league bowling decreased by 40 percent." Although small groups of people may be continuing to bowl, Putnam considers the reduction in league bowling symptomatic of "the social interaction and even occasionally civic conversations . . . that solo bowlers forgo."

A century after de Tocqueville wrote about America's impressive political vivacity, citizens have become apathetic about political rallies and speeches. The number of those working for a political party has dropped. Americans have disengaged themselves from politics. Why? Why have Americans quit working for the things they believe in?

In an article published a few years ago, Putnam blamed television for declining civic participation, saying that TV is "the only leisure activity that seems to inhibit participation outside the home." In a later article another Harvard professor, Pippa Norris, chided Putnam for missing certain regularities in TV viewing and civic participation. For example, those who regularly watch network news are *more* likely to participate in all types of political activity, not less. But she otherwise accepts Putnam's television thesis, concluding herself that in the main "the more people watched, the less active they were" and "heavy viewers . . . proved less interested in national and local community politics."

There are reasons to believe that Putnam and Norris fingered the wrong culprit. For one thing, neither provided evidence that television *causes* inactivity. Moreover, those who lack interest in participatory politics have more time to watch television. But a television set is just a lifeless box. It doesn't magically turn itself on just as we're thinking of going out for the evening.

An inanimate de-voicing machine cannot force us to spend four hours per evening sitting in front of it, with time and a half on Saturday and double time on Sunday. But there is limited merit in the television-as-cause position. When individuals live in a TV-dominated society, they unconsciously submit to the effects of television. One of these effects is acquired passivity. If there were no television, people would eventually be forced to read or play with their computers, also passive or semi-passive pursuits. Or, tiring of that—and this would evidently be Putnam's prediction—the totally tubeless might venture out into whatever communities lie outside their homes, however tentatively. But that would not assure community action. What's to keep the tubeless from stopping by a video arcade, a cyber cafe, or a sports bar?

Is TV just a substitute for other things, a filler that we turn to when we have nothing better to do? On February 27, 1975, thousands of New Yorkers found out: a fire destroyed the telephone service to a three-hundred-block area of Manhattan. In a survey of 190 affected individuals, a majority indicated that with phone service cut off they felt isolated, uneasy, or both. To compensate, about one-third spent more time watching television and listening to the radio.

I believe that desocialization and withdrawal from community life reflect several factors. One is an underlying perception that we have no functional need to affiliate with other people because we already have most of the things we need or are likely to get. Studies of social relationships indicate that the acquisition of wealth increases acquisitors' personal independence. When the financially comfortable go on vacation, they can afford a kennel for their black Labrador and a plant minder for their African violets. They don't need to ask a friend or to become a better friend so they *can* ask.

Other factors relate to the larger system of government. Robert Putnam has said that some social programs and tax policies may have created "disincentives" for civic activity, but he found it difficult to see which government policies were responsible for the decline in bowling leagues. I say lots of government policies could have had this effect if they caused individuals to feel that social capital, including relationships —the stuff of which coalitions are built—is unnecessary to personal success and joint action.

"While You're Up, Get Me a Grant"

Several decades ago there was an advertisement for a scotch whiskey in which a seated gentleman says to his paramour, "While you're up, get me a Grant's." In the federal largesse of the times, an academic remake of the ad had one professor saying to another, "While you're up, get me a grant." The recollection is relevant to issues relating to personal initiative and group effort.

For twelve years I lived in a historic seaport just north of Boston. The city decided to build and moor a replica of an ancient sailing ship in the harbor as a drawing card for tourists. To me this was an excellent opportunity to pull the community together by launching a fund drive to pay for the boat. I imagined collection canisters in all the shops. I could see where one of those large thermometers could be erected to show how much money had been collected and how much was still needed. I could imagine young people going from door to door collecting donations or operating a makeshift car wash on Saturdays. The more established members of the community might throw a $100-a-plate dinner, with the proceeds going to the boat. Others might participate in a lottery. But none of these things happened. The mayor contacted our representatives in Washington and applied for a government grant. In a single stroke, he denied his constituents new reasons to talk and work with each other, activities that would have helped unite his divided city.

Spontaneous personal assistance began to decline with large-scale urbanization, a process regretted by English writers such as Blake and Wordsworth nearly two hundred years ago. Social welfare programs were created in response. But while helping in some ways, systemic care by our government has eroded this spirit further. Richard Goodwin has written that "when the trees are cut by indirect order of the Federal Highway Administration, when the river is polluted a hundred miles away, when the new school awaits a decision in Washington or in an equally remote city hall, then community is not possible. Individuals . . . share their worries and desires only when they share in responsibility and power." Thus, although government programs may have grown up in response to public apathy, their continued operation has further eroded community spirit, and they let us off the hook when it comes to being helpful on a personal level.

Socialization and community life are impaired by something called "social loafing." I can recall from my youth occasions in which a person accidentally dropped something on the floor, but instead of bending over to pick it up, said, "Let's leave it for the sweeper," as though he'd become jobless if they exercised their responsibilities. Indeed, the presumed existence of duly-appointed others demonstrably reduces individual effort. A half-century ago a German psychologist named Ringelmann asked some workers to pull a rope as hard as they could either individually or in concert with one, two, or seven other people. Compared to solo performance, the volunteers pulled less hard when they were joined by another person, less hard still when pulling with two others, and the least hard when there were seven co-pullers.

As it turns out, to produce the social loafing effect it is not necessary to bring other people onto a task. Just the *belief*, even falsely, that there are others around to help discourages individual contributions and also potentially discourages individuals from teaming up with each other to carry out cooperative tasks. There are people whose paid employment requires them to do what used to be done by volunteers, effectively encouraging social loafing and reduced cooperative effort.

Although Americans still contribute time to community projects every year, the government reportedly finds these acts of personal voluntarism "inefficient, underfinanced, lacking in rigorous evaluation, and largely exempt from the self-policing that the market coaxes from corporations and that elections instill in government." So Washington is attempting to divert volunteers from the projects of their choice into certain government-approved ones, such as after-school programs, health care, and job training, in which the government has also provided assistance that is inefficient and underfinanced. I'm not sure it makes sense for a centralized government to divert people from the spontaneous expenditure of energy in behalf of projects they believe in, whatever the worthiness of the goal. It could snuff out the flickering spirit that remains.

Imagine that the year is 1898. Your neighbor, a man with whom you have a congenial "over-the-fence relationship," is married with three young children. One has a physical disability. The neighbor, who lives modestly, has a steady job with the largest employer in town. One day you hear from a mutual friend that your neighbor has been laid off. You go over to his house and ask if there's anything you can do to help. You take the family a loaf of homemade bread and ask if you can watch his children on Saturday morning while he looks for another job. You say you are having trouble keeping up with your yard work and wonder out loud if he'd be willing to accept payment to help you. You tell him that you lost a job once and know how it feels to be out of work.

Now suppose the year is 1998, and you live next door to an identical family. Reading in the paper that a local company has gone out of business, you surmise that your neighbor, whose car has not left the driveway in the last week, must have worked for the company and is among those now out of work. You know he can file for and get government aid until he finds another job, and you assume he is eligible for tax relief and cash payments to support the costs associated with the disabled child. The thought flickers through your mind that perhaps you ought to do something, but you do not know him. Thinking that it would be out of character to suddenly show a personal interest in your neighbor after years of not doing so, you take refuge in the knowledge that some government program will see your neighbor through his crisis. Besides, there is no way he could know for sure that you are aware of his misfortune.

I think that the contemporary scenario is uncomfortably close to the truth in many communities. You don't really know your neighbor very well. He might take advantage of your expressed willingness to help by asking for money to tide him over. Perhaps it is best to err on the safe side and leave well enough alone. Helping could get you in some sort of difficulty, but *not helping carries no risk at all.* You feel a little uncomfortable, but then you think that the government must have these social programs for a reason. Why not let them work as they're designed to?

If we needed things we couldn't buy, many of us would have more friendships. In Britain when scholars are invited to travel some distance to give a talk at a conference or university colloquium, they are commonly invited to spend a night at the home of a local academic rather than a hotel. This is done for financial reasons, but it produces familiarity and friendship, and the possibilities of something larger than the two parties individually. Wendell Berry has said that if people do not need each other, they will spend little time together telling stories to each other, and "If they do not know one another's stories, how can they know whether or not to trust one another?"

The Predictable Decline of Trust

The social prerequisites to trust probably began to slide as long as eight thousand years ago when urbanization caused the dissolution of familiar groups. The slide would have picked up momentum three to four hundred years ago when, according to Tamara Thornton, the rise of a market-based society increased wariness of strangers. In the nineteenth century, according to Thornton, "one never knew just who one's fellow city-dweller was, for he too had arrived only yesterday from parts unknown, for reasons that could not be determined."

Estrangement creates suspicion. When people don't know each other, it's hard for them to trust each other. Robert Wuthnow, a professor at Princeton University, found that when the size of small groups goes up, interpersonal trust goes down. If you ever belonged to a small group that got larger than was originally intended, you may recall the charter members lamenting that the group was "getting too big" and reminiscing about the good old days when the group was smaller.

Today, trust is in free fall. The percentage of Americans who agreed that most people can be trusted fell by two-fifths between 1960, when 58 percent did, and 1994, when only 35 percent were so trusting. At the same time there was a loss of confidence in basic institutions, from banks and businesses to governments and schools.

Distrust also works in the opposite direction. The feeling that "you can't trust anyone" also weakens confidence in the institutions that are served by people, whatever their trustworthiness. As trust dissipates, according to J. David Lewis and Andrew Weigert, "the motivation for other dependent parties to seek redress in the courts increases, further weakening trust within the class of sued parties, such as doctors, lawyers, educators, or elected officials. A spiral of distrust emerges, leading to a 'rush to the courtrooms.' " Enter the lawyers, among the least trusted of any professional group in America.

Distrust hit American politics long ago. In the 1960s a poll showed that approximately one out of three citizens felt isolated from the political process. In the mid-seventies a clear majority felt "neglected, impotent, manipulated, taken advantage of, fearful that whoever is running the country does not care what happens to them, and convinced that 'what they think does not really count.' "

Americans normally regard themselves as an open, honest, friendly lot. What was slipping here? Why the cynicism? One explanation for the decline of trust at the national level is that in the 1930s and 40s Americans began to expect things of public institutions that never actually happened. Political scandals and personal revelations damaged trust further. But co-conspiring with these factors was a growing unfamiliarity with the people who worked in public institutions.

Aware of their increasing estrangement, politicians fought back with displays of televised intimacy. But emotional pandering can backfire. "The politician opens up his or her heart," said Roderick Hart in *Seducing America,* and "we are drawn in. The politician then does something craven or stupid—an inevitability in politics. We jump back, scorned, again. We declare the lot of them toxic waste."

The underlying problem is that we don't socialize enough to know and trust each other. This is the circumstance in which we find ourselves today, and it is a costly one. Francis Fukuyama has argued that distrust is damaging the world's economies. He has pointed out, for example, that people who distrust each other cooperate "only under a system of formal rules and regulations, which have to be negotiated, agreed to, litigated, and enforced, sometimes by coercive means." These legal processes are poor substitutes for trust. They involve what economists call "transaction costs," like the cost of theft that is merely figured into the price of goods that are sold. Fukuyama concluded that "widespread distrust in a society . . . imposes a kind of tax on all forms of economic activity, a tax that high-trust societies do not have to pay."

Creeping distrust can impair long-standing business relationships. For many years Edson Spencer oversaw the corporate alliance between Honeywell, an American corporation, and Yamatake-Honeywell, a Japanese firm that made industrial and domestic control systems. Spencer gave the Japanese free rein and personally interceded whenever disagreements arose. His relationship with the Japanese was based on trust. If management teams don't trust each other, he said, "it doesn't make any difference what the percentages of ownership are or what agreements are signed." And he added, perhaps warned, "It can take decades to build up, and just moments to destroy."

For its part, Yamatake-Honeywell also trusted Spencer and therefore Honeywell. The alliance between the two firms produced prosperous results over a number of years, but it nearly collapsed in the early nineties following Honeywell's sale of Yamatake-Honeywell stock. In actuality, the sale was only part of the problem. Just months before, Edson Spencer had retired. When the troubles began, the trusted old friend and corporate troubleshooter was gone.

There are now fewer intimate social relationships than at any previous time in modern history. In consequence, unfamiliarity, suspiciousness, distrust, and loneliness are on the rise. Progressive, information-oriented societies have tested and begun to locate the psychological and biological limits of their members. "We are not equipped, like termites, to become willing members of a vast community," said Desmond Morris nearly forty years ago. "Even if startling new and at present unimagined advances in mass-communication techniques are made in the years to come, they will continue to be hampered by the bio-social limitations of our species."

Little did he know what was coming. Little do we.

SIX

The Big Chill

One day a virtual-reality game will let you enter into a virtual bar and make eye contact with, "someone special," who will note your interest and come over to engage you in conversation. You'll talk, impressing this new friend with your charm and wit.   Bill Gates, *The Road Ahead*

In 1950, Alan Turing, the English mathematician that helped launch the first "intelligent machines" during World War II, suggested a way that future technicians would be able to know when computers had reached a level of intelligence equaling that of humans. In that test a human and a computer would be interrogated by a second human. Examining the typed responses to his questions, the interrogator's task would be to figure out which set of answers came from the human and which from the machine. A half-century later, computer technicians are trying to produce machines that will pass the Turing test by virtue of their responsiveness to a human. They haven't succeeded yet but the quest is enlightening. In fact, I believe that we are on the threshold of an unintended discovery—it is that societies capable of building machines that almost pass the Turing test are in danger of producing humans that nearly fail it.

What I am suggesting is that when someone does meet Turing's challenge, the victor will not be a person but a dyad. One of the two participants will of course be the computer scientist with the technical intelligence and perspicacity to build the right sort of machine. The other will be the human interrogator who is deceived, either because of his social insensitivity or the machine-like utterances of the human speaker, which, by the time in question, may be typical, perhaps even perceptibly normal.

Electronic Communication (That Is, Writing)

... the letter is a unique form of communication. Individuals in physical proximity give each other more than the mere content of their words. Inasmuch as each of them *sees* the other, is immersed in the unverbalizable sphere of his mood, feels a thousand nuances in the tone and rhythm of his utterances, the logical or the intended content of his words gains an enrichment and modification for which the letter offers only very poor analogies. And even these, on the whole, grow only from the memories of direct personal contact between the correspondents.   Georg Simmel, *The Sociology of Georg Simmel*

We have been told how wonderful life will be when we're all expressing ourselves electronically. According to one cybernaut, "Every day, hundreds of thousands of people are communicating through the Internet —conversing, collaborating, working, playing, and letting off steam. Friendships—even marriages—are made and broken on the Internet. Clubs are formed. Problems are solved."

Lots of people are very giddy about it all, especially those who stand to profit from our purchases of computers, modems, and software. But although the "residents" of virtual communities can take advantage of unparalleled new communicative opportunities, they enter this realm inorganically. Their bodies remain behind. As Howard Rheingold said, in a virtual community "you can't kiss anybody and nobody can punch you in the nose."

With intimate talking at a new low, it is not surprising that a faceless, voiceless communication system such as e-mail should find instant appeal. Indeed, its unreflective popularity is all the more reason that we should pause and take a look at electronic writing—how it started and where it's going. And since we have all been told what it can do *for* us, let us, for the sake of a balanced perspective, take a look at what it can do *to* us. E-mail, telephone answering machines, faxes, and kindred instruments facilitate the communication of thought. But they also encourage the excommunication of our selves.

On a recent trip to London, Bill Gates extolled the virtues of e-mail. He said that it facilitates communication between parents and their children when away at college "Now I'm keen for people to use this technology effectively," said David Blunkett, the Labour party's future secretary of state for education, who happened to be in the audience, "but not for it to bypass normal human communication. What's wrong with talking?" he said.

But of course we know what's wrong with talking. By modern technostandards, it's inefficient. In some deeply biological sense, it is supposed to be. The inefficiency of talk is a product of its intimacy. One cyberwonk said that "the need to converse when all parties are available for face-to-face, telephone, or real-time conferencing can constrain the flow of information." The solution, he said, is "asynchronous computer-mediated interaction." And to think we had it right under our noses the whole time!

E-mail has skyrocketed in the last several years. Figures go out of date as fast as they are printed. According to an estimate from early 1996, sixty million people in 160 countries were using the Internet. In a separate estimate six months later, it was said that thirty-five million Americans were online and over 40 percent of those earning more than $50,000 were hooked up. By the time you read this paragraph, the true figures will be much higher. In the speech accepting his renomination for the presidency, Bill Clinton said that he wants every twelve-year-old to be able to log onto the Internet. England's prime minister, Tony Blair, is seeking to install a computer in each of Britain's 32,000 schools by 2002. The Swedish postal service is currently arranging an e-mail address and services for every Swedish citizen over the age of six.

Many e-mail "conversations" have been faulted for their lack of substance. In language reminiscent of the earlier characterization of CB radio, the humorist Dave Barry said that "most chat-area discussions revolve around the fascinating topic of who is entering and leaving the chat area. A secondary, but equally fascinating, topic is where everybody lives." In an article in the *Boston Globe*, a science writer called e-mail conversations "a vast finger-down-the-throat regurgitation of content-less palaver.... Yakkety-yak in binary bits ... bumper-to-bumper extemporaneous gab." A recent article in *The Economist* referred to the "brainless rubbish" that springs from keyboard to screen.

In my view the e-mailers are merely responding to a biological imperative by typing in a talklike way, chatting manually. As humans they retain a basic drive to connect with others but inhabit a technoculture that provides diminishing opportunities to do that. The critics seem unaware that they're evaluating a written equivalent of ordinary social talk, which is largely fact-free. They may also have been conditioned by years of experience and academic instruction to expect more propositional "heft" from written communications.

My intent here is not to ask in some sophomoric way whether e-mail is "bad" or "good." Rather, it is to ask what effect this form of communication is having on our lives, collectively and individually, and will have on us when it overtakes more personal ways of expressing ourselves. For e-mail is devoid of information about who we are. In fact, there is currently no reliable way to determine the personal identity of an e-mail correspondent, a necessity since both deception and error are growing. Attempts are being made to achieve a "digital signature" to keep con artists from setting up Web sites, doing business, then vanishing into the great ether beyond. One is tempted to say, in only slight paraphrase of Sir Walter Scott, "Oh, what a tangled Web [site] we weave, when first we practice to deceive."

Electronic writing also offers no way to convincingly show how we feel and what we are up to; as hard as we might try, it is impossible to reconstruct social intentions from inorganic letter strings. When you correspond via electronic writing, you disclose the information you want the other party to know, not facts you would prefer to keep private. Oral discourse, especially the face-to-face variety, is less inhibited in this respect. The speaker's intentions may still be message-oriented, but things come out that he hadn't planned to disclose. An expectant look, a long silence, a raised eyebrow—these things may get you to tell too much. If you want the whole story, "get it in talking."

So emotionally parched are e-mail displays, we cannot make a reasonable guess as to whether the people dealing with us are legitimate or up to no good. One authority admitted recently that on e-mail "there is no real way of discerning truth from lies. The net is a repository of facts, statistics, data: unless anything is palpably wrong, we tend to give all facts on our computer screens equal weight." When we correspond electronically, happy for the ease, speed, and economy of this kind of communication, we must accept that some of our interlocutors will be people we would not trust if we saw and heard them.

Some cyberians seem not to understand that when emotionality is drained from thoughts, unintended ambiguity rises. The resulting misinterpretations are then blamed on the recipients rather than the sender or the process. They say that *"for some reason,* people become much more sensitive when they're online, and they tend to blow things entirely out of proportion—for example, taking a couple of sentences originally meant to be humorous or sarcastic entirely the wrong way." But if one jokes voicelessly, misunderstanding is a likely outcome. "We need only deal with one side of an individual over the Net," according to cyber-cynic Clifford Stoll, "and if we don't like what we see, we just pull the plug. Or flame [verbally attack] them. There's no need to tolerate the imperfections of real people." And, Stoll asks, "is it really sensible to suggest that the way to revitalize community is to sit alone in our rooms, typing at our networked computers, and filling our lives with virtual friends?"

Cyberians say that electronic mail will help us establish new "communities" based on personal interests rather than geography. It is said that these new communities will pull us together as a nation. I think it is more likely that digital communities will Balkanize society further. First, under the steady influence of e-mail, users will probably become even more strongly entrenched in their individualistic fortresses. Second, people from certain ethnic groups and age groups are not likely to own computers and thus will be unable to hook up with those who do.

Although electronic mail is touted as the solution to societal fragmentation, telecommuting—working at home or elsewhere and communicating with others via e-mail, fax, and telephone—prevents people from seeing each other. One large advertising firm has already eliminated the traditional office environment. Its Los Angeles employees go to the office in the morning, check out a cellular phone and laptop computer, and then proceed to whatever location best suits their requirements. They do not have to socialize with or even see any of the other employees of the company.

Others don't go to work at all. Some of these solo operations have been formed from above—established corporations desocialized their staff into home offices and cars that were outfitted with pagers, cellular phones, and laptop computers. American Express has put its field sales staff in such virtual offices, compensating for the solitude with Monday morning conference calls, a telecommunicated buddy system, and monthly social events in which the people do something that, in their world, is oddly out of character—they assemble.

Those who dislike social isolation or need to collaborate on projects have discovered that being there matters, and this discovery seems to be freezing telecommuting at its present level. Others have tried to find substitutes for office levels of socialization by starting compensatory groups. A cofounder of England's "Home Alone Club" has explained that they set up the group to give themselves a sort of virtual community. "Half the stuff we talk about," he said, "is general day-to-day gossip, who's in, who's out, the rubbish that people in offices take for granted."

Unfortunately, e-mail precludes responses to the cues that define us. It does this by suppressing the cues themselves. It clips out our uniquely personal attributes while also masking our age, ethnicity, sex, social class, and geographic origin. In *The Sovereign Individual,* James Davidson and William Rees-Mogg claim that when we were all on e-mail, "it will not matter what most of the people on earth might think of your race, your looks, your age, your sexual proclivities, or the way you wear your hair. In the cybereconomy, they will never see you. The ugly, the fat, the old, the disabled will vie with the young and beautiful on equal terms in utterly color-blind anonymity on the new frontiers of cyberspace."

The reason is that unlike the setting of the old TV series "Cheers"—a neighborhood bar where everybody knows your name—on the Internet nobody knows your name or face or voice. Nor do many care. A race-looks-age-sex-hair-blind world may sound too good to be true, especially to those who consider it inappropriate to discriminate against a person based on factors irrelevant to performance. But if none of these biologically powerful characteristics matters on e-mail, then neither does any other personal characteristic.

When needed feedback is no longer readily or reliably available, aberrant behaviors get a new lease on life. If we get on our high horse, e-mail correspondents cannot bring us down a peg. If we start to take ourselves too seriously, no electronic correspondent will loosen us up. If we start kidding ourselves, we may do so unchecked by even our dearest keyboard communicants. But we humans have a biological right to, and a psychological need for, this feedback. It's been available for scores of millennia, and no being that remotely resembles a human has ever had to live without it.

Is electronic mail bringing us all together? Is e-mail a solution to office tensions? A British study of just over one thousand office workers suggests that e-mail often is the cause of new problems, some brought on by muzzling, others by emotional inflammation. Forty-six percent of the workers sampled said, predictably, that e-mail had reduced face-to-face communication at work. Thirty-six percent said that they used e-mail deliberately to avoid face-to-face interaction. This is concrete evidence of electronically induced de-voicing.

The study also turned up some evidence relevant to the claim that e-mail pacifies people, but the evidence was negative. Fifty-one percent of the respondents had received personally abusive "flame mails." Thirty-one percent had responded to these flaming messages with one of their own. Nearly an equal percentage had been forced by electronic abuse to quit responding with a colleague or experienced a desire to do so. Eighteen percent of the respondents said that the relationship had irretrievably broken down after a flaming e-mail message. If office workers are attempting to reduce personal confrontation by conversing electronically, the strategy may be backfiring.

How are we to view such statistics against cyberian claims that electronic mail is already bringing everyone together, building one large, warm, friendly "world community"? How can we be sure that verbal aggression and broken relationships won't lead to something catastrophic in the future, when flaming messages are sent simultaneously to many thousands of people *in their homes* as well as their places of work?

If this seems excessively alarming, recall that many of the existing users already knew each other before they got their communications systems. According to Francis Fukuyama, "The initial group of users was a pretty homogeneous group of scientists and engineers who socialized to a common set of fairly high professional standards. There was a high degree of trust among people in the way they interacted." But e-mailers increasingly don't know each other, do not expect to meet in the future, and may not actually care to. Without identities, a moderating factor—personal reputation—cannot operate. With no access to our species' social feedback and control mechanisms, there will be nothing to keep misunderstanding, incivility, and dishonesty from creeping into our daily life at unprecedented levels.

Messa di Voce

In operatic singing there is an instruction called *messa di voce*. It refers to a gradual increase from the softest *pianissimo* to the loudest *fortissimo*, followed by a gradual softening into silence. The term just as aptly captures societal changes in vocal prominence. In evolutionary history the role of the voice increased under biological pressures, as discussed earlier, and then decreased under the influence of a range of cultural pressures.

Progressive societies are shooshing down the back slope of vocal *crescendo*, racing toward *pianissimo* at an alarming rate. This de-voicing is indirectly fueled by the same thing that gave our species a social voice in the first place. Grooming went vocal when groups became too large to manage their social business manually. Social sound-making inched its way into speech, and to good effect. It kept our tribes together, and productively so. But unbeknownst to our newly lingual ancestors, there was always, bubbling beneath the surface, a limit on socially manageable group size. Urbanization first tested those limits, then pushed us past them. Now the only way we can maintain relationships with friends is to mass-produce our communications. And so we have invented the primate world's most exquisite form of manual grooming, a system that allows us to stroke familiars with a thousand separately controllable hands.

Our tribes have already surpassed personally manageable levels. Just as too many books produce less reading, too many acquaintances can reduce the allure of socialization. In response, some people are holing up and hunkering down. Others are trying to hang on to each of their personal associations but are turning to silicon for assistance with their basic communication needs. At its roots the dilemma is a classic conflict between biology and culture. The human need to commune with others remains steadfastly the same but cultures are on the move, and some are now challenging rather than feeding our need for intimacy.

Expanding group size, the very factor that produced social sound-making and talking in the first place, is leaching the intimacy from our personal lives. From a technical standpoint, the first accomplice was the printing press, then electricity, telephones, and increasing computerization of businesses and homes. To the extent that we can now express ourselves by keying on a computer, escalating group size has swung us *messa di voce* from manual grooming to vocal grooming and back to the manual modality again.

The manual rebound began some years ago. Remember your reactions to Christmas encyclicals, photocopies of what happened to a family since last year's account ("Bill is on the honor roll at school, Bob is doing well in his business, and I've just started working out on a rowing machine—guess there'll be no excuse for those extra pounds now!")? Recall your first reaction when you were sent a poorly veiled "personal letter" that was typed by a computer?

From form letters we rapidly progressed to computer-"personalized" letters. I still remember the ones I used to get from the *Reader's Digest* sweepstakes; these "contests" greeted me with such intimacies as "Dear Mr. John Locke" and egged me on with such phrases as "and so, Mr. Locke, why not send in your card today?" The phoniness of the personal register always seemed more obvious when they got my name wrong— some drone or machine evidently misreading my scrawled signature on something—saying, "Well, Joln Locha, when can we expect to hear from you?"

Now one can press a key on a computer and send the same message to hundreds or even thousands of people. It may be the only way we can "stay in touch" with all the people that we choose to relate to on some basis or other. Unfortunately, print is not the biologically optimal way to socialize. E-mail may be the quickest and surest way to "reach" our friends, and it effectively addresses the group size problem. But it doesn't actually have the intended effect—intimately engaging the intimate friend—and creates other, largely unrecognized problems in the process.

A great deal of social talking has already been replaced by writing, impersonal fact-oriented speaking to business colleagues and strangers, and the elective mutism associated with television, commuting, jogging, and other relatively asocial pursuits. But the would-be talkers haven't gone anywhere. They're still playing the only human games they know and ever will know, seeking the intimacy they need with a different set of tools.

Virtual Intimacy

You can talk to other people in virtual reality, and that's great. You can also turn into an octopus . . .

Jaron Lanier, "An Insider's View of the Future of Virtual Reality"

True, unpretentious, unrehearsed intimacy is on the wane. One way of making up for it is compensatory gossip. Since gossip can only be done when both parties know something about the personal life of a third party, true gossip was probably the first type of talking to suffer when social time perceptibly grew scarce. Where there's a need there's a market, of course, and our apetite for juicy facts has produced a band of hunter-gatherers who search each day for intimate news and photographic images. These "hack reporters" and "paparazzi" are the suppliers. Their customers—the middlemen—are the newspapers and magazines that specialize in people and their relationships. America has *People* magazine, Britain has *Hello!*, and France has *Paris Match*. Each is chock-full of articles about rock and film stars and other public figures such as the Kennedys and Britain's royal family.

Even an analysis of one of the world's most distinguished newspapers,

The Times of London, found that the paper concentrated on people-oriented stories. In a single day selected more or less at random, *The Times* devoted 43 percent of its primary news space to human interest stories, practically the same as its more mass-market sister, *The Sun.* Keeping these papers filled is a challenge. Britain's *Hello!* magazine runs a six-page spread each week on twelve "personalities," and the average broadsheet newspaper needs 228,000 words every single day. Television has broadcast such specifically person-oriented programs as "The Lifestyles of the Rich and Famous," and there are others, such as "Entertainment Tonight," whose only purpose is to reveal facts about the personal lives of movie stars. And there are countless talk shows in which people uninhibitedly describe their drinking problems and failed marriages.

Something strange is going on here. Several thousand years ago two old friends would never have chatted about someone they did not know. Why do we busy moderns, who juggle so many responsibilities, spend our time engaged in a discussion about people we've never met and never will meet?

Anthropologist Jerome Barkow has suggested that modern humans may not be able to avoid such behaviors completely for a biologically interesting reason. Our species evolved the psychological mechanisms for gossip thousands of years ago because our ancestors needed to share and manipulate information about the members of small tribes—people whose actions directly or indirectly affected their own lives. Needing to know about the motives of others, they required information about their status, politics, sexuality, and health—all of which provided a protective shield. There were no laws, no police, no welfare system, no government, no anything. Our ancestors could count on no entities except themselves and the people with whom they had relationships.

A dearth of relationships is forcing us to feed our Who System table scraps from "Oprah." The mass media are capitalizing on our dietary insufficiency. Strangers who, according to Barkow, are "present only on cathode ray tubes in our living rooms, or magnified many times life-size on the screens of motion picture theatres, are mistaken for important band members by the algorithms of the evolved mechanisms of our brains. We see them in our bedrooms, we hear their voices when we dine." If we come to think about these total strangers as our relatives or friends, perhaps even our rivals, Barkow suggested, it is not so illogical that we would "automatically seek information about their physical health, about changes in their relative standing, and, above all, about their sexual relationships."

In the United States a publication called *Soap Opera Weekly* reports on the romances, marriages, pregnancies, illnesses, and deaths of scores of fictitious characters who live only on American television. One headline asks, "Honeymoon in Vegas? Will Victor Be Able to Stop Nikki and Josh's Elopement on The Young and the Restless?" Another tells us that "One Life to Live's Dylan Tells Marty It's Over." A third headline announces "The Bold and the Beautiful's Ridge Proposes to Taylor and Breaks Brooke's Heart." You thus can read a factual account, illustrated with color photos, of completely fictitious stories.

If you can't wait to read about the real soaps, you can now catch a cybersoap whenever the urge arises. By accessing a Web site called "Spot," one can follow the deception, lust, love, and intrigue of characters on such programs as "Ski Vixens from the X-Dimension," a mixture of myth, musical, and science fiction. On some sites the audience can even join the cast, interacting with the characters and actively influencing the outcome.

Some people have apparently given up on "real-life" experiences altogether. There is a very large Usenet newsgroup devoted purely to discussion of daytime soap operas. Since its address is rec.arts.tv.soaps, this newsgroup is called, simply, r.a.t.s. According to Nancy Baym, a communication professor at Wayne State University, r.a.t.s. exists to provide information about what has happened and what will happen next on these shows, and to interpret them. In July 1993, r.a.t.s. processed more messages than any other such group, typically about 150 new messages each day.

This kind of participation is hardly an idle pastime. Some of the soap fans that participate have watched the same shows for over twenty years. Soap operas are their life. They read several soap opera magazines, belong to dozens of fan clubs, tune in to prime-time awards shows, attend celebrity public appearances and charity events, and go on cruises with the stars. When soap opera fans are brought together on r.a.t.s., said Baym, they pool their information from these various sources. This makes viewing all the more pleasurable and adds to their incentive to watch daytime TV, for what they learn increases their sense of belonging when they get on r.a.t.s. So there they are, hapless souls, induced by a computer to watch a television series in which actors portray real people's unbelievable lives. Does the expression "Get a life" come to mind?

Reduced socialization contributes to our fascination with the virtual lives of unknown people. We personally know too few people to gossip about with the other people that we also know, and we spend too little time engaged in these kinds of interactions. To fill our daily quota of gossip, we have no alternative but to consult artificial sources and therefore must turn on the TV or open a newspaper or magazine. But once again we are spectators; we sit back and watch personal facts fly through the air like the tennis balls at Wimbledon.

"What Is Time For?"

Although actual time counts indicate that there is more free time than ever, television eats up the difference, causing viewers to "stack time," that is, do three or four things simultaneously in order to complete their self-assigned chores. These time pressures affect the way we speak to each other. I used to work with a business type of guy who asked me one day to "bottom-line" him. If we are seen to be dawdling, someone may ask us to "cut to the chase." More and more people nowadays use strategies such as these to verbally click their way through social encounters, much as we remotely change television channels. With their stock of verbal (and nonverbal) clickers, these "channel changers" can delete the normally gradual openings and closings from what might have been a complete human interaction. When we are hurried along our verbal way, personal remarks become little different from unwanted commercials, or programs that have lost their grip on our attention.

Children are harmed more than anyone. A British father wrote that when he was on an outing with his family, his wife implored their daughter Molly to hurry up because there was "no time to stop and blow dandelions." In response Molly raised what may be for a child— perhaps for all of us—the major philosophical issue of the new millennium. "Mummy," she said, "what is time for?"

When life gets intolerably heavy, the first things to be thrown over-board are those that are not perceptibly critical to our survival. But in our diagnostic naïveté, the danger is that we will jettison "little things" like small talk, whose name implies its perceived value—perhaps it's the adult version of dandelion blowing—instead of something *less necessary* to our social and personal survival.

The second thing to go is any type of discourse with people who know nothing that we need to know and can do nothing that we need to have done for us. In the provident economies and socially responsive governments of today, there are few unsatisfied personal needs. The first people to be ignored are those who are unconnected with our work and unconnected with our domestic well-being—those who may be more interested in talking to us as a person than telling us something as an employee, family member, or citizen.

Adrift in a Voiceless Society

How does it feel to be adrift in a voiceless society? Some people already know. For several years I trudged back and forth from my research lab at the Massachusetts General Hospital to an academic office I had been given at the Institute of Health Professions. What I failed to realize at the time was that the site of my daily zigs and zags—a veritable Stonehenge of unsightly high-rise apartment buildings—had been a complete, utterly wholesome neighborhood some years earlier. All twenty-seven hundred residents of this patch of Boston's West End had been forced to evacuate the area and had scattered throughout the city. Urban renewal wiped out the neighborhood. A report written later indicated that "for the majority it seems quite precise to speak of their reactions as expressions of grief. These are manifest in the feelings of painful loss, the continued longing, the general depressive tone, fre-quent symptoms of psychological or social or somatic distress."

All normal humans have a basic drive to form and maintain significant relationships. This requires pleasant interactions with a few other peo-ple at a satisfying level of frequency and in the context of a stable framework in which concern for each other's welfare is freely express-ible. A series of helter-skelter interactions will be less satisfactory than repeated ones with the same persons. Without the feeling of belonging that springs from stable relationships, people experience deprivation and may be susceptible to a variety of ailments, as lonely people are.

Those who lose contact with their friends and close neighbors illustrate this. Years ago "detribalization," a specific case of such loss, demonstrably increased rate of mental collapse in urbanizing Africans. Surveys generally reveal a higher rate of suicide among immigrants to a new country than the rate in the countries from which they came. But individuals with few close relationships generally report feeling less socially supported than those awash in intimacy, and typically experience poorer physical and mental health. Women with few intimate relationships are more likely to break down following a crisis. And people of both sexes are more likely to die at any given age than more "connected" people.

Ironically, friendships—the preventative cure—involve little more than talking. Those with too little time or disposition to "just talk" have too little time to be a friend. Removed from emotional and social friendship, we may well ask what it means to be human—asking not in intellectual curiosity but in exasperation or despair. Stripped of the social interactions that define us as individuals and give meaning to our lives, we become efficient automatons with plenty of money and no wasted time but little that connects us either to others or to our own selves.

What if we were prevented from interacting with friends? What is it like to be physically voiceless? Consider the locked-in life of the late Jean-Dominique Bauby, the editor in chief of Paris's *Elle* magazine. At forty-two, Bauby suffered a massive stroke that destroyed the lower part of his brain, the brainstem, but left his higher cortical areas intact. When Bauby regained consciousness three weeks later, he reentered life full of bright ideas but physically paralyzed and speechless—able to move little more than his left eyelid. This he used to blink out the letters needed to "talk."

Socially de-voiced people don't have to blink the alphabet, they can say sounds and words, but there is a sense in which they, too, are locked in. For without the company of kindred souls, there are no opportunities to express their innermost thoughts and feelings, and it is frequently in self-expression that our mental and emotional lives become comprehensible.

You say, Okay, I get your point, but the people you describe had no choice. They couldn't walk away from their voiceless worlds, but for me, a day of e-mail, or a night of television, these are choices I make. I can still socialize with my friends anytime I want. I can chat with an elderly person, catch up with an old school friend, spend an afternoon talking with a child, visit my next-door neighbor. Yes, you can, at least if they're also willing and available, but how often do you? And how certain are you that these experiences will always be available to you? Good hearing and a serviceable larynx may matter little if the opportunities to express yourself vocally grow fewer by the day.

It's one thing to have lost your voice in a group or organization, perhaps because your temper got the best of you or you said something foolish or spoke out too often. You might drop out of that group, or if that were impossible—say, because it happened at work—you would keep a low profile: you would sit quietly, minding your own business. But what if you lost your voice *everywhere?* What if you were universally blackballed, disenfranchised, left in a state of permanent laryngeal paralysis? What business would remain to be minded?

Loss of speech normally conjures up thoughts about the threat to free speech of repressive political regimes such as the Soviet Union or contemporary China. In free and democratic societies one has no fear of such punishment, of course. One need not worry that he will be caught talking about subjects that are too significant for his own good. But too many of us are being squeezed by an inverted culture that has begun to restrict opportunities to talk about *insignificant* things, the perfectly forgettable things that cement us together.

Going It Alone

When people begin to "go it alone," a variety of potential ills present themselves. First, they of course miss out on the feeling of belonging, the affirmations of their own worth. A person in good social contact can see a reflection of himself on the faces of his friends, can see the way *he* is. A person with friends has what is arguably the most valuable feeling that a social being can have: that he is a worthwhile member of a worthwhile group.

Some of the people who will be hit the hardest are the ones that

David Riesman called "other-directed" people. Lacking the "psychic gyroscope" of inner-directed people, the other-directeds are unusually sensitive to the expectations and preferences of others. In the early 1950s they were most easily found in the business and professional classes of the larger cities, groups that have steadily enlarged in the last half-century. Since other-directed people derive feelings of self-worth from their environment, their psychological well-being is compromised by a society with fewer and fewer appropriate opportunities.

Any person who operates from the periphery of social frameworks is prone to a disconnected, isolated feeling and also lacks constant feedback about his or her behavior. If one of your strengths is a talent for witty remarks, in social isolation you may forget this, and then you'll have just one less reason to feel good about yourself.

Relationships can also be a big help to those who experience serious stress. And within relationships, self-disclosure is known to reduce stress, thereby also reducing the harmful effects of stress on physical and mental health. When we "unburden" ourselves, "we do for nothing in the street or the parlour," said Auden, "what we should have to pay two guineas an hour for doing in the consulting room." Stress tends to draw people closer together, and this is adaptive, for the antidote is, or is in, the relationship.

We saw in the previous chapter that Americans have increasingly ignored their neighbors over the past twenty years. Unfortunately, this leaves the neighbors in the lurch, for many live alone. According to a U.S. Census Bureau survey taken in March 1995, solitaries now comprise one-fourth of American households. This is up from 1970 when one-sixth of the households were singly occupied, and 1950, when one-eleventh were. Solo dwelling is equally common in the United Kingdom. In 1995, 27 percent of households contained one person, a near doubling since 1961 when just 14 percent did.

Although everyone is susceptible to de-voicing, women and men are unequally affected at different ages. Among the youngish Sinmoos, males predominate, but among the older set, women are less likely to share their home with an adult talker. Thirty-five percent of the sixty- to seventy-four-year-old women live alone or with children, compared to 20 percent of men. Sixty-eight percent of the women over seventy-five are completely alone. To socialize they either must leave their home

—not a straightforward proposition if some fairly high percentage is infirmed—receive a visit, or make unusually heavy use of the telephone.

Cohabitation with a sympathetic spouse or partner may help but does not guarantee feelings of connectededness and support. That feeling usually rests in part on solid same-sex relationships. Lacking intimacy in those associations, a de-voicing man may become increasingly "masculine"—the strong silent type is prototypically male, after all—more deeply entrenched in his info world, reading the papers, watching football on TV, handling his investments. A de-voicing woman may plunge more deeply into people-oriented magazines, books, and television shows, but lost intimacy cannot be restored through these second-order experiences.

Solo dwellers have less access to caring experiences. They cannot have an intimate adult conversation under their own roof. They can pipe soap operas and other forms of social vocalization into their homes, but if they wish to interact, they must reach outside. The immediate benefit of intimacy is in the emotional experience. The "solution" to many of our problems—indeed, their prevention—lies not in the action we take but in the cathartic relief that comes from social and emotional talking. Frequently there isn't anything we can actually do about the things that trouble us. We cannot have our old job back. Our parents may be in irreversible physical and mental decline. We can't even rein-hale the words we uttered so flippantly at an office party. But that doesn't mean we have to take these things lying down. We can discuss them with a friend.

These talking experiences work, but we cannot simply snap our fingers and have them. We can't just hit our social channel changers and watch new friends file into our lives. The groundwork has to have been laid in advance. The problem for many members of our society is that the groundwork isn't there; without ever explicitly thinking about it, they were subtly encouraged to put security above intimacy. Those who spend long hours at work and perpetually feel rushed or tired have fewer alliances to service by way of talking and have trouble finding the time to service those who do exist. Intimacy thus declines. When intimacy is lost, our society circles back to the insecurity its members originally sought to avoid, for with loss of intimacy there is loneliness and vulnerability to strangers who offer an infusion of affection.

When did we begin to put security ahead of intimacy? Undoubtedly the desire to become secure—or to equate security with monetary wealth—has a long history. But there is tangible evidence that in the early 1970s American values were changing. A longitudinal study showed that college students began then to prefer the goal of "being very well off financially" to the goal of "developing a meaningful life philosophy." In 1978 the former goal passed the latter one and continued to gain ground for at least ten years thereafter. Actor Alan Alda proclaimed that "it isn't necessary to be rich and famous to be happy. It's only necessary to be rich." "Dallas" and "Dynasty" beat "The Waltons" and "Little House on the Prairie" in the television ratings. Cars were seen sporting a bumper sticker proclaiming "He who dies with the most toys wins."

Many of us have toys, and now we fill our time playing with them and working with them. We take small television sets out on our patio or watch TV while moored in our sailboat. Before venturing out on the links, we throw a cellular phone in with our golf clubs. On a drive in the country we pull into a parking lot and fax a message to the office over the communications system in our car. While on vacation we use a telephone hookup on our laptop to hear a text-to-speech system convert the e-mail messages on our office computers. We *are* dying with the most toys, but perched atop our silicon silo, the view is magnificent. We can see all the way to our new lives in The Autistic Society.

SEVEN

The Autistic Society

With social interactions you have to have confidence that the rest of the world will be nice to you. You can't control how the rest of the world is going to react to you. But with computers you are in complete control, the rest of the world cannot affect you. Anthony, computer hacker, quoted in Sherry Turkle, *The Second Self*

Personal relationships are something I don't really understand.... I've remained celibate because doing so helps me to avoid the many complicated situations that are too difficult for me to handle. Temple Grandin, *Thinking in Pictures and Other Reports from My Life with Autism*

Imagine a person who is afraid of your face. He flinches at the sound of your voice, withdraws from your touch. Very little about you makes sense to him. Your humor is uninterpretable. He does not know you and lacks the capacity to learn who you are. He is unaware of your feelings and thoughts. This poor soul is even biologically incapable of contemplating the idea that you have your own mental and emotional experiences. Anything, anything that his mind can imagine would be better than a conversation with you. This unfortunate individual is suffering from an unremitting lifelong genetic disorder. He has autism.

Years of research have not brought us any closer to a cure for autism, but there is, oddly, some good news for autists, the victims of this condition. A massive herd of like-minded people is marching their way.

Society no longer requires the social stimulation that autists fear and cannot interpret. Now, to be successful in business, one need not interact with others. Increasingly one can "converse" without speaking and comprehend without listening. A voiceless society is the autist's dream come true.

Autistic individuals are known for an obsession with mechanical objects. Many of them love computers. Do they love machines because machines are not human, or are the autistic simply unconcerned about this? The answer is unclear. Some research indicates, however, that normal people who make unusually heavy social use of computers do not perceive their machines as low in "social presence."

In Newcastle, Australia, there is a whole family of autists. This is quite unusual because people who shun social relationships are unlikely to mate. The mother, Carolyn Baird, is classified as a high-functioning autist, as her maternal status attests. Her oldest son, Chris, is also unusual; unlike the typical autist, he has friends. But he didn't meet them the old-fashioned way—at school, in the neighborhood, on the athletic field. He "met" *all* of them on the Internet.

There is much that we do not know about the private lives and personal experiences of autistic people. Few autists have described their problems; most have serious linguistic deficits and cannot write to a commercial standard. But one high-functioning autist, Temple Grandin, has written and lectured widely on her autistic life. She also has been described by Oliver Sachs in his book *Anthropologist on Mars*.

Temple was diagnosed with autism in early childhood. She was a loner. Symptomatic of her syndrome, she fixated on various tasks all too easily and was fascinated by mechanical objects. As a child, Temple became aware of a device called a "squeeze chute" that is used when injections or other procedures are administered to livestock. The squeeze chute had side panels that were hinged at the bottom. The unsuspecting animal is first led into an enclosure, and its head is then secured in a device. The chute operator pulls a rope, and the panels press against the sides of the animal. This immobilizes the animal and also tends to calm it.

Fascinated by this machine, Temple asked if she could try the cattle chute on herself, reasoning that it might calm her, too. In a literal enactment of the prescription to "pull your own strings," Temple pulled her own rope from inside the machine. Years later she wrote about this experience. Once she was in the squeeze chute, Temple said, she found the experience "both stimulating and relaxing at the same time. But most importantly for an autistic person, I was in control."

Temple was way ahead of her time. When the only kind of reality was what was real, she invented the virtual hug. By pulling a rope she got an experience that offered some of the same benefits one derives from a real hug. But unlike a real hug, Temple controlled when the experience started and stopped, and the amount of pressure she felt.

When I learned about Temple Grandin's interest in controlled hugging, it brought to mind some things I had read about computer hackers. Sherry Turkle, a sociologist at the Massachusetts Institute of Technology, has written that hackers typically grew up as loners. Many always thought of themselves as "different." For them, hacking represented a way to escape from isolation without having to engage in what they saw as complicated relationships with other people.

Turkle has observed that unlike the unpredictable human, computers "offer companionship without the mutuality and complexity of a human relationship. They seduce because they provide a chance to be in complete control, but they can trap people into an infatuation with control, with building one's own private world." She also noticed that far from using machines as time-saving tools, for the typical hacker "the fascination is with the machine itself. Contact with the tool is its own reward."

One university student interviewed by Sherry Turkle said she knew a hacker that "never had a friendship at Harvard. He'd come to breakfast saying that he'd stayed up all night with his terminal and he got frustrated and burned out but he seemed to enjoy it somehow. It was better for him, I guess, than staying up all night talking to a friend."

If hackers prefer controlled experiences with machines to unpredictable experiences with humans, it is not surprising that Temple Grandin, prompted by an article in *The New Yorker*, should see a connection between autism and hacking—a connection, more specifically, between her and Bill Gates, the head of Microsoft. Gates "has some autistic traits," she noted, including "repetitive rocking and poor social skills. Gates rocks during business meetings and on airplanes; autistic children and adults rock when they are nervous. Other autistic traits he exhibits are lack of eye contact and poor social skills. . . . As a child, Gates had remarkable savant skills. He could recite long passages from the Bible without making a single mistake. His voice lacks tone. . . . Clothes and hygiene are low on his list of important things."

Gates does have some interesting habits. Recently he told an interviewer that he combs his hair before sending e-mail messages in order to "appear attractive." But he is not unique in his desire to be alone. Recently, one of America's most prominent computer experts and theorists, Esther Dyson, admitted that she had been "a lonely and socially inept child who preferred learning Russian to playing games." "She was happy to be left alone," according to her father. "We hardly noticed her."

Although any connection between autism and an affinity for computers may seem metaphorical, evidence is emerging to support a genetic basis for such a connection. Simon Baron-Cohen and his colleagues at the University of Cambridge report that the fathers and grandfathers of children with autism are more than twice as likely to work in the field of engineering than the fathers and grandfathers of normal children and children with other (nonautistic) kinds of cognitive and linguistic delays. These findings suggest that there is a characteristic cognitive profile of fathers of autistic children, according to which the ability to understand the causal and mechanical properties of objects exceeds the ability to understand other people's social intentions.

The characteristic cognitive profile of fathers extends to mothers, too. In a second study, Baron-Cohen and a colleague, Jessica Hammer, found that in children with Asperger's syndrome—a problem resembling autism though usually milder in severity—both parents did worse than other male and female adults on a "mind reading" task involving interpretation of mental states associated with the eyes; autists typically perform poorly on this task. They also were better at locating shapes embedded in complex designs; autists typically do well on this task.

This research makes it easy to see why some of the inventors and advocates of computerized communication systems might fail to appreciate the reductions of intimacy associated with computers, and also to see why autistic individuals are reported to enjoy using those systems. In fact, everyone from the fearful and the shy to the speech-impaired can now cast aside their inhibitions and begin to celebrate the new choices awaiting them in a voiceless society. When speech is no longer the leading social currency, the pressure is off those who stutter, vocalize strangely, or speak unintelligibly. The literate deaf will immediately find themselves in a better position to cope. In a voiceless society, new personalities can poke through; no one need fear unscheduled episodes of intimacy.

When Mutism Becomes the Norm

Muds are not just games, they are *real*!!! My mud friends are my best friends, they are the people who like me most in the entire world. Maybe the only people who do. . . . They are my family, they are not just some dumb game. Player of multi-user dimension computer games (muds) quoted in Elizabeth Reid, *Virtual Worlds*

In 1956 psychiatrist Erich Fromm asked a simple but powerful question: how do we know that we are sane? He pointed out that in the last century we in the Western world have achieved more material wealth than any other society in history and yet have managed to kill off millions of bright young people in periodic wars. And during our wars, "every participant firmly believed that he was fighting in his self-defense, for his honor, or that he was backed up by God." The combatants are typically viewed as "cruel, irrational fiends, whom one must defeat to save the world from evil. But a few years after the mutual slaughter is over," said Fromm, "the enemies of yesterday are our friends, the friends of yesterday our enemies." Domestically, "a particularly good crop is often an economic disaster, and we restrict some of our agricultural productivity in order to 'stabilize the market,' although there are millions of people who do not have the very things we restrict, and who need them badly." If an *individual* acted in this fashion, according to Fromm, "serious doubts would be raised as to his sanity. . . . Yet many psychiatrists and psychologists refuse to entertain the idea that society as a whole may be lacking in sanity."

I originally trained as a speech and language pathologist. For over thirty years I have been concerned with individuals who lose or fail to achieve satisfying levels of social communication. But why should a clinician be less concerned with a deficit—in this case, an intimacy deficit arising from social de-voicing—when it is experienced by an entire society?

When a practicing physician enters the field of public health, the "unit" of treatment increases from the individual to an entire population. At the same time, the concern may shift from the amelioration of individual complaints to their prevention, with a parallel shift of goals from the reversal of pathology to optimization of health.

Speech and language clinicians have always accepted that the optimal number of individuals to be treated simultaneously could vary from one to a small group of a half-dozen or so. But what if some very large group is involved, not as the optimal treatable unit but as the *cause* of the problem? That is, what if the group—the culture, in this case—is causing a problem for individuals? What if the individual finds himself increasingly incognito just by living in a de-voicing society?

We are now living in a computer-dominated world that changes by the day. But the movement is not driven by functions that will obviously improve our lives. Rather, it seems to have a zany, inward-looking, cybermanic quality. According to Ian Pearson, a futurologist for British Telephone, artificial cats and dogs will replace computers by 2010. He already has his own electronic cat, he said, and "it would not take much to add robotic legs and a furry covering, and replace the insides with a radio link to a powerful computer. The pet could then become your link to the global information superhighway. . . . The rest of the time it could be a cute family pet."

Pearson's colleagues at BT have already developed a computer that supposedly can tell whether someone is happy or sad from his or her facial expression, and can recognize whether people are indicating yes and no by the way they nod or shake their head. BT is also working on a computerization of the paper messages that people stick on their refrigerators. "Within a year or two we will be talking to our fridges," said Dr. Pearson, seemingly oblivious of the fact that in his own society husbands talk too little to wives and parents too little to children. Are refrigerated listeners a response to consumer demand?

We may soon be able to reinvent the voices of dead people. With a prototype of the new technology, voice samples have been copied, decomposed, and synthesized by computer, thereby producing songs never sung by the deceased singer. The method has been illustrated with samples from Maria Callas and Ella Fitzgerald. But some people are objecting. One jazz performer said that "redistributing notes is not what singing is all about. The difference between man and machine is emotion and feeling, and that is what Ella has and no box can ever match."

In the popular films *Forrest Gump* and *Contact*, American presidents are seen making statements that they never made in real life. The producer of *Contact*, Steve Starkey, says that technology now makes it possible to make anyone say anything. "You can actually sample all of the vowel and consonant sounds of a particular person's voice into a computer. Then you can form an entirely new sentence—and re-animate the face to fit the words."

Is it a response to consumer demand that cybernauts are now at work on a system that senses and displays human emotions on a computer screen along with our typed messages? A professor at the University of Geneva is doing exactly that, and prospective vendors are interested. To do this a computer scans facial muscles to see which of several basic emotions the user may be experiencing. Then a face and virtual body, called an "avatar," is animated with these emotions. In addition to displaying the emotions, the avatar wags its tail for intensely happy emotions and gets red in the face for anger. The inventor believes that "humans will react positively when they find virtual humans are clever, polite, capable of learning, and helpful. We will accept them," she declared, "because they will be helpful to us."

Imagine Cyber City, U.S.A., a community in which every resident is on the Net. Blacksburg, Virginia, is a town of thirty-five thousand in the Blue Ridge Mountains. Several years ago it became Blacksburg Electronic Village, a joint project of a local university, the town, and a regional telephone company. It now has a dubious distinction: it's the "most wired town" in the United States. Several years ago the fourteen thousand users received more than 110,000 e-mail messages per day. They ordered food and merchandise with their computers. This made Blacksburg residents feel pretty special, but some residents aren't convinced that the specialness is all positive. One thinks that boasting of its "most wired" status is not so different from claiming it has the most TV addicts.

Some of this has a *Brave New World* feeling; some resembles the parallel play of children. For example, a group of political scientists recently held a roundtable discussion at a Los Angeles–based Web site called Aapornet. "We were sitting alone staring into our computer screens," said the Web site's moderator, a communications professor, "but we were bonding together." Those describing the event said that "while communicating on the Internet isn't exactly like attending a town-hall meeting or a speech on the village green, it is not being alone either. It is being alone together, which will increasingly be a form of togetherness."

Get it? If you are alone at the same time as some other people, it gives you a feeling of togetherness with those people if your reasons for being alone are the same as theirs.

Some universities are seeking this sort of togetherness. One, the University of Phoenix, grants undergraduate and graduate degrees to cyberstudents who take their studies at an online campus. In June 1996 the governors of ten western states announced their intention to cooperate to create an entire virtual university in the following year. This new offering should please administrators and state legislators alike, for "at Virtual U., there is no need for costly land, buildings, or roads. There are no books, no protests, no students griping about food, parking, or surly roommates. And space is never a problem."

The fear, of course, is that there will be no one on the other end of the line to ensure that cyberstudents push themselves to think in new ways, learn to observe and interpret what they see, and change their views in the face of new evidence. One of the first cybergraduates of the State University of New York's Empire State College said she was "concerned that feedback will be limited to course work itself, and that the fuller relationships that develop between students and teachers on a college campus will be missing."

When they graduate, whether from a virtual university or a real one, students can interview for their first job on the Internet. Recently, over twenty national companies interviewed about a thousand students during a five-day "virtual job fair." The recruiters, who never left their corporate offices, talked with applicants over high-speed fiber-optic telephone lines, their images transmitted by personal computers mounted with tiny cameras. These virtual interviews cost no more than a dollar a minute, a real bargain considering the usual travel and hotel costs associated with recruitment. But personal reactions were mixed.

One of the recruiters said, "I missed the sense of that face-to-face encounter where I can shake the hands and read a little bit into nonverbal cues."

Okay, you say, some unusual, even odd things are happening under the name of improved communications, but isn't "cybermania" a pretty pejorative name for this kind of activity? No, not really. Evidence is accumulating that a sizable proportion of those who cannot wait to turn on their computers every morning are unable to turn them off at night. This new mania—which psychologists call Internet Addiction Syndrome, or IAS—is apparently affecting hundreds if not thousands of the cybercrazed. The syndrome was named by Dr. Ivan Goldberg, a psychopharmacologist from New York, and its effects are not limited to the young geeks from MIT. Rather, the affected include middle-aged and elderly housewives and husbands, many of whom were actually afraid of computers until they got seriously hooked. Symptoms are said to include "recurring dreams and fantasies about the Internet and a need to access it first thing in the morning . . . followed by lying to spouses about the time spent online and unsuccessful attempts to cut down." Some addicts experience "voluntary or involuntary typing movements of the fingers." Perhaps they're talking to themselves.

Some American addicts confess to spending twelve hours per day on the Net. One said, "I've been thinking of getting a second home phone installed in order to be able to talk to my family once in a while. I currently subscribe to eighty-nine news groups." At the University of Maryland in College Park there's a counseling service for students called "Caught in the Net." One American mother's Net addiction is so extreme that she was recently charged with neglecting her three young children.

In a study of one hundred Glaswegian cyberians conducted at the University of Glasgow, 16 percent claimed that they were irritable, tense, depressed, or restless if they were prevented from using the Internet; 27 percent felt guilty about the time they spent online; 10 percent admitted they had neglected a partner, child, or their work because of overuse; and 4 percent said excessive time on the Net had impaired their mental or physical health. A survey in New York revealed that seventeen percent of the cyberians spent more than forty hours a week on the Internet.

In a study conducted by Kimberly Young, a psychologist at the University of Pittsburgh, nearly four hundred Internet addicts—most with impoverished personal lives—were found to use the Internet for social support and sexual fulfillment, and for the opportunity to live through personas of their own creation. "In cyberspace," said Dr. Young, "a shy person can become outgoing, a nonsexual person can be sexual, a nonassertive person can be forceful, or an aloof person can be gregarious." The dependency of these pathological Internet users resembled that of alcoholics and gamblers.

Whatever is causing this level of mania is unknown, although the opportunity to assume false identities is apparently behind many of the addictions. But help is on the way. If the cybersick need assistance, they can contact the Center for On-Line Addiction at the University of Pittsburgh or a specialized netaholic clinic at McLean Hospital in Boston. Or they can log onto the Internet—taking a hair of the dog that bites them—and access "Internets Anonymous," "Webaholics," or Dr. Goldberg's group, the "Internet Addiction Support Group." One psychiatrist recommends that addicts not try to go "cold turkey" but limit use to a set number of hours per week. If that fails, psychotherapy is thought to be advisable.

Psychotherapy is called "the talking cure," but nowadays patients are increasingly encouraged to do their talking to a machine. Psychiatrists are beginning to tinker with the Internet for the evaluation and treatment of patients who at one time would have been candidates for psychotherapy. In America there is an e-mail system called Shrinklink. Individuals who are experiencing psychological problems can log on, ask a personal question (for $20), and, if necessary, be referred to a psychologist, psychiatrist, or therapist. There is also a human-free computerized screening service. Troubled telephonists hear a voice say, "I have crying spells" or "I get tired for no reason," and press a number between one and four to indicate how often they experience those feelings. A computer then analyzes their responses. At the moment, economic pressures are encouraging some psychiatrists to experiment with computer-assisted therapies for depression and anxiety.

In England, a mental hospital just inaugurated the country's first computerized self-help treatment for psychiatric patients. With this telephone service, it is now possible to "treat" thousands of patients in their own homes (many patients say they prefer to talk to a computer about their problems). Patients with obsessive-compulsive disorder simply call the hospital and request the telephone treatment. Those with other obsessive conditions (agoraphobia, claustrophobia) can ask for the Fear Fighter program. Individuals suffering from general anxiety are encouraged to apply for Worrytel. According to press reports, patients are assigned a PIN number and sent a manual that explains what to do. The manual has a nine-step treatment plan and a list of the different problems patients may encounter, each with its own code number. The patient rings a toll-free number, enters the identification number, and then follows pre-recorded instructions that are suggested by the computers. If something additional is needed, the patient is sent a fax. So don't say nobody cares about you!

Churches have no intention of missing the boat to Cyberia. At this writing over 400,000 home pages on the World Wide Web mention God; 146,000 refer to Christ. The priest at one of these sites, a Catholic church in Milwaukee, Wisconsin, says he regards the Web as "a contemporary version of making one's self available and accessible." The Web site of a nearby Orthodox Jewish congregation promises "an island of Yiddishkeit in the desert of suburbia." According to a study by Barna Research in California, churches that continue to do clerical business the old-fashioned way may soon be in difficulty. It "sends an important signal about the church's ability to advise people in an era of technological growth," Barna says.

The diocese of one French bishop, Jacques Gaillot, exists *only* in cyberspace. It is undeniably the most catholic of all Catholic churches. When Gaillot was dismissed from a diocese near Paris for opposing the Church hierarchy, the Vatican gave him the diocese of Partenia, which was last known as a specific place in Algeria during the fifth century. A computer-wise supporter suggested that Partenia become the host site of the bishop's diocese. And so it did. By accessing http://www.partenia.org you can get Gaillot's electronic catechism, a newsletter on rare or lost causes, and an e-mail number for people in need of advice or blessings. But at last report the bishop was still resisting online confessions.

The Internet is bringing about a change in church activity, but it also is causing a reexamination of God. William Gibson, coiner of the term "cyberspace," says that the Net "may regard itself as God. And it may *be* God on its own terms." According to a professor of religion at Temple University, to remain viable the concept of God must change along with the times. "If God doesn't change," he said, "we are in danger of losing God. . . . If you believe in an eternal, unchanging God, you'll be in trouble."

Electronic butlers that interpret your facial expressions, computer villages, addictions to e-mail, psychiatrists and clergy on the Net—these things are strange enough. But they pale in comparison to the romantic applications of computers. If you want to see weirdness in its purest form, consider the many wonderful benefits of "virtual dating," surely the most effective means of birth control yet developed.

The president of Microsoft, Bill Gates, apparently considers himself something of a virtual romantic. He says that he "used to date a woman who lived in a different city. We spent a lot of time together on e-mail. And we figured out a way we could sort of go to the movies together. We'd find a film that was playing at about the same time in both our cities. We'd drive to our respective theaters, chatting on our cellular phones. We'd watch the movie, and on the way home we'd use our cellular phones again to discuss the show." And then we may presume they jumped back on their computers for a good-night kiss. A certified doubter, Clifford Stoll, has said that "the networks are certainly great places to meet men. There are several guys online for every woman. But, like the outlook for women in Alaska, the odds are good, but the goods are odd."

Some people use the Net not as a means of getting to know another person but for more explicitly cybersexual purposes with a person they are hoping never to know. One woman "used interactive soft pornography to hold her marriage together," according to a recent article in *The Times* of London, "but she had a contract with her husband that she wouldn't actually see the man on the end of the computer link in real life. Dull marriages are often preserved today by one partner's cruising of the Net for sexual adventure." According to American anthropologist Helen Fisher, "A computer love match can be just as time-consuming and disruptive as a regular adulterous affair. You are very secretive, you hide information and you can—and these people do—actually reach orgasm."

Unless, of course, the electronic lovers' ardor is cooled by a misspelling. Humorist Dave Barry says that he could not have a satisfying bout of cybersex "with someone who misused apostrophes." No lover, according to Barry, should have to think about punctuation or spelling while having sex, whether he does so on the Net or in bed.

In at least one case, e-mail's impersonal nature made it seem exactly the right modality for ending a relationship. Recently, just as a San Francisco man was readying himself for a long-anticipated march down the matrimonial aisle, his computer began to blink out a four-page Dear John letter. "I couldn't believe that after six and a half years she ended our relationship by e-mail," he said.

A fifty-year-old lawyer in Sheffield, England, had less difficulty believing that his extramarital affair had come to an end. The Dear John letter from his young lover was waiting in his electronic mail when he returned from a business trip. The computer in his office impersonally blinked out the reasons. Distraught, the lawyer went home to gas himself. While in the garage, he left a suicide message to his wife on a Dictaphone. His very last act was to change the message on his office voicemail system from his mobile phone. It was high-tech to the bitter end.

In another case a man claimed in court to have been electronically cuckolded over the Internet. His wife, he alleged, sent increasingly affectionate messages from her New Jersey home to an electronic lover in North Carolina who signed himself "The Weasel." Although they had never met, the two arranged for a romantic liaison in a hotel in New Hampshire. But the husband discovered their plans when he came home early from work one day. His surprised wife hurriedly switched off the computer and tore paper from the printer. But the husband called up his wife's old e-mail message on to the screen—and was shocked at what he read. He asked her to stop the electronic liaison, but in vain. The grounds for divorce were unprecedented: the husband alleged that his wife and her admirer "got it on" through e-mail.

We have all heard of cross-dressing, but since the Internet became popular, there has also been an outbreak of cross-talking. The following story offers a glimpse of this:

> Sue lived in South Wales, which is some distance away from the rest of the MUD-playing community, long phone calls

away. And Sue got all the way up to game administrator level, "Arch Witch." She used to write letters to everybody, great long old-fashioned letters on paper. She enclosed photographs. She's quite good-looking. As far as we were concerned, Sue was a female. One of our wizzes fell quite heavily in love with Sue and sent photographs and gifts and so on, flowers, and he even proposed marriage. Then Sue started behaving out of character. And all of a sudden Sue said she was going to Sweden to be an au pair and that was that. We never heard any more, so we thought something seemed suspicious here. So a group of the wizzies put together facts from Sue's letters, like her father ran some kind of a factory and you know she lives in South Wales and we've got the address that we write to, and went around—I wasn't there—but they went around to see Sue, knocked on the door, this woman opens the door. "Hello, we've come to see Sue." The woman says, "I think you better come in. Unfortunately, Sue's name is Steve and he's been arrested for defrauding the Department of Transport. He's presently in prison. I'm his wife."

In a survey carried out as long as ten years ago, some 150,000 males had already confessed to masquerading as women on one Internet server. Why men pose as females on the Net is unclear, but the tendency to "ventriloquize" female voices is nothing new. According to a book by Elizabeth Harvey, it's been happening in literature since the English Renaissance.

I suppose it is only "natural" that some of the "romantic" relationships that develop on the Net would lead to "virtual marriage," and they do. But first, in keeping with the times, many just "live together." When a relationship becomes serious, wrote Elizabeth Reid, as a doctoral student in Melbourne, Australia, it is not uncommon for them to

set up virtual house together. They quite literally create a home together, using the MUD program to arrange textual information in a way that simulates a physical structure which they can then share and invite others to share. These relationships may even be consummated through virtual sex, enacted as cowritten interactive erotica. More technically gifted players may also create objects, which other players can interact with, that textually mimic the behavior of pets and children. Such creations act as a virtual affirmation and imaginative realization of players' emotions.

Reid also provides us with an intimate glimpse of a "wedding ceremony" in this unusual Net culture:

> MUD weddings are simple in conception. The virtual bride and groom are married by another player who virtually reads, and actually types, the wedding ceremony. Tokens are often exchanged, virtual representations of flowers and rings attached to a player's virtual manifestations through the manipulation of the textual description of the character. The wedding is usually attended by a number of fellow players, whose participation in the event bolsters its imaginative reality in the shared minds of the MUD community. The forthcoming nuptials are often publicized in the communications media.

When love and friendship flourish over a computer network, when marriages are decided and terminated electronically, or have no extra-electronic reality, it is time to ask what social interaction is *for*. In the words of the song recorded years ago by the actress Lola Albright, "What are these arms for, what are these charms for, use your imagination." Apparently some people use their imaginations very well indeed. They take pleasure in a society that is virtual, controlled, unthreatening. In *The Virtual Community*, Howard Rheingold wrote about a party he attended in which all the invitees were people he had corresponded with by e-mail but had never met:

> I looked around at the room full of strangers when I walked in. It was one of the oddest sensations of my life. I had contended with these people, shot the invisible breeze around the electronic watercooler, shared alliances and formed bonds, fallen off my chair laughing with them, become livid with

anger at some of them. But there wasn't a recognizable face in the house. I had never seen them before.

Computer-assisted communication is coming on like a steamroller, flattening intimate forms of self-expression. Justifying the cost and time associated with business trips will get harder, especially when the available communication systems were bought in order to obviate such travel. Eventually, meeting or knowing someone with whom we work will be viewed as a coincidence.

A clock is ticking on our personal lives, our communities, and our civic institutions. How much longer can we and our communities prosper with so little personal warmth and trust? What are the chances of vocal warming?

EIGHT

Vocal Warming?

A people cannot restore the vivacity of its earlier times, any more than a man can return to the innocence and the bloom of childhood: such things may be regretted, but they cannot be renewed. Alexis de Tocqueville, *Democracy in America*

No one questions de Tocqueville's characterization of nineteenth-century America, but when he wrote the paragraph above, the place he had in mind was Europe. There, he said, "the inhabitants . . . set too high a value upon their time to spend it on the interests of the community; and they prefer to withdraw within the exact limits of a wholesome egotism, marked out by four sunk fences and a quickset hedge."

Now, over a century later, de Tocqueville's description sadly fits America, too. Self-interest pulled even with and then overtook community needs. Neighborliness went out of fashion. Social infrastructure shriveled.

The critical question before us, wrote social and political commentator Max Lerner, "is not whether the small town can be rehabilitated in the image of its earlier strength and growth—for clearly it cannot—but whether American life will be able to evolve any other integral community to replace it." This sounds remarkably like a challenge, one not met in the thirty years since Lerner issued it. Can we begin to meet it now?

When I was a graduate student, a sage remarked one day that it was inhumane to diagnose a condition that could not be treated, that doing so just puts the patient in an uncomfortable position. At base I am a meliorist. I want to help make things better, but it is unclear just what we individuals, mere dots on the larger technoscape, can do to re-voice ourselves. And with staggering environmental problems—traffic jams, fuel shortages, unbreatheable air—it may only be a matter of time before virtual offices in our homes replace the real ones in which people gather to work cooperatively.

Reheating the Voice

We cannot reverse vocal cooling any more easily than readers of *Future Shock* could go out and slow down societal change. But we can begin to respond reflectively, a process abetted to some degree by having the concept "de-voicing" in our lexicon. For it is when we learn to recognize society-level disorders and their causes that we potentially reduce our personal bewilderment.

If you begin to feel vaguely disconnected, lonely, or isolated, it might be beneficial to ask yourself how much time you've spent lately talking and laughing with close friends.

If you find that as you walk down the street you scan the faces of passersby to see if you recognize them, or they you; or if you look into the eyes of all people, familiar or unfamiliar, as though to seek "connection," then you may be missing socially intimate interactions.

If at the end of a day of speaking you still haven't emotionally connected with anyone, you may be suffering from society's newest form of "locked-in syndrome"—selective loss of intimate communication with preserved ability to produce words and sentences.

We have seen that business and government depend on trust, which is in free fall in America and other progressive nations. This decline is a condition that needs to be treated. The catch is that trust can only be restored through personal action. There is nothing that government can do except perhaps to increasingly remove itself from our lives. Unfortunately, there is a vicious cycle. On the one hand, personal contact—the only means to deal effectively with declining trust—is also subsiding rapidly. On the other hand, the probability of people suddenly beginning consistently to exchange personal views and attitudes with others is unlikely under conditions of serious mistrust.

How easily the tide can be reversed I do not know, but there are some positive signs here and there. Seventy-seven percent of the thousand-plus Americans responding to a *Time*/CNN poll in July 1996 said, understandably, that they wished they could have more contact with other members of their communities. Thirty-six percent said they already take part in volunteer organizations; and in low-income areas there has been a tremendous upsurge in the number of people who want to help out in their own communities. Even teenagers—57 percent, no less—participate in some form of community service.

Much to the astonishment of Ben Brantley, chief drama critic of the *New York Times*, a British play named *Skylight* has been well received by the tough-minded theater audiences on Broadway. The surprise is because the central theme of the play pits capitalistic selfishness against community altruism, an issue that would normally be guaranteed to keep Americans at home in front of their TVs. One applause-garnering line was "Do you know what social workers do? Every day? They try to clear out society's drains. They clear out the rubbish. They do what no one else is doing, what no one else is willing to do. And for that, oh Christ, do we thank them?"

Should we be hopeful? Certainly not on the basis of these fragments. And yet for all the desocialization that has occurred over the past decades, there is every reason to believe that time-honored social principles live on in some quarters. Diplomats, for example, have never forgotten that harmonious relations among nations require personal ties among the leaders of those nations. The language of international diplomacy includes *rapprochement*, the reestablishment of harmonious relations, and *deténte*, a means of managing adversarial powers through conscious and deliberate reduction in tension. In pursuit of "shuttle diplomacy," President Nixon's Secretary of State, Henry Kissinger, flew to all corners of the earth to conduct negotiations in a face-to-face fashion rather than trust the process to cable and telephone. In business, important deals are still negotiated in a heavily personal and social climate. Sociality may be slipping, but it is surely not dead.

In *The Broken Heart*, James Lynch wrote that "the best hope of changing the Type A behavior pattern," a documented threat to cardiac health, "rests in revitalizing human companionship and the pleasure derived from social intercourse." How to do this is, of course, another matter. We cannot change society, but we may be able to change our own personal priorities.

Altered Priorities Ahead

The possibility of change depends on the existence of people who have the power to change . . . not from the outside by the instruction of visiting experts, but from the inside by the ancient rule of neighborliness.

Wendell Berry, *What Are People For?*

When driving through the south of England in 1994, I came across a road sign that said "Altered Priorities Ahead." Later I was to learn from British friends that this sign merely advised motorists that at some place up the road the normal rights-of-way had been changed. But the phrase stuck in my mind because I had just begun to think that it was time for me to restructure my life in certain ways.

We must alter our priorities if we are to get our voices back. Just as each of us participated in the process that led to our de-voicing, so must we re-voice ourselves through individual action. Some people are already beginning to do precisely that. They're "putting their emotional investment into values and lifestyles that depend less on work and money," says Daniel Yankelovich, the public opinion analyst. "It's going to be the political issue of the future." According to Inferential Focus, a New York trend-analysis firm, the desire "to take flight from current employment predicaments has become pandemic." Some people are doing this by staying put—rejecting corporate relocations, even if they mean faster advancement or more money. These "rooted workers," according to a recent article in *USA Today*, "are becoming a major obstacle for employers, who once rearranged personnel as easily as push pins on a map.

Others are "downshifting." Downshifting ranges from complete retirement to accepting a less demanding job. It could also include more or longer holidays. At the 1996 Reform Party Convention in Long Beach, California, the official planks of the party's political platform were ticked off one by one. But a television camera that had been panning the audience fixated on a delegate with an additional candidate for plankhood neatly printed on a letter-size envelope:

4-WEEK VACATIONS?

In Bohematea, a restaurant in Victoria, British Columbia, I saw a sign in a window:

WE ARE NOW CLOSED ON MONDAYS BECAUSE IT'S SMART
TO TAKE A DAY OFF AND DO OTHER STUFF.

There are economic implications to working fewer hours, of course. Unless there is a commensurate decrease in pay, the cost of our products goes up, and we become less competitive. But who says we can't have a reduction in pay? Did you personally insist that you be allowed to work forty hours per week, or was that just what happened to be available at the time?

If we get more time to socialize, that by itself would not guarantee more repersonalization. How do we socialize with our fellows when our environment is littered with privatizing devices? Visitors to the 1933 World's Fair in Chicago were greeted by a sign over the entryway that said,

SCIENCE EXPLORES: TECHNOLOGY EXECUTES: MAN CONFORMS.

Man does indeed conform, even deluding himself into thinking that the possibilities inherent in various inventions were actually something he had always wanted. Little wonder: the Madison Avenue ad agencies present new products as "solutions" to people's problems (such as deodorant for underarm odor) even if the need was previously unnoticed.

Recently, Prince Charles claimed that technology was becoming a "virtual reality god . . . the eventual murderer" of the human soul. How, then, do we keep technology in its place? It begins with the determination to do something about it. Some years ago, according to Marshall McLuhan, "UNESCO installed water pipes in some Indian villages. But soon after the water began to flow, the villagers requested that the pipes be removed, for it seemed to them that the whole social life of the village had been impoverished when it was no longer necessary for all to visit the communal well."

I believe that in one sense, the cybercrowd is doing us all a favor. By touting the wonders of virtual communities, they are psychologically freeing us to see that real community is something we lack, and we can at least ask how it might be regained.

Virtual communities are not biological ones of course, so they cannot fill the need of which their existence, paradoxically, makes us aware. At most they abstractly unite dissociated people. The psychological nature of the hookup—the humanity of it—falls far short of any kind of human experience to which our grandparents were accustomed.

Other people craving community think that urban planning is the answer. They think that we can be stitched into a quilt of relationships when we have wider sidewalks, and more places that we can walk to. But we have to *want* to do these things, to make the time, to crawl out of our technocopias. Some things we are currently doing, such as vegetating, will have to be abandoned.

To win back our voices, we will need to use certain technologies judiciously. Where their children are concerned, some people already make and apply rules to limit technical and other self-absorbing pursuits and extend familial companionship. They limit the amount of television, VCR, and computer time, and insist that their children eat dinner at the family dining table instead of on the floor in front of the TV set. Adults need to make and apply rules to their own behaviors as well, to spend a certain amount of time talking without extraneous interference whether it originates within or without their domestic environment.

People give up smoking to avoid losing years from their life but if one gave up television they would probably gain a day a week. Over a sixty-five-year period one could add more than nine years of usable time to one's life. In Chicago there is a quarterly magazine, *The White Dot*, that is explicitly directed to people who have rid themselves of their television sets. The magazine prints tips on how TV-less parents can entertain their children while taking a shower or cooking. Recently a spokesman for the White Dot Society was in London to promote "National Turn Off Your Television Week." He expressed sadness that people would watch an American television program like "Cheers," which advertises that everyone knows your name, instead of actually going out and mingling with friends and neighbors.

One solution is to throw your TV out the window, as at least one White Dotter did, but less theatrical viewers can simply reduce their tube time. They also can use it differently. Instead of staring in social isolation at a film on one's VCR, friends and neighbors can be invited over for a mini-film fest.

Most of us feel strongly that artificial substances should not be used in such a way as to foul the environment or harm animals and plants. But we human animals inhabit a social environment that is being harmed by devices that are so aggressively assistive that they completely replace us. How are we to deal with domestic technology? In an essay on why he planned not to buy a computer, Wendell Berry said that he wished to replace neither his Royal standard typewriter, bought new in 1956, nor his wife, who patiently typed his handwritten essays, catching errors as she went. A new tool, Berry declared, "should not replace or disrupt anything good that already exists, and this includes family and community relationships."

Kurt Vonnegut, obviously agrees. Asked in an interview how he feels about life in a computerized world, Vonnegut took the question as an opportunity to say exactly how he normally operates. "I use a typewriter," he said,

> and afterwards I mark up the pages with a pencil. Then I call up this woman named Carol out in Woodstock and say: "Are you still doing typing?" She is, and her husband is trying to track bluebirds out there and not having much luck, and so we chitchat back and forth, and I say, "Okay, I'll send you the pages." . . . So I go to this newsstand across the street where they sell magazines and lottery tickets and stationery. I have to get in line because there are people buying candy and all that sort of thing, and I talk to them.

When Vonnegut finally gets to the woman behind the counter, he said,

I ask her if there have been any big winners lately. I get my envelope and seal it up and go to the postal convenience center down the block at the corner of 47th Street and 2nd Avenue, where I'm secretly in love with the woman behind the counter. I keep absolutely poker-faced, I never let her know how I feel about her. . . . Anyway, I address the envelope to Carol in Woodstock. I stamp the envelope and mail it in a mailbox in front of the post office, and I go home.

Vonnegut concluded by offering up his philosophy of life: "We are here on Earth to fart around, and don't let anybody tell you any different."

Kurt Vonnegut is one person that is neither aided nor hindered by technology. He is an extraordinarily talented writer with a strong international reputation. He can afford to do things his own way. But even if computers were destroying his life, could we really say that technology was at fault? People have always had to actively avoid the domination and damage of technology. They can do this if, like Vonnegut, they ask what they want life to be for, and recognize that the resources needed to secure that life are in them and available to them—time, energy, self-discipline, and imagination.

If people cannot break away from the screens in their life—TV, VCR, e-mail, computer—I see little hope for their resocialization. But for those who are able to de-tube themselves, what can they do with the new time that becomes available? Should they rush out and join a group? Formal groups, with a regular meeting time and place, are designed to do for their members what life in neighborhoods and communities used to do. They exist in large measure as compensations for societal changes that reduce the frequency and intimacy of personal interactions.

If small groups are thought of as a solution to desocialization, I'm afraid the news isn't very good. Few think they work, at least on a personal level. Richard Goodwin has pointed out that all the clubs, associations, citizens' groups, and recreation leagues "are not a substitute for the regular contact of people who share an environment and its concerns." Princeton's Robert Wuthnow has found that small groups mainly "provide occasions for individuals to focus on themselves in the presence of others. The social contract binding members together asserts only the weakest of obligations. Come if you have time. Talk if you feel like it. Respect everyone's opinion. Never criticize. Leave quietly if you become dissatisfied." These groups, he concluded, do not really substitute for families, neighborhoods, and broader community attachments.

In *Overcoming Loneliness in Everyday Life,* two Boston psychiatrists, Jacqueline Olds and Richard Schwartz, suggest that because of their episodic nature, groups "fail to replicate the sense of belonging we have lost. Attending weekly meetings, dropping in and out as one pleases, shopping around for a more satisfactory or appealing group—all of these factors work against the growth of true community."

Nearly thirty years ago a lecturer in sociology in Harvard's community psychiatry program, Robert Weiss, published a paper on "The Fund of Sociability." In this paper Weiss toyed with the idea that individuals have an interaction quota that may be filled in various ways. Weiss hypothesized that people "may with equal satisfaction have a few intense relationships or have a large number of relationships of lesser intensity. They would experience stress," Weiss ventured, "only if the total amount of relating to others was too little or too great."

Weiss proceeded to test out his "fund" concept by looking at what group membership did for two categories of people who were experiencing stress. One category, which included people who were divorced, separated, or widowed, belonged to the local chapter of Parents without Partners. The other category included married couples who were experiencing personal or marital stress because of relocation, and they belonged to a group operated by Weiss himself. In the end, Weiss found that participation in these groups did very little to meet or restore the sense of personal well-being that had been lost. He surmised that "just as friendships do not provide the functions ordinarily provided by marriage, neither does marriage provide the functions ordinarily provided by friendship."

To affiliate is to become a member of a group. It is not to connect with individual members. There is thus a great difference between intimacy and affiliation, and one cannot be substituted for the other. Humans need both. Without personal intimacy, affiliation becomes, in Weiss's words, "little more than a means of dulling the sense of emptiness in our lives. Lacking affiliation, intimacy becomes overburdened even as it risks the dullness of restricted human contact."

Since we get different things from different types of relationships, each of us needs a number of different relationships to achieve a feeling of well-being. Relationships give us that feeling through the specific actions of our friends. They assure us that we have worth, and they affirm that we have specific competences and characteristics that make us worthy of respect. As Pete Hamill said, friends "understand that at its dark secret root, friendship is a conspiracy."

I believe satisfying types of socialization are most likely to be found when people take the time to engage in cooperative efforts, frequently those that—like the topics of small talk—are of less than earth-shattering significance. Several years ago I spent a sabbatical at the University of Cambridge. Each day I rode my bicycle to the laboratory, which was located in a tiny village several miles from the city. One chilly morning I noticed a sign that said:

TOADS' CROSSING

PLEASE BE CAREFUL

Initially it seemed preposterous, but I learned from an English friend that every March the people of the village help toads across the road so they can lay their eggs in a nearby pond. When the biological deed is done the following month, the toad brigade again assembles to carry the toads back to whence they came.

The reason this amused and intrigued me is the reason that it is odd: most of us fast-trackers think we don't have enough time to do something so insignificant. Who cares about toads? They're not on the endangered species list, are they? And if they're so valuable, why not pressure the government into doing something or, failing that, chip in a few bucks and hire some kids to help out? We could then use the toad-helping time to . . . to . . .

Notes

Chapter One   The Articulate Heart

PAGE

22 *Anthropologist Polly Wiessner learned:* The ! symbol means that the first sound is made by forcibly pushing the tip of the tongue off from the roof of the mouth with a loud click.

23 *Although Wiessner's immediate interest:* Wiessner (1983).

23 *"Your car locates you":* "Type of Car Can Reveal Exactly What Drives You," *The Daily Telegraph,* London, April 21, 1997.

23 *There were strong correlations between:* Newhagen and Ancell (1995).

24 *They call attention to our existence:* Derber (1983).

25 *Although there are many connections:* Kramer (1963).

25 *Not just anger and contempt:* Ross, Duffy, Cooker, and Sargeant (1973); Scherer, Koivumaki, and Rosenthal (1972).

25 *For this reason the voice of the squirrel monkey:* Larson (1988); Jürgens (1995).

26 *In Stanislavski's school of:* Stanislavski (1990).

26 *Within a few hours of birth:* Berntson and Boysen (1989).

27 *Human children and adults require:* Linnankoski, Laakso, Aulanko, and Leinonen (1994).

27 *In the uterus, despite noisy:* DeCasper and Fifer (1980); DeCasper, Lecanuet, Busnel, Granier-Deferre, and Maugeais (1994).

27 *When loud sounds occur:* Birnholz and Benacerraf (1983).

27 *Once, in the middle of a delivery:* Blair (1965), p. 1165.

27 *In laboratories, too, electronic filtering:* Ross, Duffy, Cooker, and Sergeant (1973); Scherer, Koivumaki, and Rosenthal (1972).

28 *Cambridge psychologist Nicholas Humphrey:* Humphrey (1996).

28 *If a speaker's tone conflicts:* Argyle, Salter, Nicholson, Williams, and Burgess (1970); Mehrabian and Wiener (1967).

28 *If people physically approach:* Kozlowski and Cutting (1977).

29 *In one study it was found:* Bahrick, Bahrick, and Wittlinger (1975).

29   *Recently, two neuroscientists in San Diego:* Hirstein and Ramachandran (1997).
29   *In one experiment, volunteers were unable:* Van Lancker, Kreiman, and Emmorey (1985); Van Lancker, Kreiman, and Wickens (1985).
29   *In a more appropriately designed study:* Cf. Ladefoged and Ladefoged (1980).
30   *Even discrimination of handwritten samples:* Hamilton (1991).
30   *When combined in a single analysis:* Farringdon (1996).
30   *Then an unrelated analysis showed:* "Primary Suspect Is Trapped by His Own Hand," *The Times,* London, July 18, 1996.
30   *Ensnared by the consistency:* "Media Nail Author of Clinton Expose," *The Independent,* London, July 19, 1996.
30   *This requires that we mine:* Labov (1984, 1990); Shipp and Hollien (1969); Walton and Orlikoff (1994).
30   *The benefits to our ancient ancestors:* Dunbar (1988); Plutchik (1981).
31   *Although the environmental playing field:* Baumeister and Tice (1990).
31   *Members of any subgroup:* Coates (1986).
31   *One of the goals of psychotherapy:* Ludwig (1997, p. 157).
32   *Thus, regardless of what we believe:* Zajonc (1980) has reported that the emotion associated with events often persists even after their cognitive basis has been invalidated.
32   *"A glance, a few spoken words":* Asch (1946).
32   *Nearly a century ago:* Cooley (1902).
33   *Over time, the word* persona: Beare (1964); Moses (1954).
33   *As might be expected, they observed:* Zuckerman and Driver (1989); Zuckerman, Hodgins, and Miyake (1990).
33   *In females, an attractive voice:* D. S. Berry (1990).
33   *And these attributes will be revealed:* Davitz (1964).
33   *One prominent public relations executive:* "Your Number's Up: The Phone That Can Tell the Ring of Truth," *The Times,* London, July 13, 1997.
34   *People were not surprised:* "The Making of a Contender," *Newsweek,* March 12, 1984; "A Talk with Gary Hart," and "In Search of the Real Hart," *Newsweek,* March 26, 1984.
34   *An eminent graphologist declared:* Thornton (1996), p. 84.
35   *Specifically, he misarticulated:* Tanford, Pisoni, and Johnson (1990).
35   *The Vocalyser, another device:* "Telling Test for Drink Drivers," *The Sunday Times,* London, September 29, 1995.
36   *In the typical case, one of the parties:* Cappella and Greene (1982); Giles (1984); Giles, Mulac, Bradac, and Johnson (1987); Giles and Coupland (1991).
36   *Analyses of transcripts:* Levin and Lin (1988).
37   *There was a general trend:* Gregory and Webster (1996).
38   *One of the reasons we can risk:* Haith, Bergman, and Moore (1977); Keating and Keating (1982, 1993); Mendelson, Haith, and Goldman-Rakic (1982).
38   *Other cells are tuned to direction:* Desimone (1991); Perrett and Mistlin (1990).
38   *In view of the generally close connection:* Raushecker, Tian, and Hauser (1995).
38   *Like those of monkeys:* Creutzfeldt, Ojemann, and Lettich (1989a, b); Ross (1981); Tranel, Damasio, and Damasio (1988); Van Lancker, Cummings, Kreiman, and Dobkin (1988).
38   *This set of neural and cognitive:* Brothers (1990); Karmiloff-Smith, Klima, Bellugi, Grant, and Baron-Cohen (1995); Locke (1992; 1993).

38   *And there are gross anatomical similarities:* Hamilton and Vermeire (1988); Hauser (1993); Ross, Duffy, Cooker, and Sergeant (1973).

38   *Much to the astonishment:* Geiselman (1979); Geiselman and Bellezza (1976, 1977); Goldinger (1992); Schacter and Church (1992); Speer, Crowder, and Thomas (1993).

39   *"For anyone who regards* language": Miller (1990, pp. 113 and 115; italics his).

40   *Essentially the same level of prediction:* Ambady and Rosenthal (1993).

40   *"As soon as a strong current":* Stevenson (1897, p. 187).

40   *Infants begin to track:* Scaife and Bruner (1975).

40   *The speaker's glance at the listener:* Kendon (1967, 1973); Argyle and Dean (1965); Argyle and Cook (1976): gaze and emotions and language; Eibl-Eibesfeldt (1974): eyebrow movements.

41   *Tests reveal that we usually know:* Gibson and Pick (1963).

41   *One of the suggestions:* "Highway Code to Advise on Road Rage," *The Times*, London, May 26, 1996.

42   *And when, caught by Ehrlichman's gaze:* Hearings before the Select Committee on Presidential Campaign Activities (1973, pp. 2106–107).

42   *According to a media watcher:* "He Smiled but His Eyes Conveyed Fear," *The Daily Telegraph*, London, April 8, 1997.

42   *Four days later Mr. Blair's opponent:* "How Major Got His Smile Back," *The Times*, London, April 12, 1997.

42   *In Iraq, Saddam Hussein:* Hart (1994), p. 72.

42   *Remarkably, Gottman found:* Gottman (1994)

42   *The last found:* Argyle and Cook (1976, pp. 164–65).

43   *In this "bible" of diplomacy:* Callières (1983/1716, p. 145).

43   *Bill Raduchel, of Sun:* "All You Need to Know," Tom Peters, *Forbes ASAP*, June 3, 1996.

Chapter Two   Duty and Pleasure

45   *Examples of pure sound-making:* Samarin (1972).

45   *The rhythmic and melodic aspects:* Locke (1997); in the vast majority, the left hemisphere is rather more strongly given over to linguistic processing than the right, but both hemispheres play a role, and from an early age the right hemisphere is capable of taking on all linguistic operations if the left is damaged or even surgically removed.

45   *KLM 4805:The KLM four eight zero five is now ready for takeoff:* Cushing (1994, pp. 9–10).

46   *Later, Malinowski reflected:* Malinowski (1923, p. 316).

47   *Inquiries about health:* Malinowski (1923, p. 313).

47   *In* The Language Instinct: Pinker (1994).

48   *He said that "great freedom is allowed":* Carothers (1959, p. 308).

48   *The women sit near the chiefs:* Sherzer (1990).

49   *Their conversation, said Malinowski:* Malinowski (1922, p. 214).

49   *Among the Nharo people:* Barnard (1992).

49   *Each story told by the Limba:* Finnegan (1967, p. 93).

49   *Anthropologist Lorna Marshall:* Marshall (1961, p. 232).

49 *Other characterizations indicate:* Lee (1979, p. 372).
50 *While poisoning an arrow:* Obituary of Marjorie Shostak, *The Economist*, October 19, 1996.
50 *This includes laws:* Ong (1982).
50 *A researcher at the University of Canterbury:* Kuiper (1996).
51 *In fact, an analysis of nearly two thousand:* Soskin and John (1963).
51 *Several decades ago, Warren:* Fay (1975).
52 *The kvetching mother:* Birdwhistell (1974, p. 213).
52 *A reviewer observed:* Rose (1985, p. 126).
52 *Rather, talking usually begins:* Schegloff and Sacks (1974).
53 *It is interesting to note in this connection:* Settle (1977).
54 *The data were not gathered:* Dunbar (1993).
54 *"In their talk and thought":* Harding (1975, pp. 286–87).
55 *Complaints about people who hoarded:* Wiessner (1981).
55 *But a great deal of their car talk:* Folb (1980, p. 84).
55 *They were the instruments:* Thomas (1992).
56 *In 1930, before telephone eavesdropping:* French, Carter, and Koenig (1930).
56 *But the inhabitants of industrialized societies:* Miller (1996).
57 *Blind children do not necessarily:* See Landau and Gleitman (1985).
57 *When Sweden's rulers:* Oldenburg (1989); in 1675, King Charles II attempted to suppress English coffeehouses where "false, malicious, and scandalous reports are devised and spread abroad" (Sommerville, 1997).
58 *In the last stage of the opening phase:* Laver (1975).
58 *He: Night, darling:* Dempster and Evans (1994).
59 *If you were the ideal applicant: The Guardian*, London, May 21, 1997.
59 *At least twenty thousand Brits:* "20,000 Apply to Be Spies for MI5," *The Daily Telegraph*, London, June 5, 1997.
59 *And every bit as important:* Rymer (1994, p. 227).
60 *Children with hydrocephalus:* Landau and Kleffner (1957); Tew (1979).
60 *Talkers are thus limited:* Morris (1967, pp. 204–5).
61 *The desire for intimacy:* Linder (1970, p. 90).
61 *V. H. Friedlaender said:* Friedlaender (1922, p. 73).
61 *"It is not what is said":* Sapir (1933, p. 160).
61 *Another geographically displaced wife:* Gerstel and Gross (1984, p. 54).
62 *"I replied stiffly":* Kissinger (1979, p. 9).
62 *Viewing this with understandable alarm:* The book is *The Conversation Piece: Creative Questions to Tickle the Mind;* the column is "Hello Dollies, Everywhere," *The Sunday Times*, London, October 27, 1996.
62 *Although many of us associate:* Cowlan (1979)
62 *In an analysis of verbal:* Powell and Ary (1979, p. 124; quote below from p. 125).
63 *Therapist: so this is where they adapt cars:* Wilkinson (1995, pp. 278–79).
64 *Anyone who doubts this:* Sirica (1979).
64 *In* The Man Who Mistook: Sacks (1985, p. 76).
65 *The aphasia evidence pointed me:* Locke (1996).
65 *Since the newly lexical:* Furrow (1992).
65 *I concluded that the true motive:* Locke (1996); also see Trevarthen (1993).
65 *The speaker must mean something:* Wittgenstein (1973, p. 457).
65 *For his part, the listener must understand:* Bakhtin (1986, p. 68; quotation written in 1953).

Chapter Three   Social Work

PAGE

68 *But these infants usually vocalize:* Dennis (1941); Ferrier, Johnston, and Bashir (1991); MacKain (1984); Marchman, Miller, and Bates (1991); O'Gara and Logemann (1988); Sachs, Bard, and Johnson (1981); Schiff (1979).

68 *Even profound deafness fails:* Lenneberg, Rebelsky, and Nichols (1965).

68 *And when congenitally deaf mothers:* Mills and Coerts (1990).

68 *Intentional communication involves:* MacKay (1972).

68 *They were mathematicians:* Shannon and Weaver (1949).

69 *Those who use ambiguity:* Brenneis (1987).

69 *One reason for believing so:* Brown (1981).

69 *These dissociations of language:* See, for example, Blank, Gessner, and Esposito (1979).

69 *clinicians recently discovered:* The first example is from Bishop and Adams (1989), the second from Perkins (in press).

70 *Recently, the English archeologist Steven Mithen:* Mithen (1996, pp. 49–50).

71 *Nevertheless, within a year:* Ardrey (1961, p. 44).

71 *These are as obvious:* Fortes (1945); Short and Strodtbeck (1965).

72 *But these signals are usually audible:* Harcourt, Stewart, and Hauser (1993).

72 *Dian Fossey heard them:* Fossey (1972).

72 *Their calls, like our talking:* Cheney and Seyfarth (1980, 1990); Symmes and Biben (1985); Waser (1977).

73 *Since manual grooming has little to do:* Goosen (1981); Sade (1966) provides a detailed account of all the manual movements used in grooming.

73 *it is usually referred to as social grooming:* van Lawick-Goodall (1975).

73 *In a study of female baboons:* Cheney (1977).

73 *Similar findings have been reported:* Simpson (1973).

73 *As animal behaviorist Andrew Whiten:* Whiten (1993, p. 719; italics his).

74 *When our premodern ancestors:* Aiello (1996).

74 *In nonhuman primates:* Dunbar (1996).

74 *These calls meet certain requirements:* Biben, Symmes, and Bernhards (1989); Boinski (1991); Cheney and Seyfarth (1982).

75 *The human conversational speaking rate:* Anthoney (1968); rate of human syllable production is from Deese (1984), cited by Levelt (1989).

75 *The sound is made:* Redican (1975); van Hoof (1962).

75 *Tongue smacking may have signaled:* Marler and Tenaza (1977).

75 *the smacks acting not so very differently:* Richard Meier and his colleagues (Meter, McGarvin, Zakia, and Willerman, 1997) have observed "jaw wags" in nine- and 10-month-old infants that make a lip-smacking sound and have been called "lipsmacks" by at least one vocal development researcher (Stark, 1980). We human primates thus share the disposition to lip smack with the other primates to some extent.

75 *But smacking arises:* Redican (1975).

76 *It is the girney:* Much of my information about girneys comes from a personal discussion with Marc Hauser, who played samples for me.

76 *They resemble the subdued murmur:* Hauser (1992).

76 *For as one rhetorician observed:* Brummett (1980, p. 294).

76 *A study by Steven Green:* Green (1975).

77 *Similarly, a professor at the City University:* Dore (1974, 1975).

77   *This may be all they can use:* Moynihan (1970); also see Smith (1977, pp. 170–72) for a discussion of this point.

77   *These include changes:* Smith, Chase, and Lieblich (1974).

78   *When word of this got out:* Warwick (1983).

78   *For example, only women deloused:* Le Roy Ladurie (1978).

78   *Manual grooming occurred:* Just as, in parallel, rhesus males groom unrelated females primarily during the mating season (Goosen, 1981).

78   *According to Malinowski's account:* Malinowski (1929, p. 327).

78   *Manual grooming was documented:* Sugawara (1984, 1990).

78   *Sugawara's analysis revealed:* The women of Madagascar also share a number of intimacies with other women. In doing so, according to Elinor Keenan (1989), they talk intimately, bathe together, and "dig into each other's hair looking for fleas" (p. 141).

79   *In our own species:* Kimura (1973).

79   *In apes, face-touching movements:* Dimond and Harries (1984); the force of this comparison is weakened somewhat by evidence that nonhuman primates tend to be left-handed more generally (Westergaard, Champoux, and Suomi, 1997).

79   *It is also responsible:* Van Lancker (1987).

79   *There is a synonymous interchangeability:* Jones and Yarbrough (1985).

80   *Additional analyses indicated:* Jones and Yarbrough (1985).

80   *Similar research by Judith Hall:* Hall (1996).

80   *Following Darwin's lead:* Morton (1977).

80   *One might expect similar patterns:* Nonhuman primates' grin face—which is displayed when animals are disposed to share, assemble, groom, and play, and is never associated with aggression—sometimes co-occurs with a *high-pitched*, soft twittering sound (van Hoof, 1962, 1967).

80   *This is why listeners can tell:* Tartter (1980); Tartter and Braun (1994).

80   *He also noted a connection:* Ohala (1983, 1984).

81   *They also produce groups:* Hatfield, Cacioppo, and Rapson (1994).

81   *What struck the professor most:* Heaton (1992).

82   *The professor concluded:* McNeill (1995, p. 2).

82   *If the conversation lagged:* Hall (1977, p. 78).

82   *Seventy-five years ago:* Malinowski (1935).

83   *Sugawara noted "the joyful enthusiasm":* Sugawara (1984, pp. 18, 36–37).

83   *Likewise, when rhesus monkeys:* Sade (1966, p. 6).

83   *Suzanne Langer seemed to suggest:* Langer (1960, pp. 43–44).

84   *And as parents might guess:* Raffaelli and Duckett (1989).

84   *In a normal day, adults use:* Wagner (1985).

84   *In an hour of relaxed conversation:* Mines, Hanson, and Shoup (1978).

84   *"We may like to think":* Nydegger and Mitteness (1988, p. 704); of course, talk is a tool with which we accomplish a great deal of personal and social work.

84   *With a one-word modifier:* Stross (1989).

84   *By my calculations the typical member:* I base this estimate on data contained in various word-count studies, according to which the first decade of life runs gradually from zero words per day in year one to forty thousand per day in year ten. All other decades assume production of forty thousand words per day.

84   *Twenty-eight percent of the respondents:* Katcher (1981).

84 *In another survey, 90 percent:* Stallones, Marx, Garrity, and Johnson (1988).

85 *While out dog walking:* Rogers, Hart, and Boltz (1993).

85 *Only later did the supersleuths:* Well, It Sounded Like Heavy Petting to the CIA," *The Independent*, London, May 11, 1997.

85 *The research of Jaak Panksepp:* Panksepp, Siviy, and Normansell (1985, p. 25).

85 *Thus the positive feeling:* Fabre-Nys, Meller, and Keverne (1982).

86 *Indirectly, they cause a fall:* Martel, Nevison, Rayment, Simpson, and Keverne (1993, p. 307).

86 *In one human, removal of:* Scott, Young, Calder, Hellawell, Aggleton, and Johnson (1997); after the surgery, the patient was insensitive not just to emotion but to several types of vocal information that is unrelated to word identification.

86 *This rhythmicity has never been explained:* Hayes and Cobb (1982).

86 *After the lights go out:* Elbers and Ton (1985); Kuczaj (1983); Nelson (1992); Weir (1970).

86 *One thing learned in those experiments:* Heron, Doane, and Scott (1956).

87 *Although Marshall McLuhan is famous:* McLuhan and Fiore (1967); italics mine.

87 *Robin Dunbar has suggested:* Dunbar (1993).

87 *Investigators digging around:* Arensburg, Schepartz, Tillier, Vandermeersch, and Rak (1990); Arensburg, Tillier, Vandermeersch, Duday, Schepartz, and Rak (1989).

87 *Unfortunately, as critics were quick:* Lieberman (1993).

87 *In related research:* Lieberman and Crelin (1971); Lieberman, Crelin, and Klatt (1972).

88 *Of course this argument:* Mithen (1996).

88 *Like monkeys and apes, we humans:* Comuzzie and Wilcox (1993).

89 *"Would it be a great advantage":* Premack (1986, pp. 281–82).

89 *University of Hawaii's linguist:* In fact, Bickerton (1995, in press) argued that language evolved to facilitate internal cognitive operations such as reasoning *rather than* public communicative and social processes.

90 *I think it is theoretically less adventurous:* Also see Catania (1991).

90 *Each of these registers:* Kochman (1969, 1981); also see Abrahams (1989).

90 *Rapping is probably the best known:* Rose (1994).

91 *A black teenage girl:* Folb (1980, p. 91 and 101).

91 *The physically combative subject loses face:* Berdie (1947).

91 *It is "Good Talking":* Abrahams (1970, p. 506).

91 *Over a half-century ago W. J. Cash:* Cash (1941, pp. 71–72); apparently, it would be a mistake to link this weakness for flowery rhetoric specifically to blacks, for it was shared to some degree with the larger southern culture. According to Cash, "The politics of the Old South was a theater for the play of the purely personal, the purely romantic, and the purely hedonistic. It was an arena wherein one great champion confronted another or a dozen, and sought to outdo them in rhetoric and splendid gesturing. It swept back the loneliness of the land, it brought men together under torches, it filled them with the contagious power of the crowd, it unleashed emotion and set it to leaping and dancing, it caught the very meanest man up out of his tiny legend into the gorgeous fabric of the legend of this or that great hero." [p. 73]

92   *"The concept," said Edith Folb:* Folb (1980, pp. 88–89).

92   *Perfectly normal people experience:* Friedmann, Thomas, Kulick-Ciuffo, Lynch, and Suginohara (1982); Liehr (1992); Tardy, Thompson, and Allen (1989).

92   *Men who monopolize and dominate:* Houston, Babyak, Chesney, Black, and Ragland (1997).

92   *According to Joel Sherzer:* Sherzer (1990, p. 37).

92   *And so it was in ancient China:* Garrett (1993, p. 306).

93   *"Who you are":* Folb (1980, p. 89 and 90–91).

93   *Geneva Smitherman noted:* Smitherman (1986, p. 76).

93   *Likewise, in the telling of Limba tales:* Finnegan (1967, p. 13).

93   *Much the same has been said:* Sherzer (1990).

93   *The deeper biological links have yet to be:* Dabbs and Ruback (1984); Kendon and Cook (1969); Mulac (1989).

94   *Countless generations of selective mating:* Locke (1998); I should point out that some scholars think the capability for language was created by a chance convergence of genes. For example, Piatelli-Palmarini (1989) has suggested that whatever separate pieces of genetic material are needed for a linguistic grammar more or less found themselves, through happenstance, on the same chromosome. In this view, the incorporation of language into our species' repertoire was an accident.

94   *Successful businessmen spend:* Goddard (1973).

94   *To this day the chief executive officers:* "Welcome to the Wired World," *Time,* February 3, 1997.

94   *W. J. Cash called rhetoric:* Cash (1941, p. 72).

95   *"Even the impending impeachment":* Quotes from Hart (1987, p. 46 and xxiii; italics his).

95   *The power of words was well known:* Malinowski (1935).

95   *According to an article in the* Boston Globe: "Japan Spoke the Word Quietly: Leader's 'Apology' Seems Not to Reflect Nation's Sentiment," *The Boston Globe,* August 16, 1995.

95   *The speeches of the Maoris:* Salmond (1975, p. 54).

96   *If a Tshidi politician:* Comaroff (1975, p. 143).

96   *Indeed, the "weekly Hogg-fight":* "It's Fiesta Time as Commons Lives High on the Hogg," *The Times,* London, March 13, 1997.

97   *The Limba people themselves:* Finnegan (1967, p. 70).

97   *Marjorie Shostak commented:* Shostak (1981).

97   *The same is true:* Firth (1975, p. 41).

97   *One of them is "lames":* Labov (1972).

97   *Anthropological studies indicate:* Keenan (1989); Sherzer (1990).

97   *In the Maori culture:* Salmond (1975).

97   *This is also true:* Strathern (1975, p. 187).

97   *It is unknown whether:* Jamieson (1988) has written that with the rise of public speaking in America, women were distinctly disadvantaged because their voices didn't carry as well as men's.

97   *when Edith Folb tested:* Folb (1980).

97   *The reason for this sex bias:* Abrahams (1962).

97   *Instead of taking the floor:* Finnegan (1967, p. 70).

97   *For decades, evidence has converged:* Maccoby and Jacklin (1974); infant references include Huttenlocher, Haight, Bryk, Selzer, and Lyons (1991) and Morisset, Barnard, and Booth (1995).

97 *For example, in Anne Machung's study:* Machung (1988, p. 73).

98 *These differences have been affirmed:* Larson, Richards, Monete, Holmbeck, and Duckett (1996); Raffaelli and Duckett (1989); Youniss and Smoker (1985).

98 *They have also long been evident:* Rubin (1976).

98 *Just over twenty years ago Lillian Rubin:* Barnard (1993, p. 231); quoting from Rubin (1976, p. 114).

98 *In conversation women:* Duncan and Fiske (1977); Frances (1979); Ickes and Barnes (1977).

99 *Men's talk, called* bavarder: Bailey (1971, p. 1).

99 *Certainly no evidence for the latter:* See references cited by James and Drakich (1993).

99 *Some other studies seem to show:* Frances (1979); Simkins-Bullock and Wildman (1991).

99 *When females are free to choose:* Aries and Johnson (1983).

99 *The sixteen hours each week:* Raffaelli and Duckett (1989).

99 *Among adults there is also evidence:* Child studies include Jersild and Ritzman (1938) and Smith and Connolly (1972); preadolescent and adolescent studies include Raffaelli and Duckett (1989); Larson, Richards, Moneta, Holmbeck, and Duckett (1996): studies of adults include Aries and Johnson (1983); Ickes and Barnes (1977); and Street and Murphy (1987).

100 *According to Penelope Eckert:* Eckert (1993, p. 34).

100 *"There are elements of all three":* Sally Quinn, "Party protocol: confessions of a Washington hostess," *The New Yorker,* September 29, 1997.

100 *One recent study indicates that females:* Denton and Zarbatany (1996).

100 *Although alliances determine the outcome:* Lee and Johnson (1992).

101 *Interestingly, Marc's data showed:* Hauser and Locke (in preparation); field observations suggest that it may even be possible to guess the sex of a monkey from tape recordings, with roars and screams coming disproportionately from males and females, respectively (Gautier and Gautier, 1977).

101 *Some recent neuropathological research:* Harasty, Double, Halliday, Kril, and McRitchie (1997).

101 *Recently Richard Wrangham:* Wrangham and Peterson (1996).

101 *Talking is among the human activities:* Though propositional speech may be among those forces that, through its capacity to promote cooperation and planning, enable war.

102 *In diplomacy, according to Cohen:* Cohen (1987, p. 21).

102 *In some societies several different:* Watson-Gegeo and White (1990).

102 *The following day Mr. Hull:* Hull (1948, p. 1098).

Chapter Four   Lip Service

103 *As Harvard professor Robert Putnam:* Putnam (1993, p. 38).

104 *"As familiarity grows":* Bateson (1988, p. 28).

104 *But clues to reputation:* Goffman (1959).

104 *Avoiding gossip, Auden said:* Mendelson (1996, p. 427), quoting from a 1937 radio broadcast.

105 *If Penelope Eckert is correct:* Eckert (1993, p. 40).

105   *That is why it is illegal:* Rosenberg (1986, p. 3).

105   *And that is why in England:* Schilling (1991, p. 171).

105   *Recently an English physician:* "Drunk GP Told Couple's Secret," *The Daily Telegraph*, London, April 23, 1997; "Doctor Banned for Gossiping in Pub About IVF Couple," *The Daily Telegraph*, London, April 24, 1997; "GP's Drunken Betrayal Left Our Lives in Tatters," *The Daily Telegraph*, London, April 25, 1997.

105   *The coroner's jury brought in:* Rosnow (1977).

106   *Its poor public image notwithstanding:* Suls (1977).

106   *A truly personal fact is something:* Berg (1987).

107   *In a large, hierarchically organized group:* Slobin, Miller, and Porter (1968).

107   *The main exceptions occur:* Stiles (1987).

107   *Thirty years ago members:* Slobin, Miller, and Porter (1968).

107   *Years ago Rose Coser:* Coser (1959).

108   *Neuroscientist Robert Provine commented:* Provine (1993, p. 296).

108   *It occurs contagiously:* Provine (1992).

108   *Once a whole village:* Rankin and Philip (1963).

109   *When a man from one clan:* Fortes (1945, p. 91).

110   *Trust is like the air:* Fried (1981, p. 8).

110   *Recently, Ronald Noë and:* Noë and Bshary (1997); also see Dunbar (1997).

110   *Like monkeys, we humans:* Sacks (1997).

111   *We know the rules:* Coleman (1990, p. S102).

111   *A gift or an act of kindness:* Clark and Mills (1979).

111   *In such a relationship:* Sahlins (1974, p. 186).

111   *Consider the food:* Wiessner (1982).

112   *In time, today's "haves":* Wiessner (1982).

112   *After all, they only spend:* Wiessner (1982, p. 68).

113   *Unlike physical capital:* Coleman (1990, pp. S11–101).

113   *Intimate talking promotes:* Barnes and Duck (1994, pp. 178, 179).

114   *This competitiveness has produced:* Gomes-Casseres (1996).

114   *According to Benjamin Gomes-Casseres:* Gomes-Casseres (1996, p. 41).

114   *For if a diamond merchant:* Coleman (1988); Powell and Smith-Doerr (1994).

115   *"The widespread preference":* Granovetter (1985, p. 490).

115   *Often, this offers greater security:* Macaulay (1963).

115   *Indeed, as Pierre Bourdieu pointed out:* Bourdieu (1977, p. 174).

115   *It gets conspiratorial:* Baker (1983, p. 117).

115   *One veteran broker said:* Quoted in Baker (1983), which source was consulted in the preparation of this section.

116   *Salesmen pass along gossip:* Macaulay (1963).

116   *European countries that lack:* Lewis (1996).

116   *The need for trust:* Dalton (1959).

116   *Business managers join:* Carroll and Teo (1996).

116   *But as Edward Lorenz said:* Lorenz (1988, p. 209).

116   *You cannot have an "arm's length":* "Now Listen, Net Freaks, It's Not Who You Know, but Who You Trust," *Forbes ASAP*, December 4, 1995, an interview with Francis Fukuyama.

116   *"The visitor in the City is impressed":* Wechsberg (1966, p. 40).

116   *The contracts based on oral agreements:* Kunihiro (1972, p. 164).

117   *Defamation suits are down:* Rosenberg (1986).

Chapter Five   De-Voicing

PAGE

119   *About eight thousand years ago:* Morris (1969, p. 26).

119   *Every person had continuous:* Phillips and Metzger (1976).

119   *When two islanders meet:* Wayne (1995, p. 145).

120   *Their conversations would have dealt:* I base this on the fact that the need for explicit statements can rob speech of its emotionally binding qualities (Hall, 1977).

120   *"It was this change":* Morris (1967, p. 20).

120   *"Above all," he said:* Wordsworth (1971, p. 256).

121   *In New England the larger villages:* Gilmore (1989).

121   *Very few individuals could read:* Stedman and Kaestle (1991).

121   *A decade later American handwriting expert:* Thornton (1996, p. 103).

121   *Thanks to the supremacy of print:* Toffler (1981, p. 164).

121   *In the courtroom the most valued:* Hibbitts (1992).

122   *Even those who use toll-free numbers:* "With Phones Everywhere, Everyone Is Talking More." *The New York Times*, October 11, 1989.

122   *My father grew up before:* Toffler (1970, p. 164).

123   *Studies conducted afterward:* Naremore (1989); for a more in-depth analysis see Cantril (1940).

123   *Live radio and television dramas:* Boorstin (1971)

124   *Rather than finding that:* Newhagen and Ancell (1995, p. 322).

124   *By recognizing and amplifying:* Turow (1997).

124   *Here, finally, we find that:* Weiss (1988, p. 2).

125   *Before that, according to Alexis de Tocqueville:* Alexis de Tocqueville, 1856, *L'Ancient Regime et la Revolution,* taken from Lukes (1973, p. 14).

125   *And yet fifty years earlier:* Rousseau (1782); quoted in Lukes (1973, p. 67).

125   *In* Individualism Reconsidered: Riesman (1954); quoted in Lukes (1973, p. 65).

125   *Our "ideology of individualism":* Goodwin (1974, part 1, p. 60).

126   *Americans cannot easily describe:* Yankelovich (1975, p. 772).

126   *I wish my life and decisions:* Berlin (1969, p. 131).

126   *A British newspaper article:* "Thomson Offers Aegean Tourists Free-Drinks Deal," *The Times*, London, August 22, 1996.

127   *The number under forty-five:* "Rise of the Home-Alone Generation," *The Daily Telegraph*, London, May 9, 1997.

127   *A man of the same age:* "Space, Privacy and No Flatmates from Hell," *The Daily Telegraph*, London, May 9, 1997.

127   *The ads were based on:* "Listening to Khakis," *The New Yorker,* July 28, 1997.

128   *In 1994 it was estimated:* Turow (1997).

128   *In recent years many of Velez's:* "Communities barricade themselves against crime", *The Seattle Times*, November 24, 1996.

128   *Fully shielded from view:* Hynek (1972, p. 177).

128   *These systems require:* "Sound Barrier Can Silence Neighbours," *The Daily Telegraph*, London, April 26, 1997.

129   *Moreover, according to Slater:* Slater (1970, p. 9).

130   *They come and go:* Phillips and Metzger (1976, p. 86).

131   *The result of this globalization:* Toffler (1981, p. 167).

131   *When author Umberto Eco:* Eco (1994, p. 69).

131   *No wonder there is now a book:* Shenk (1997).

131   *This is why a writer:* pp. 46 and 49, "Interrupt-Driven," *Wired,* June 1994.

131   *Unfortunately, according to Berry:* W. Berry (1990, pp. 158, 159).

132   *But in 1994 there was:* National Opinion Research Center at the University of Chicago.

132   *Wendell Berry lamented:* W. Berry (1990, p. 159).

132   *Ten years later:* Robinson and Godbey (1997).

132   *There is no contact:* Oldenburg (1989, p. 4).

132   *It can never be said that:* "Years After Neighbors Last Saw Her, Worcester Woman Found Died in Home," *Boston Globe,* reproduced in Olds, Schwartz, and Webster (1996, pp. 28–29.)

133   *One professor commented:* Latané and Darley (1970, p. 3).

133   *"Detectives were reluctant":* "150 Cars Fail to Stop for Roadside Rape Victim," *The Times,* London, December 19, 1996; quote from "Why Did Drivers Ignore Screams of Rape Victim?", *The Times,* London, December 20, 1996.

134   *According to the article, Galczynski:* "Bloomfield Street's Good Neighbor," *The Boston Globe,* February 3, 1995

134   *The article struck two psychiatrists:* Olds, Schwartz, and Webster (1996, p. 166).

134   *The people who go there:* Oldenburg (1989, p. 43).

135   *"They play dominoes":* Wilson (1969, p. 80).

135   *Among the !Kung:* p. 104, Draper (1975, p. 104).

135   *New Zealand's Maoris hold public discussions:* Salmond (1975).

135   *This saved scrubbing laundry:* According to an American writer, Richard Sclove; see "Seduced by technology," *New Internationalist,* December 1996.

135   *"When the village bakery opened":* Harding (1975, p. 300).

135   *In that year over one-third:* Scitovsky (1976).

135   *Then, according to Richard Sennett:* Sennett (1973, p. 81); also see Sommerville (1997).

136   *The English pub, according to:* Oldenburg (1989, p. 47).

136   *These kinds of oases:* Slater (1970, p. 8).

136   *"They peel labels":* Oldenburg (1989, p. 34).

136   *Little wonder, since the very rationale:* Kunstler (1993, p. 189).

137   *This hapless soul:* Oldenburg (1989, p. 6).

137   *"Most kids just hang out":* "Safety Is Our Top Priority," *USA Today* (International Edition), September 11, 1996; italics mine.

137   *But "a community is not":* Kunstler (1993, pp. 185–86), italics in the original.

138   *"The most stopped-up":* Hamill (1969, p. 222).

139   *In America the number of:* Redelmeier and Tibshirani (1997).

139   *The injunction was evidently issued:* "Can You Hear Me? I'm at the Theatre," *The Times,* London, 1996.

139   *A Finnish university student explained:* "Finns Take Digital Dialogue to Heart," *The Guardian,* London, February 11, 1997.

139   *"We can be quite talkative":* "Nordic Nations Lead the Way in Upward Mobility," *The European,* April 19, 1997.

140   *"It was getting ridiculous":* "Train Ban Proves Mobile Phone Is Turn-off in Tokyo," *The Daily Telegraph,* London, April, 1997.

140   *Recently a city councilman:* "Tel Aviv Man Is Calling for Zones Barring Cell Phones." *The Seattle Times,* November 24, 1996.

141 *Israelis can order a refrigerator:* "It's Hard to Imagine Buying Something as Significant as a Refrigerator Online," *The Jerusalem Post Magazine*, August 23, 1996.

141 *You choose the car:* "Shoppers Soon Can Cyber-kick the Car Tires," *USA Today*, October 9, 1996.

141 *From a computer in their homes:* "Stop Squeezing the Cyber Melons!" *The New York Times*, June 14, 1997.

142 *"This is everybody's dream":* "What Runs the Store, Doesn't Talk, and Won't Smash Your Sushi?" *International Herald Tribune*, May 19, 1997.

142 *People "would rather deal":* "British Computer Talks Its Way to Intelligence Prize," *The Daily Telegraph*, London, May 16, 1997.

142 *With this advance:* Temple (1995, p. 424).

142 *Indications are that:* "Habit of Walking Comes to a Halt," *The Daily Telegraph*, London, April 10, 1996.

142 *According to one commentator:* Oldenburg (1989, p. 12).

143 *Daughters say the same:* Leto (1988).

143 *Few seem to mind:* "Voice of the Cyber Cabbie," *The Times*, London, March 25, 1996; "The New (Yorker's) Voice in the Back Seat of the Taxi," *The New York Times*, June 30, 1996; also "Everyone Has an Opinion on 'That Voice,'" *The New York Times*, July 3, 1996.

143 *The American home, now a technocopia:* Oldenburg (1989, p. 12).

144 *Extras include projection TV:* "Why It Takes 12,000 Watts to Get a College Degree," *The Boston Globe*, October 9, 1996.

144 *A young lady at Vassar:* "Computers Can Unify Campuses, but Also Drive Students Apart," *The New York Times*, November 11, 1996.

145 *"In Britain," according to a recent article:* "Message Received . . . ," *The Times*, London, December 5, 1996.

145 *British businessmen recently voted:* "Where No One Can Hear You Scream," *The Guardian*, London, June 3, 1997.

146 *The president said:* "Voice Mail," *Waterloo-Cedar Falls Courier*, October 13, 1996; italics mine.

146 *Finally, according to The Times:* "Message Received . . . ," *The Times*, London, December 5, 1996; italics mine.

147 *"Everybody talks about freedom of speech":* "No Place to Hide from Ubiquitous TV," *The International Herald Tribune*, May 6, 1997.

147 *The average American actively watches:* Putnam (1996); "Life Too Serious? Cue the Pudding Racers," *The International Herald Tribune*, March 10, 1997.

147 *In Britain those in the age group:* From Table 13.4 in *Social Trends* (1996).

147 *In Japan the average person over seven:* "Life Too Serious?" *The International Herald Tribune*, May 6, 1997.

147 *This is consistent with:* Putnam (1996).

147 *A study of the routine activities:* Larson, Richards, Moneta, Holmbeck, and Duckett (1996)

148 *Norberg-Hodge concluded:* Norberg-Hodge (1991, pp. 123–24, 134).

148 *As one observer put it:* Putnam (1994, p. 31).

148 *In his book Hot Air:* Kurtz (1996).

148 *Proponents say that these shows bring:* Coleman (1997, p. 128).

149 *Nearly half of the seven- and eight-year-old:* "Bedroom TV Sets Free Children to Watch Adult Shows," *The Times*, London, June 20, 1996.

149   *Currently in Britain there is a battle:* "A Spot of Tubby Trouble," *The Guardian*, London, May 21, 1997.

149   *Unfortunately, we find at second blush:* "American Children Switch Screens," *The Times*, London, April 10, 1996.

149   *A recent poll indicates:* "Video Game Time," *USA Today*, November 21, 1996.

150   *"If we don't understand":* "Internet boom 'is threat to future of TV,' " *The Times*, London, September 20, 1997

150   *A recent market survey has projected:* "On-line Games Net More Fans," *USA Today*, December 23, 1996.

150   *Before computer games came along:* Raffaelli and Duckett (1989).

150   *Recent surveys indicate:* "A Full-Throttle Lifestyle Signifies the Harried '90s," *USA Today*, May 27, 1997.

150   *One major American newspaper has decried:* "Nation of Strangers: A Danger to Democracy," *Chicago Tribune*, December 29, 1995.

151   *Similar reductions have occurred:* In reality, some of this inactivity represents a shift in interests, as was pointed out in a later article ("Bowling Together," *Time*, July 22, 1996), but I think Putnam's point is still valid.

151   *Recently, a team of reporters:* "Nation of Strangers: Suburbia Comes to the City," *Chicago Tribune*, December 28, 1995.

151   *Those who donated their time:* Verba, Schlozman, and Brady (1995).

151   *Memberships in fraternal organizations:* Putnam (1995a).

151   *Robert Putnam uses bowling:* Putnam (1995a, p. 24).

152   *In an article published:* Putnam (1995b, p. 678).

152   *In a later article another Harvard professor:* Norris (1996, p. 476).

153   *To compensate, about one-third spent:* Wurtzel and Turner (1977).

153   *Studies of social relationships indicate:* Kidder, Fagan, and Cohn (1981).

153   *Robert Putnam has said:* Putnam (1995b).

154   *Richard Goodwin has written:* Goodwin (1974, part 2, p. 37).

154   *A half-century ago a German psychologist:* Latané, Williams, and Harkins (1979)

154   *Just the belief, even falsely:* Ingham, Graves, and Peckham (1974)

155   *So Washington is attempting:* "Is 'Summit' Asking Too Much of Volunteers?" *The International Herald Tribune*, April 28, 1997.

156   *Wendell Berry has said:* W. Berry (1990, p. 157).

156   *In the nineteenth century, according to Thornton:* Thornton (1996, p. 99).

157   *Robert Wuthnow, a professor:* Wuthnow (1994).

157   *The percentage of Americans:* Putnam (1995a).

157   *At the same time there was a loss:* Coleman (1990).

157   *As trust dissipates:* p. 979, Lewis and Weigert 1985

157   *In the mid-seventies a clear majority:* Yankelovich (1975, p. 762).

157   *"The politician opens up":* Hart (1994, p. 29).

158   *Fukuyama concluded:* Fukuyama (1995, pp. 27–28).

158   *If management teams don't trust each other:* Gomes-Casseres (1996); quote from p. 66.

158   *"We are not equipped":* Morris (1969, pp. 37–38).

Chapter Six   The Big Chill

PAGE

160   *In 1950, Alan Turing:* Turing (1950).

161   *According to one cybernaut:* LaQuey (1994, p. 45).

161   *As Howard Rheingold said:* Rheingold (1994, p. 3).

162   *"Now I'm keen":* "A Mind on the Revolution," *The Times Education Supplement*, January 3, 1997.

162   *One cyberwonk said:* Steinfield (1986, p. 780).

162   *According to an estimate from early 1996:* "Whose Internet Is It?" *Newsweek*, April 22, 1996.

162   *In a separate estimate:* "On-line's Elusive Face," *USA Today*, October 9, 1996.

162   *over 40 percent of those earning:* "High-tech Comfort Level," *USA Today*, October 14, 1996.

162   *England's prime minister, Tony Blair:* "Blair Asks Gates to Link Schools to Internet," *The Times*, London, October 7, 1997.

162   *The Swedish postal service:* "Snail Mail to 'Die Within a Decade,' " *The Times (Interface)*, September 3, 1997.

163   *In language reminiscent of:* Barry (1996, p. 127).

163   *In an article in the* Boston Globe: "Beware: Electronic Logorrhea Looms," *The Boston Globe*, May 22, 1995

163   *Attempts are being made:* "Sign Here," *The Economist*, July 27, 1996.

164   *One authority admitted recently:* "Getting the Measure of Hate," *The Times*, London, October 25, 1995.

164   *They say that "for some reason":* LaQuey (1994, p. 80).

164   *"We need only deal with":* Quotes from Stoll (1995, pp. 58 and 52).

164   *Second, people from certain ethnic groups:* Anderson, Bikson, Law, and Mitchell (1995).

165   *They do not have to socialize:* Temple (1995).

165   *Others don't go to work at all:* "The Growing Appeal of Working Home Alone," *The Times*, London, March 6, 1996.

165   *American Express has put:* "You, Inc.," *U.S. News & World Report*, October 28, 1996.

165   *Those who dislike social isolation:* "Telecommuting Honks Own Horn; Few Hop Aboard," *USA Today*, November 25, 1996.

165   *A cofounder of England's "Home Alone Club":* "Home Alone," *The Times*, London, January 14, 1997.

165   *In* The Sovereign Individual: Davidson and Rees-Mogg (1997, p. 15).

166   *Eighteen percent of the respondents:* Shaming, blaming and flaming (1997).

167   *According to Francis Fukuyama:* "Now Listen, Net Freaks, It's Not Who You Know, but Who You Trust," *Forbes ASAP*, December 4, 1995.

170   *In a single day selected:* Dunbar (1996).

170   *Britain's* Hello! *magazine:* "Small Talk with Big Names," *The Daily Telegraph Magazine*, London, March 15, 1997.

170   *Strangers who, according to Barkow:* Barkow (1992, p. 630).

171   *On some sites the audience can:* "24 Hours in Cyberspace," *U.S News & World Report*, October 21, 1996 (from the book by the same name, published by Macmillan in 1996).

171   *This makes viewing all the more pleasurable:* Baym (1995)

172   *Although actual time counts indicate:* Robinson and Godbey (1997).
172   *A British father wrote:* "Time to spare—but not for the children," *The Daily Telegraph* of London, May 26, 1997.
173   *A report written later:* Packard (1972, p. 230).
174   *Without the feeling of belonging:* Baumeister and Leary (1995).
174   *Years ago "detribalization":* Carothers (1947, 1953).
174   *But individuals with few close relationships:* Sarason, Pierce, and Sarason (1990).
174   *Women with few intimate relationships:* Brown and Harris (1978).
174   *And people of both sexes:* Berkman and Syme (1979).
174   *Consider the locked-in life:* Bauby (1997).
175   *Loss of speech normally:* Bauer and Gleicher (1953).
176   *Since other-directed people:* Riesman (1950).
176   *And within relationships, self-disclosure:* Pennebaker, Barger, and Tiebout (1989).
176   *When we "unburden" ourselves:* Mendelson (1996, p. 428). Auden was right; talk with a trained psychotherapist and a personal friend are equally effective (Berman and Norton, 1985; House, Landis, and Umberson, 1988; Solano, Baten, and Parish, 1982; Stiles, 1987).
176   *Stress tends to draw people:* Miller and Ingham (1976).
176   *This is up from 1970:* " 'Typical' family is a modern-day oxymoron," *USA Today*, November 27, 1996; "Shifts in families reach a plateau, study says," *The New York Times*, November 27, 1996.
176   *Solo dwelling is equally common:* From data reported in *Social Trends* (1996).
178   *Cars were seen sporting:* Myers (1992).

Chapter Seven   The Autistic Society

PAGE
180   *Some research indicates, however:* Steinfield (1986).
180   *In Newcastle, Australia:* Smolan and Erwitt (1996).
181   *Once she was in the squeeze chute:* Quotes from Grandin and Scariano (1986, pp. 91 and 105); other material taken from Grandin (1995).
181   *Turkle has observed:* Quotes from Turkle (1984, pp. 10 and 206).
181   *One university student interviewed:* Turkle (1988, p. 47).
181   *Gates "has some autistic traits":* Grandin (1995, p. 184); the tendency to rock has also been noted by at least two interviewers, as well as the lack of eye contact ("What Will Microsoft Be Like in 10 Years?" *USA Today*, October 14, 1996; Seabrook, 1997).
182   *Recently he told an interviewer:* Seabrook (1997).
182   *Recently, one of America's most prominent computer experts:* The first quote is from "Wordless Author Poised to Scoop Book Million," *The Sunday Times*, London, September 29, 1996; the second quote is from "Wired at heart," *Vanity Fair*, November, 1997.
182   *These findings suggest:* Baron-Cohen, Wheelwright, Stott, Bolton, and Goodyer (1997).
182   *In a second study, Baron-Cohen:* Baron-Cohen and Hammer (1997).
183   *If an* individual *acted:* Fromm (1956, pp. 4–6).
184   *"Within a year or two":* "Bionic Man Shows Us the Future," *The Daily Telegraph*, London, April 26, 1997.

185   *One jazz performer said:* "Dead Singers Given New Voice by Hi-tech Clone," *The Sunday Times,* London, May 11, 1997.

185   *"You can actually sample":* "Technology Puts Fiction in 'Contact' with Reality," *USA Today,* July 31, 1997.

185   *The inventor believes:* "Computers Have Feelings Too," *The Times,* London, July 10, 1996.

185   *One thinks that boasting:* "The Most Wired Town in America," *Reader's Digest* (condensed from *USA Weekend*), July 1996, pp. 54-58.

186   *Those describing the event said:* "Bowling Together," *Time,* July 22, 1996.

186   *This new offering should please:* "When the Alma Mater Ends with '.edu,' " *The New York Times,* July 7, 1996.

186   *One of the first cybergraduates:* "Reflections of an On-line Graduate," *The New York Times,* August 4, 1996.

187   *One of the recruiters said:* "Campus Job Interviews on a Virtual Path," *The New York Times,* November 27, 1996.

188   *The dependency of these pathological:* "Internet 'Is as Addictive as Gambling or Alcohol,' " *The Daily Telegraph,* London, April 15, 1997.

188   *If that fails, psychotherapy:* "Internet Traps 'Surfers' in Addictive Web" and "Internet Users Risk Addiction to Computers," *The Times,* London, June 9, 1996; "Just Click No," *The New Yorker,* January 13, 1997. According to *The New Yorker* article, Dr. Goldberg (described as a psychiatrist) now thinks that the condition should be called "pathological Internet-use disorder" since electronic communications systems are not truly addictive like heroin.

188   *At the moment, economic pressures:* "A Virtual Shoulder to Cry On," *New Scientist,* December 9, 1995.

189   *According to press reports:* "Computer offers patients online analysis," *The Times,* London, October 7, 1997.

189   *But at last report the bishop:* "Wired to God," *The Milwaukee Journal Sentinel,* November 30, 1996.

190   *"If God doesn't change":* "Finding God on the Web," *Time,* December 16, 1996; my italics.

190   *He says that he "used to date":* Gates (1995, p. 206).

190   *A certified doubter, Clifford Stoll:* Stoll (1995, p. 24).

190   *According to American anthropologist Helen Fisher:* "Caught in the Net," *The Times,* London, February 11, 1996.

191   *Humorist Dave Barry says:* For On-line Absurdity, Dave Barry's Your Guy," *USA Today,* October 16, 1996.

191   *"I couldn't believe":* "Jilted by an E-mail," *The Times,* London, July 18, 1996.

191   *A fifty-year-old lawyer in Sheffield:* "Tragedy of Lover Ditched by E-mail," *The Star,* Sheffield, England, June 24, 1997.

191   *In another case a man claimed:* Internet Betrays Virtual Affair," *The Times,* London, February 3, 1996.

191   *Sue lived in South Wales:* Rheingold (1994, p. 164; story attributed to Richard Bartle).

192   *In a survey carried out:* "Choose Your Sex in Cyberspace," *The Times,* London, November 15, 1995.

192   *According to a book by Elizabeth Harvey:* Harvey (1992).

193   *MUD weddings are simple:* Reid (1995, pp. 175–76).

193   *I looked around at the room:* Rheingold (1994, p. 2).

Chapter Eight   Vocal Warming?

PAGE

195 *There, he said, "the inhabitants":* de Tocqueville (1862, p. 293).

195 *The critical question before us:* Lerner (1957).

197 *Even teenagers — 57 percent:* "Bowling Together," *Time*, July 22, 1996.

197 *One applause-garnering line:* "We're Finally Speaking Their Language," *The Sunday Times*, London, October 27, 1996.

197 *The language of international diplomacy:* Bell (1977).

198 *In* The Broken Heart: Lynch (1977, p. 66).

198 *These "rooted workers":* "70% say family ties are reason they won't move," *USA Today*, September 30, 1997.

199 *Visitors to the 1933 World's Fair:* Sale (1995, p. 209).

199 *Recently, Prince Charles claimed:* "Technology Is Killing the Soul, Warns Prince," *The Daily Telegraph*, London, April 30, 1997.

200 *Some years ago, according to Marshall McLuhan:* McLuhan (1964, p. 86).

200 *They think that we can be stitched:* A Lonely Road, *"Chicago Tribune*, December 29, 1996.

200 *The magazine prints tips:* "Readers Write Off TV Viewing," *The Times*, New York, May 13, 1996.

201 *A new tool, Berry declared:* Berry (1988, p. 38).

202 *Vonnegut concluded by offering:* "Having a Hell of a Good Time," *The Times*, London, December 16, 1996; from an interview in the November issue of *Inc. Technology*.

202 *Richard Goodwin has pointed out:* Goodwin (1974, part 2, p. 38).

203 *These groups, he concluded:* Wuthnow (1994).

203 *In* Overcoming Loneliness in Everyday Life: Olds, Schwartz, and Webster (1996, p. 90).

203 *Without personal intimacy:* Weiss (1969, p. 63).

204 *As Pete Hamill said:* Hamill (1969, p. 151).

References

Abrahams, R. D. (1962). "Playing the Dozens." *Journal of American Folklore*, July–September.

———. (1970). "Traditions of Eloquence in the West Indies." *Journal of Inter-American Studies and World Affairs*, 12, 505–27.

———. (1989). "Black Talking on the Streets." In Bauman, R., and J. Sherzer, eds. *Explorations in the Ethnography of Speaking*. Cambridge, England: Cambridge University Press.

Aiello, L. C. (1996). "Terrestriality, Bipedalism and the Origin of Language." *Proceedings of the British Academy*, 88, 269–89.

Ambady, N., and R. Rosenthal (1993). "Half a Minute: Predicting Teacher Evaluations from Thin Slices of Nonverbal Behavior and Physical Attractiveness." *Journal of Personality and Social Psychology*, 64, 431–41.

Anderson, R. H., T. K. Bikson, S. A. Law, and B. M. Mitchell (1995). *Universal Access to E-mail: Feasibility and Societal Implications*. Santa Monica, CA: RAND (National Book Network, Inc.).

Anthoney, T. R. (1968). "The Ontogeny of Greeting, Grooming and Sexual Motor Patterns in Captive Baboons (Superspecies *Papio cynocephalus*)." *Behaviour*, 31, 358–72.

Ardrey, R. (1961). *African Genesis: A Personal Investigation into the Animal Origins and Nature of Man*. London: Collins.

Arensburg, B., L. A. Schepartz, A-M. Tillier, N. B. Vandermeersch, and Y. Rak (1990). "A Reappraisal of the Anatomical Basis for Speech in Middle Paleolithic Hominids." *American Journal of Physical Anthropology*, 83, 137–46.

Arensburg, B., A-M. Tillier, N. B. Vandermeersch, H. Duday, L. A. Schepartz, and Y. Rak (1989). "A Middle Paleolithic Hyoid Bone." *Nature*, 338, 758–60.

Argyle, M., and M. Cook (1976). *Gaze and Mutual Gaze*. Cambridge, England: Cambridge University Press.

Argyle, M., and J. Dean (1965). "Eye-contact, Distance and Affiliation." *Sociometry*, 28, 289–304.

Argyle, M., V. Salter, H. Nicholson, M. Williams, and P. Burgess (1970). "The Communication of Inferior and Superior Attitudes by Verbal and Non-Verbal Signals." *British Journal of Social and Clinical Psychology*, 9, 222–31.

Aries, E., and F. L. Johnson (1983). "Close Friendship in Adulthood: Conversational Content Between Same-Sex Friends. *Sex Roles*, 9, 1183–96.

Asch, S. E. (1946). "Forming Impressions of Personality." *Journal of Abnormal and Social Psychology*, 41, 258–90.

Bahrick, H. P., P. O. Bahrick, and R. P. Wittlinger (1975). "Fifty Years of Memory for Names and Faces: A Cross-Sectional Approach." *Journal of Experimental Psychology: General*, 104, 54–75.

Bailey, F. G. (1971). *Gifts and Poison: The Politics of Reputation*. Oxford: Blackwell.

Baker, W. E. (1983). "Floor Trading and Crowd Dynamics." In Adler, P. A., and P. Adler, eds. *Social Dynamics of Financial Markets*. Greenwich, CT: JAI.

Bakhtin, M. M. (1986). *Speech Genres and Other Late Essays*. Austin, TX: University of Texas Press.

Barkow, J. H. (1992). "Beneath New Culture Is Old Psychology: Gossip and Social Stratification." In Barkow, J. H., L. Cosmides, and J. Tooby, eds. *The Adapted Mind: Evolutionary Psychology and the Generation of Culture*. Oxford: Oxford University Press.

Barnard, A. (1992). *Hunters and Herders of Southern Africa: A Comparative Ethnography of the Khoisan Peoples*. Cambridge, England: Cambridge University Press.

Barnes, M. K., and S. Duck (1994). "Everyday Communicative Contexts for Social Support." In Burleson, B. R., T. L. Albrecht, and I. G. Sarason, eds. *Communication of Social Support*. Thousand Oaks, CA: Sage.

Baron-Cohen, S., and J. Hammer (1997). "Parents of Children with Asperger Syndrome: What Is the Cognitive Phenotype? *Journal of Cognitive Neuroscience*, 9, 548–54.

Baron-Cohen, S., S. Wheelwright, C. Stott, P. Bolton, and I. Goodyer (1997). "Is There a Link Between Engineering and Autism?" *Autism*, 1, 101–9.

Barry, D. (1996). *Dave Barry in Cyberspace*. New York: Crown Publishers.

Bateson, P. (1988). "The Biological Evolution of Cooperation and Trust." In Gambetta, D., ed., *Trust: Making and Breaking Cooperative Relations*. Oxford: Basil Blackwell.

Bauby, J.-D. (1997). *The Diving Bell and the Butterfly*. Translated by Jeremy Leggatt. London: Fourth Estate.

Bauer, R. A., and D. B. Gleicher (1953). "Word-of-Mouth Communication in the Soviet Union." *Public Opinion Quarterly*, 15, 297–310.

Baumeister, R. F., and M. R. Leary (1995). "The Need to Belong: Desire for Interpersonal Attachments as a Fundamental Human Motivation." *Psychological Bulletin*, 117, 497–529.

Baumeister, R. F., and D. M. Tice (1990). "Anxiety and Social Exclusion. *Journal of Social and Clinical Psychology*, 9, 165–95.

Baym, N. K. (1995). "The Emergence of Community in Computer-Mediated Communication." In Jones, S. G., ed. *Cybersociety: Computer Mediated Communication and Community*. Newbury Park, CA: Sage.

Beare, W. (1964). *The Roman Stage: A Short History of Latin Drama in the Time of the Republic.* London: Methuen & Co.

Bell, C. (1977). *The Diplomacy of Detente: The Kissinger Era.* London: Martin Robertson and Company Ltd.

Berdie, R. F. (1947). "Playing the Dozens." *Journal of Abnormal and Social Psychology*, 42, 120–21.

Berg, J. H. (1987). "Responsiveness and Self-disclosure." In Derlega, V. J., and J. H. Berg, eds., *Self-disclosure: Theory, Research, and Therapy.* New York: Plenum.

Berkman, L. F., and S. L. Syme (1979). "Social Networks, Host Resistance, and Mortality: A Nine-Year Follow-up Study of Alameda County Residents." *American Journal of Epidemiology*, 109, 186–204.

Berlin, I. (1969). *Four Essays on Liberty.* Oxford: Oxford University Press.

Berman, J. S., and N. C. Norton (1985). "Does Professional Training Make a Therapist More Effective?" *Psychological Bulletin*, 98, 401–7.

Berntson, G. G., and S. T. Boysen (1989). "Specificity of the Cardiac Response to Conspecific Vocalizations in Chimpanzees." *Behavioral Neuroscience*, 103, 235–45.

Berry, D. S. (1990). "Vocal Attractiveness and Vocal Babyishness: Effects of Stranger, Self, and Friend Impressions." *Journal of Nonverbal Behavior*, 14, 141–53.

Berry, W. (1988). "Against PCs." *Harper's Magazine*, September.

———. (1990). *What Are People For?* London: Rider Books.

Biben, M., D. Symmes, and D. Bernhards (1989). "Contour Variables in Vocal Communication Between Squirrel Monkey Mothers and Infants." *Developmental Psychobiology*, 22, 617–31.

Bickerton, D. (1995). *Language and Human Behaviour.* London: UCL Press.

———. (in press). "Catastrophic Evolution: The Case for a Single Step from Protolanguage to Full Human Language." In Hurford, J. R., M. Studdert-Kennedy, and C. Knight, eds. *Approaches to the Evolution of Language: Social and Cognitive Bases.* Cambridge, England: Cambridge University Press.

Bierig, J., and J. Dimmick (1982). "The Late Night Radio Talk Show as Interpersonal Communication." *Journalism Quarterly*, 56, 92–96

Birdwhistell, R. L. (1974). "The Language of the Body: The Natural Environment of Words." In Silverstein, A. ed. *Human Communication: Theoretical Explorations.* New York: John Wiley.

Birnholz, J. C., and B. R. Benacerraf (1983). The Development of Human Fetal Hearing. *Science*, 222, 516–18.

Bishop, D. V. M., and C. Adams (1989). "Conversational Characteristics of Children with Semantic-Pragmatic Disorder. II: What Features Lead to a Judgement of Inappropriacy?" *British Journal of Disorders of Communication*, 24, 241–63.

Blair, R. G. (1965). "Vagitus Uterinus: Crying in Utero." *Lancet*, 11, 1164–65.

Blank, M., M. Gessner, and A. Esposito (1979). "Language Without Communication: A Case Study. *Journal of Child Language*, 6, 329–52.

Boinski, S. (1991). "The Coordination of Spatial Position: A Field Study of the Vocal Behavior of Adult Female Squirrel Monkeys." *Animal Behaviour*, 41, 89–102.

Boorstin, D. J. (1971). *The Image: A Guide to Pseudo-events in America*. New York, Harper Colophon Books.

Bourdieu, P. (1977). *Outline of a Theory of Practice*. Cambridge, England: Cambridge University Press.

Brenneis, D. (1987). "Talk and Transformation." *Man*, 22, 499–510.

Brothers, L. (1990). "The Social Brain: A project for Integrating Primate Behavior and Neurophysiology in a New Domain." *Concepts in Neuroscience*, 1, 27–51.

Brown, G. W., and T. Harris (1978). *Social Origins of Depression: A Study of Psychiatric Disorders in Women*. London: Tavistock Publications.

Brown, J. W., ed. (1981) *Jargonaphasia*. New York: Academic Press.

Brummett, B. (1980). "Towards a Theory of Silence as a Political Strategy." *The Quarterly Journal of Speech*, 66, 289–303.

Callières, F. de (1716/1983). *The Art of Diplomacy*. Edited by H. M. A. Keens-Soper and Karl W. Schweizer. New York: Holmes & Meier.

Cantril, H. (1940). *The Invasion from Mars: A Study in the Psychology of Panic*. Princeton, NJ: Princeton University Press.

Cappella, J. N., and J. O. Greene (1982). "A Discrepancy-Arousal Explanation of Mutual Influence in Expressive Behavior for Adult and Infant-Adult Interaction." *Communication Monographs*, 49, 89–114.

Carlson, R. (1997). *Slowing Down to the Speed of Life*. San Francisco, CA: Harper San Francisco.

Carothers, J. C. (1947). "A Study of Mental Derangement in Africans, and an Attempt to Explain Its Peculiarities, More Especially in Relation to the African Attitude to Life." *Journal of Mental Science*, 93, 548–97.

———. (1953). *The Africa Mind in Health and Disease: a Study in Ethnopsychiatry*. Geneva: World Health Organization.

———. (1959). "Culture, Psychiatry, and the Written Word." *Psychiatry*, 18–20, 307–320.

Carroll, G. R., and A. C. Teo (1996). "On the Social Networks of Managers." *Academy of Management Journal*, 39, 421–40.

Cash, W. J. (1941/1971). *The Mind of the South*. Harmondsworth, Middlesex, England: Penguin Books.

Catania, A. C. (1991). "The Phylogeny and Ontogeny of Language Function." In Krasnegor, N. A., D. M. Rumbaugh, R. L. Schiefelbusch, and M. Studdert-Kennedy, eds., *Biological and Behavioral Determinants of Language Development*. Hillsdale, NJ: Lawrence Erlbaum.

Cheney, D. (1977). "The Acquisition of Rank and the Development of Reciprocal Alliances Among Free-Ranging Immature Baboons." *Behavioral Ecology and Sociobiology*, 2, 303–18.

Cheney, D. L., and R. M. Seyfarth (1980). "Vocal Recognition in Free-Ranging Vervet Monkeys." *Animal Behaviour*, 28, 362–67.

———. (1982). "How Vervet Monkeys Perceive Their Grunts: Field Playback Experiments." *Animal Behaviour*, 30, 739–51.

———. (1990). *How Monkeys See the World: Inside the Mind of Another Species*. Chicago: University of Chicago Press.

Clark, M. S., and J. Mills (1979). "Interpersonal Attraction in Exchange and Communal Relationships." *Journal of Personality and Social Psychology*, 37, 12–24.

Coates, J. (1986). *Women, Men and Language: A Sociolinguistic Account of Sex Differences in Language*. London: Longman.

Cohen, R. (1987). *Theatre of Power: The Art of Diplomatic Signalling*. London: Longman.

Coleman, J. S. (1988). "Social Capital in the Creation of Human Capital." *American Journal of Sociology*, 94, S95-S120.

———. (1990). *Foundations of Social Theory*. Cambridge, MA: Harvard University Press.

———. (1997). *Stilled Tongues: From Soapbox to Soundbite*. London: Porcupine Press.

Comaroff, J. (1975). "Talking Politics: Oratory and Authority in a Tswana Chiefdom." In Bloch, M., ed., *Political Language and Oratory in Traditional Society*. London: Academic Press.

Comuzzie, D. K. C., and K. A. Wilcox (1993). *The Localizability of Human Alarm Calls*. Unpublished manuscript.

Cooley, C. H. (1902). *Human Nature and the Social Order*. New York: Scribner's

Coser, R. L. (1959). "Some Social Functions of Laughter: A Study of Humor in a Hospital Setting." *Human Relations*, 12, 171–82.

Cowlan, B. (1979). "A Revolution in Personal Communications: The Explosive Growth of Citizens Band Radio." In Gumpert, G., and R. Cathcart, eds., *Inter/media: Interpersonal Communication in a Media World*. Oxford: Oxford University Press.

Creutzfeldt, O., G. Ojemann, and E. Lettich (1989a). "Neuronal Activity in the Human Lateral Temporal Lobe. I. Responses to speech." *Experimental Brain Research*, 77, 451–75.

———. (1989b). "Neuronal Activity in the Human Lateral Temporal Lobe. II. Responses to the Subjects' Own Voice. *Experimental Brain Research*, 77, 476–89.

Cushing, S. (1994). *Fatal Words: Communication Clashes and Aircraft Crashes*. Chicago, IL: University of Chicago Press.

Dabbs, J. M., and R. B. Ruback (1984). "Vocal Patterns in Male and Female Groups." *Personality and Social Psychology Bulletin*, 10, 518–25.

Dalton, M. (1959). *Men Who Manage*. New York: John Wiley.

Davidson, J. D., and W. Rees-Mogg, W. (1997). *The Sovereign Individual: The Coming Economic Revolution, How to Survive and Prosper in It*. London: Macmillan.

Davitz, J. R. (1964). *The Communication of Emotional Meaning*. New York: McGraw-Hill.

DeCasper, A., and W. P. Fifer (1980). "On Human Bonding: Newborns Prefer Their Mothers' Voices." *Science*, 208, 1174–76.

DeCasper, A., J. P. Lecanuet, M.-C. Busnel, C. Granier-Deferre, and R. Maugeais (1994). Fetal Reactions to Recurrent Maternal Speech. *Infant Behavior and Development*, 17, 159–64.

Dempster, N., and P. Evans (1994). *Behind Palace Doors*. London: Orion.

Dennis, W. (1941). "Infant Development Under Conditions of Restricted Practice and of Minimum Social Stimulation." *Genetic Psychology Monographs*, 23, 143–189.

Denton, K., and L. Zarbatany (1996). "Age Differences in Support Processes in Conversations Between Friends." *Child Development*, 67, 1360–73.

Derber, C. (1983). *The Pursuit of Attention: Power and Individualism in Everyday Life.* Oxford: Oxford University Press.

de Selincourt, E. (1927/1964). "The Art of Conversation." In de Selincourt, E., ed., *Wordsworthian and Other Studies.* New York: Russell & Russell.

Desimone, R. (1991). "Face-Selective Cells in the Temporal Cortex of Monkeys." *Journal of Cognitive Neuroscience,* 3, 1–8.

de Tocqueville, A. (1862). *Democracy in America.* London: Longman, Green, Longman, and Roberts.

Dimond, S., and R. Harries (1984). "Face Touching in Monkeys, Apes and Man: Evolutionary Origins and Cerebral Asymmetry." *Neuropsychologia,* 22, 224–33.

Dore, J. (1974). "A Pragmatic Description of Early Language Development." *Journal of Psycholinguistic Research,* 3, 343–50.

———. (1975). "Holophrases, Speech Acts and Language Universals." *Journal of Child Language,* 2, 21–40.

Draper, P. (1975). "!Kung Women: Contrasts in Sexual Egalitarianism in Foraging and Sedentary Contexts." In Reiter, R., ed., *Toward an Anthropology of Women.* New York: Monthly Review Press.

Dunbar, R. I. M. (1988). *Primate Social Systems.* Ithaca, NY: Cornell University Press.

———. (1993). "Coevolution of Neocortical Size, Group Size and Language in Humans." *Behavioral and Brain Sciences,* 16, 681–94.

———. (1996). *Grooming, Gossip and the Evolution of Language.* London: Faber and Faber.

Dunbar, R. (1997). "The Monkeys' Defence Alliance." *Nature,* 386, 555, 557.

Duncan, S., and D. W. Fiske (1977). *Face-to-face Interaction.* Hillsdale, NJ: Lawrence Erlbaum.

Eckert, P. (1993). "Cooperative Competition in Adolescent 'Girl Talk.'" In Tannen, D., ed., *Gender and Conversational Interaction.* New York: Oxford University Press.

Eco, U. (1994). "The Future of Literacy." In Lumley, R., ed., *Apocalypse Postponed.* Bloomington, IN: Indiana University Press.

Eibl-Eibesfeldt, I. (1974). "Similarities and Differences Between Cultures in Expressive Movements." In Weitz, S., ed., *Nonverbal Communication.* New York: Oxford University Press.

Elbers, L., and J. Ton (1985). "Plan Pen Monologues: The Interplay of Words and Babbles in the First Words Period." *Journal of Child Language,* 12, 551–65.

Fabre-Nys, C., R. E. Meller, and E. B. Keverne (1982). "Opiate Antagonists Stimulate Affiliative Behaviour in Monkeys." *Pharmacology, Biochemistry & Behaviour,* 16, 653–59.

Farringdon, J. (1996). *Analyzing for Authorship.* Cardiff: University of Wales Press.

Fay, W. H. (1975). "Occurrence of Children's Echoic Responses According to Interlocutory Question Types." *Journal of Speech and Hearing Research,* 18, 336–45.

Ferrier, L. J., J. J. Johnston, and A. S. Bashir (1991). "A Longitudinal Study of the Babbling and Phonological Development of a Child with Hypoglossia." *Clinical Linguistics & Phonetics,* 5, 187–206.

Finnegan, R. (1967). *Limba Stories and Story-telling.* Oxford: Oxford University Press.

Firth, J. R. (1937). *The Tongues of Men.* Reprinted as *The Tongues of Men and Speech.* Westport, CT: Greenwood Press, 1986.

Firth, R. (1975). "Speech-making and Authority in Tokopia." In Bloch, M., ed., *Political Language and Oratory in Traditional Society.* London: Academic Press.

Folb, E. (1980). *Runnin' Down Some Lines: The Language and Culture of Black Teenagers.* Cambridge, MA: Harvard University Press.

Fortes, M. (1945). *The Dynamics of Clanship Among the Tallensi: Being the First Part of an Analysis of the Social Structure of a Trans-Volta Tribe.* London: Oxford University Press.

Fossey, D. (1972). "Vocalizations of the Mountain Gorilla *(Gorilla Gorilla Beringei)."* *Animal Behaviour,* 20, 36–53.

Frances, S. J. (1979). "Sex Differences in Nonverbal Behavior." *Sex Roles,* 5, 519–535.

French, N. R., C. W. Carter, and W. Koenig (1930). "The Words and Sounds of Telephone Conversations." *Bell System Technical Journal,* 9, 290–324.

Fried, C. (1981). *Contract as Promise: A Theory of Contractual Obligation.* Cambridge, MA: Harvard University Press.

Friedlaender, V. H. (1922). "Small-talk." In Friedlaender, V. H., *Pied Piper's Street and Other Essays.* Bristol, England: J. W. Arrowsmith.

Friedmann, E., S. A. Thomas, D. Kulick-Ciuffo, J. J. Lynch, and M. Suginohara (1982). "The Effects of Normal and Rapid Speech on Blood Pressure." *Psychosomatic Medicine,* 44, 545–53.

Fromm, E. (1956). *The Sane Society.* London: Routledge & Kegan Paul.

Fukuyama, F. (1995). *Trust: The Social Virtues and the Creation of Prosperity.* New York: The Free Press.

Furrow, D. (1992). "Developmental Trends in the Differentiation of Social and Private Speech." In Diaz, R. M., and L. E. Berk, eds., *Private Speech: From Social Interaction to Self-Regulation.* Hillsdale, NJ: Lawrence Erlbaum.

Garrett, M. M. (1993). "Wit, Power, and Oppositional Groups: A Case Study of 'Pure Talk.' " *Quarterly Journal of Speech,* 79, 303–18.

Gates, B. (1995). *The Road Ahead.* New York: Penguin.

Gautier, J.-P., and A. Gautier (1977). "Communication in Old World Monkeys." In Sebeok, T. A., ed., *How Animals Communicate.* Bloomington, IN: Indiana University Press.

Geiselman, R. E. (1979). "Inhibition of the Automatic Storage of Speaker's Voice." *Memory & Cognition,* 7, 201–4.

Geiselman, R. E., and F. S. Bellezza (1976). "Long-term Memory for Speaker's Voice and Source Location." *Memory & Cognition,* 4, 483–89.

———. (1977). "Incidental Retention of Speaker's Voice." *Memory & Cognition,* 5, 658–65.

Gerstel, N., and H. Gross (1984). *Commuter Marriage: A Study of Work and Family.* New York: The Guilford Press.

Gibson, J. J., and A. D. Pick (1963). "Perception of Another Person's Looking Behavior." *American Journal of Psychology,* 76, 386–94.

Giles, H., ed. (1984). "The Dynamics of Speech Accommodation." *International Journal of the Sociology of Language,* 46, 1–155.

Giles, H., and N. Coupland (1991). *Language: Contexts and Consequences.* Pacific Grove, CA: Brooks/Cole Publishing Company.

Giles, H., N. Coupland and J. Wiemann (1992). " 'Talk Is Cheap . . .' but 'My Word Is My Bond': Beliefs About Talk." In Bolton, K., and H. Kwok, eds., *Sociolinguistics Today: International Perspectives*. New York: Routledge.

Giles, H., A. Mulac, J. J. Bradac, and P. Johnson (1987). "Speech Accommodation Theory: The Next Decade and Beyond." In McLaughlin, M., ed., *Communication Yearbook*. Oxford: Blackwell.

Gilmore, W. J. (1989). *Reading Becomes a Necessity of Life: Material and Cultural Life in Rural New England, 1780–1835.* Knoxville, TN: University of Tennessee Press.

Goddard, J. B. (1973). "Office Linkages and Location: A Study of Communications and Spatial Patterns in Central London." In Diamond, D. R., and J. B. McLoughlin, eds., *Progress in Planning*, vol. 1. Oxford: Pergamon Press.

Goffman, E. (1959). *The Presentation of Self in Everyday Life*. Garden City, NY: Doubleday.

Goldinger, S. D. (1992). "Words and Voices: Implicit and Explicit Memory for Spoken Words." *Research on Speech Perception. Technical Report No. 7*. Speech Research Laboratory, Department of Psychology, Indiana University, Bloomington, Indiana.

Gomes-Casseres, B. (1996). *The Alliance Revolution: The New Shape of Business Rivalry*. Cambridge, MA: Harvard University Press.

Goodwin, R. (1974). "Reflections: The American Condition." *The New Yorker*, part 1: January 21; part 2, January 28; part 3, February 4.

Goosen, C. (1981). "On the Function of Allogrooming in Old-World Monkeys." In Chiarelli, A. B., and R. S. Corruccini, eds., *Primate Behaviour and Sociobiology*. Berlin: Springer.

Grandin, T. (1995). *Thinking in Pictures: and Other Reports from My Life with Autism*. New York: Doubleday.

Grandin, T., and M. M. Scariano (1986). *Emergence: Labeled Autistic*. Turnbridge Wells, Kent, England: Costello.

Granovetter, M. (1985). "Economic Action and Social Structure: The Problem of Embeddedness." *American Journal of Sociology*, 91, 481–510.

Green, S. (1975). "Variation of Vocal Pattern with Social Situation in the Japanese Monkey *(Macaca Fascata)*: A Field Study." In Rosenblum, L. A., ed., *Primate Behavior: Developments in Field and Laboratory Research*. New York: Academic Press.

Gregory, S. W., and S. Webster (1996). "A Nonverbal Signal in Voices of Interview Partners Effectively Predicts Communication Accommodation and Social Status Perceptions." *Journal of Personality and Social Psychology*, 70, 1231–40.

Haith, M. M., T. Bergman, and M. J. Moore (1977). "Eye Contact and Face Scanning in Early Infancy." *Science*, 198, 853–55.

Hall, E. T. (1977). *Beyond Culture*. Garden City, NY: Anchor Books.

Hall, J. A. (1996). "Touch, Status, and Gender at Professional Meetings." *Journal of Nonverbal Behavior*, 20, 23–44.

Hamill, P. (1969). "A Hangout 'Is a Place . . . the Great Good Place that Every Man Carries in His Heart, the Place of Safety . . .' " *Mademoiselle*, November.

Hamilton, C. (1991). *The Hitler Diaries: Fakes that Fooled the World*. Lexington, KY: University Press of Kentucky.

Hamilton, C. R., and B. A. Vermeire (1988). "Complementary Hemisphere Specialization in Monkeys." *Science*, 242, 1691–94.

Harasty, J., K. L. Double, G. M. Halliday, J. J. Kril, and D. A. McRitchie (1997). "Language-Associated Cortical Regions are Proportionally Larger in the Female Brain." *Archives of Neurology*, 54, 171–76.

Harcourt, A. H., K. Stewart, and M. D. Hauser (1993). "The Social Use of Vocalizations by Gorillas: I. Social Behaviour and Vocal Repertoire." *Behaviour*, 124, 89–122.

Harding, S. (1975). "Women and Words in a Spanish Village." In Reiter, R. R., ed., *Toward an Anthropology of Women*. New York: Monthly Review Press.

Hart, R. P. (1987). *The Sound of Leadership: Presidential Communication in the Modern Age*. Chicago: University of Chicago Press.

———. (1994). *Seducing America: How Television Charms the Modern Voter*. Oxford, England: Oxford University Press.

Harvey, E. D. (1992). *Ventriloquized Voices: Feminist Theory and English Renaissance Texts*. London: Routledge.

Hatfield, E., J. T. Cacioppo, and R. L. Rapson (1994). "Emotional Contagion." Cambridge, England: Cambridge University Press.

Hauser, M. (1993). Right Hemisphere Dominance for the Production of Facial Expression in Monkeys. *Science*, 261, 475–77.

Hauser, M. D. (1992). "A Mechanism Guiding Conversational Turn-taking in Vervet Monkeys and Rhesus Macaques." In Nishida, T., F. B. M. de Waal, W. McGrew, P. Marler, and M. Pickford eds., *Topics in Primatology*, vol. 1. *Human Origins*. Tokyo: Tokyo University Press.

Hayes, D. P., and L. Cobb (1982). "Cycles of Spontaneous Conversation Under Long-term Isolation." In Davis, M., ed., *Interaction Rhythms: Periodicity in Communicative Behavior*. New York: Human Sciences Press.

Heaton, C. P. (1992). "Air Ball: Spontaneous Large-Group Precision Chanting." *Popular Music and Society*, 16, 81–83.

Heron, W., B. K. Doane, and T. H. Scott (1956). "Visual Disturbances After Prolonged Perceptual Isolation." *Canadian Journal of Psychology*, 10, 13–18.

Hibbitts, B. J. (1992). "Coming to Our Senses": Communication and Legal Expression in Performance Cultures." *Emory Law Journal*, 41, 873–960.

Hirstein, W., and V. S. Ramachandran (1997). "Capgras Syndrome: A Novel Probe for Understanding the Neural Representation of the Identity and Familiarity of Persons." *Proceedings of the Royal Society B*, 264, 437–44.

Hollien, H. (1990). *The Acoustics of Crime: The New Science of Forensic Phonetics*. New York: Plenum.

House, J. S., K. R. Landis, and D. Umberson (1988). "Social Relationships and Health." *Science*, 241, 540–45.

Houston, B. K., M. A. Babyak, M. A. Chesney, G. Black, and D. R. Ragland (1997). "Social Dominance and 22-Year All-Cause Mortality in Men." *Psychosomatic Medicine*, 59, 5–12.

Hull, C. (1948). *The Memoirs of Cordell Hull*, vol. 2. New York: Macmillan.

Humphrey, N. (1996). "The Thick Moment." In Brockman, J., ed., *The Third Culture*. New York: Simon & Schuster.

Huttenlocher, J., W. Haight, A. Bryk, M. Selzer, and T. Lyons (1991). "Early Vocabulary Growth: Relation to Language Input and Gender. *Developmental Psychology*, 27, 236–48.

Hynek, J. A. (1972). *The UFO Experience: A Scientific Inquiry*. London: Corgi Books.

Ickes, W., and R. D. Barnes (1977). "The Role of Sex and Self-monitoring in Unstructured Dyadic Interactions." *Journal of Personality and Social Psychology*, 35, 315–30.

Ingham, A. G., G. Levinger, J. Graves, and V. Peckham (1974). "The Ringelmann Effect: Studies of Group Size and Group Performance." *Journal of Experimental Social Psychology*, 10, 371–84.

James, D., and J. Drakich (1993). "Understanding Gender Differences in Amount of Talk: A Critical Review of Research." In Tannen, D., ed., *Gender and Conversational Interaction*. New York: Oxford University Press.

Jamieson, K. H. (1988). *Eloquence in an Electronic Age: The Transformation of Political Speechmaking*. Oxford: Oxford University Press.

Jersild, A. T., and R. Ritzman (1938). "Aspects of Language Development: The Growth of Loquacity and Vocabulary." *Child Development*, 9, 243–59.

Jones, S. E., and A. E. Yarbrough (1985). "A Naturalistic Study of the Meanings of Touch." *Communication Monographs*, 52, 19–56.

Jourard, S. M. (1968). *Disclosing Man to Himself*. Princeton, NJ: Van Nostrand.

Jürgens, U. (1995). "Neuronal Control of Vocal Production in Non-human and Human Primates." In Zimmermann, E., J. D. Newman, and U. Jürgens, eds., *Current Topics in Primate Vocal Communication*. New York: Plenum Press.

Karmiloff-Smith, A., E. Klima, U. Bellugi, J. Grant, and S. Baron-Cohen (1995). "Is There a Social Module? Language, Face Processing, and Theory of Mind in Individuals with Williams Syndrome." *Journal of Cognitive Neuroscience*, 7, 196–208.

Katcher, A. H. (1981). "Interactions Between People and Their Pets: Form and Function." In Fogle, B., ed., *Interrelations Between People and Pets*. Springfield, IL: Charles C. Thomas.

Keating, C. F., and E. G. Keating (1982). "Visual Scan Patterns of Rhesus Monkeys Viewing Faces." *Perception*, 11, 211–19.

———. (1993). "Monkeys and Mug Shots: Cues Used by Rhesus Monkeys *(Macaca Mulatta)* to Recognize a Human Face." *Journal of Comparative Psychology*, 107, 131–39.

Keenan, E. (1989). "Norm-Makers, Norm-Breakers: Uses of Speech by Men and Women in a Malagasy Community." In Bauman, R., and J. Sherzer, eds., *Explorations in the Ethnography of Speaking*. Cambridge, England: Cambridge University Press.

Kendon, A. (1967). "Some Functions of Gaze Direction in Social Interaction." *Acta Psychologica*, 26, 22–63.

———. (1973). "The Role of Visible Behaviour in the Organization of Face-to-Face Interaction." In von Cranach, M., and I. Vine, eds., *Social Communication and Movement: Studies of Interaction and Expression in Man and Chimpanzee*. New York: Academic Press.

Kendon, A., and M. Cook (1969). "The Consistency of Gaze Patterns in Social Interaction." *British Journal of Psychology*, 60, 481–94.

Kidder, L. H., M. A. Fagan, and E. S. Cohn (1981). "Giving and Receiving: Social Justice in Close Relationships." In Lerner, M. J., and S. C. Lerner, eds., *The Justice Motive in Social Behavior: Adapting to Times of Scarcity and Change*. New York: Plenum.

Kimura, D. (1973). "Manual Activity During Speaking I. Right-handers." *Neuropsychologia*, 11, 45–50.

Kissinger, H. (1979). *White House Years*. Boston: Little, Brown.

Kochman, T. (1969). " 'Rapping' in the Black Ghetto." *Trans-action*, 6, 26–34.

———. (1981) *Black and White Styles in Conflict*. Chicago: University of Illinois Press.

Kozlowski, L. T., and J. E. Cutting (1977). "Recognizing the Sex of a Walker from a Dynamic Point-Light Display." *Perception & Psychophysics*, 21, 575–80.

Kramer, E. (1963). "Judgment of Personal Characteristics and Emotions from Nonverbal Properties of Speech." *Psychological Bulletin*, 60, 408–20.

Kuczaj, S. A. (1983). *Crib Speech and Language Play*. New York: Springer.

Kuiper, K. (1996). *Smooth Talkers: The Linguistic Performance of Auctioneers and Sportscasters*. Mahwah, NJ: Lawrence Erlbaum.

Kunihiro, M. (1972). U.S.–Japan Communications. In Rosovsky, H., ed., *Discord in the Pacific*. Washington, D.C.: Columbia Books.

James, H. K. (1993). *The Geography of Nowhere: The Rise and Decline of America's Manmade Landscape*. New York: Simon & Schuster.

Kurtz, H. (1996). *Hot Air: All Talk, All the Time*. New York: Times Books.

Labov, W. (1972). *Sociolinguistic Patterns*. Philadelphia: University of Pennsylvania Press.

———. (1990). "The Intersection of Sex and Social Class in the Course of Linguistic Change." *Language Variation and Change*, 2, 205–54.

———. ed. (1984). *Locating Language in Time and Space*. New York: Academic Press.

Ladefoged, P., and J. Ladefoged (1980). "The Ability of Listeners to Identify Voices." *UCLA Working Papers in Phonetics*, 41, 43–51.

Landau, B., and L. R. Gleitman (1985). *Language and Experience: Evidence from the Blind Child*. Cambridge, MA: Harvard University Press.

Landau, W. M., and F. R. Kleffner (1957). "Syndrome of Acquired Aphasia with Convulsive Disorder in Children." *Neurology*, 7, 523–30.

Langer, S. K. (1960). *Philosophy in a New Key: A Study in the Symbolism of Reason, Rite, and Art*. Cambridge, MA: Harvard University Press.

Lanier, J. (1992). An Insider's View of the Future of Virtual Reality. *Journal of Communication*, 42, 150–72.

LaQuey, T. (1994). *The Internet Companion: A Beginner's Guide to Global Networking*. Reading, MA: Addison-Wesley.

Larson, C. R. (1988). "Brain Mechanisms Involved in the Control of Vocalization." *Journal of Voice*, 2, 301–11.

Larson, R. W., M. H. Richards, G. Moneta, G. Holmbeck, and E. Duckett (1996). "Changes in Adolescents' Daily Interactions with Their Families from Ages 10 to 18: Disengagement and Transformation." *Developmental Psychology*, 32, 744–54.

Latané, B., and J. M. Darley (1970). *The Unresponsive Bystander: Why Doesn't He Help?* New York: Appleton-Century-Crofts.

Latané, B., K. Williams, and S. G. Harkins (1979). "Many Hands Make Light the Work: The Causes and Consequences of Social Loafing." *Journal of Personality and Social Psychology*, 37, 822–32.

Laver, J. (1975). "Communicative Functions of Phatic Communion." In Kendon, A., R. M. Harris, and M. R. Key, eds., *Organization of Behavior in Face-to-Face Interaction*. The Hague: Mouton.

Lee, P. C., and J. A. Johnson (1992). Sex Differences in Alliances, and the Acquisition and Maintenance of Dominance Status Among Immature Primates." In Harcourt, A. H., and F. B. M. de Waal, eds. *Coalitions and Alliances in Humans and Other Animals*. Oxford: Oxford University Press.

Lee, R. B. (1979). *The !Kung San: Men, Women, and Work in a Foraging Society*. Cambridge, England: Cambridge University Press.

Lenneberg, E. H., F. G. Rebelsky, and I. A. Nichols (1965). "The Vocalizations of Infants Born to Deaf and to Hearing Parents." *Human Development*, 8, 23–37.

Lerner, M. (1957). *America as a Civilization*. New York: Simon & Schuster.

Le Roy Ladurie, E. (1978). *Montaillou: Cathars and Catholics in a French Village, 1294–1324*. London: Scolar Press.

Leto, V. (1988). " 'Washing, Seems It's All We Do': Washing Technology and Women's Communication." In Kramarae, C., ed., *Technology and Women's Voices: Keeping in Touch*. London: Routledge & Kegan Paul.

Levelt, W. J. M. (1989). *Speaking: From Intention to Articulation*. Cambridge, MA: MIT Press.

Levin, H., and T. Lin (1988). "An Accommodating Witness." *Language and Communication*, 8, 195–98.

Lewis, J. D., and A. Weigert (1985). Trust as a Social Reality. *Social Forces*, 63, 967–85.

Lewis, R. D. (1996). *When Cultures Collide: Managing Successfully Across Cultures*. London: Nicholas Brealey.

Lieberman, P. (1993). "On the Kebara KMH 2 Hyoid and Neanderthal Speech." *Current Anthropology*, 34, 172–75.

Lieberman, P., and E. S. Crelin (1971). "On the Speech of Neanderthal Man." *Linguistic Inquiry*, 2, 203–22.

Lieberman, P., E. S. Crelin, and D. H. Klatt (1972). "Phonetic Ability and Related Anatomy of the Newborn and Adult Human, Neanderthal Man, and the Chimpanzee." *American Anthropologist*, 74, 287–307.

Liehr, P. (1992). "Uncovering a Hidden Language: The Effects of Listening and Talking on Blood Pressure and Heart Rate." *Archives of Psychiatric Nursing*, 6, 306–11.

Linder, Staffan B. (1970). *The Harried Leisure Class*. New York: Columbia University Press.

Linnankoski, I., M. Laakso, R. Aulanko, and L. Leinonen (1994). "Recognition of Emotions in Macaque Vocalizations by Children and Adults." *Language & Communication*, 14, 183–92.

Locke, J. L. (1992). "Neural Specializations for Language: A Developmental Perspective." *Seminars in the Neurosciences*, 4, 425–31.

———. (1993). *The Child's Path to Spoken Language*. Cambridge, MA: Harvard University Press.

———. (1996). "Why Do Infants Begin to Talk? Language as an Unintended Consequence." *Journal of Child Language*, 23, 251–68.

———. (1997). "A Theory of Neurolinguistic Development." *Brain and Language*, 58, 265–326.

———. (1998). Social Sound-making as a Precursor to Spoken Language." In Hurford, J. R., M. Studdert-Kennedy, and C. Knight, eds., *Approaches to the Evolution of Language: Social and Cognitive Bases*. Cambridge, England: Cambridge University Press.

Locke, J. L., and M. Hauser (in preparation). *Parallel Sex and Status Effects in the Volubility of Human and Nonhuman Primates.*

Lorenz, E. H. (1988). "Neither Friends nor Strangers: Informal Networks of Subcontracting in French Industry." In Gambetta, D., ed., *Trust: Making and Breaking Cooperative Relations.* Oxford: Basil Blackwell.

Ludwig, A. M. (1997). *How Do We Know Who We Are? A Biography of the Self.* Oxford: Oxford University Press.

Lukes, S. (1973). *Individualism.* Oxford: Basil Blackwell.

Lynch, J. J. (1977). *The Broken Heart: The Medical Consequences of Loneliness.* New York: Basic Books.

Macaulay, S. (1963). "Non-contractual Relations in Business: A Preliminary Study." *American Sociological Review,* 28, 55–67.

Maccoby, E. E., and C. M. Jacklin (1974). *The Psychology of Sex Differences.* Stanford, CA: Stanford University Press.

Machung, A. (1988). " 'Who Needs a Personality to Talk to a Machine?': Communication in the Automated Office." In Kramarae, C., ed., *Technology and Women's Voices: Keeping in Touch.* London: Routledge & Kegan Paul.

MacKain, K. S. (1984). "Speaking Without a Tongue." *Journal of the National Student Speech Language Hearing Association,* 12, 46–71.

MacKay, D. M. (1972). "Formal Analysis of Communicative Processes." In Hinde, R. A., ed., *Non-verbal Communication.* Cambridge, England: Cambridge University Press.

Malinowski, B. (1922). *Argonauts of the Western Pacific: An Account of Native Enterprise and Adventure in the Archipelagoes of Melanesian New Guinea.* Prospect Heights, IL: Waveland Press (reprinted in 1984).

———. (1923). "The Problem of Meaning in Primitive Languages." In Ogden, C. K., and I. A. Richards, eds., *The Meaning of Meaning.* London: Routledge and Kegan Paul.

———. (1929). *The Sexual Life of Savages in North-Western Melanesia: An Ethnographic Account of Courtship, Marriage and Family Life Among the Natives of the Trobriand Islands, British New Guinea.* New York: Halcyon House.

———. (1935). *Coral Gardens and Their Magic: A Study of the Methods of Tilling the Soil and of Agricultural Rites in the Trobriand Islands.* Vol 2: *The Language of Magic and Gardening.* New York: American Book Company.

Marchman, V. A., R. Miller, and E. A. Bates (1991). "Babble and First Words in Children with Focal Brain Injury." *Applied Psycholinguistics,* 12, 1–22.

Marler, P., and R. Tenaza (1977). "Signaling Behavior of Apes with Special Reference to Vocalization." In Sebeok, T. A., ed., *How Animals Communicate.* Bloomington: Indiana University Press.

Marshall, L. (1961). "Sharing, Talking and Giving: Relief of Social Tensions Among !Kung Bushmen." *Africa,* 31, 231–49.

Martel, F. L., C. M. Nevison, F. D. Rayment, M. J. A. Simpson, and E. B. Keverne (1993). "Opioid Receptor Blockade Reduces Maternal Affect and Social Grooming in Rhesus Monkeys." *Psychoneuroendocrinology,* 18, 307–21.

McLuhan, M. (1964). *Understanding Media: The Extensions of Man.* London: Routledge and Kegan Paul.

McLuhan, M., and Q. Fiore (1967). *The Medium Is the Massage.* New York: Bantam Books.

McNeill, W. H. (1995). *Keeping Together in Time: Dance and Drill in Human History.* Cambridge, MA: Harvard University Press.

Mehrabian, A., and M. Wiener (1967). "Decoding of Inconsistent Communications." *Journal of Personality and Social Psychology*, 6, 109–14.

Meier, R. P., L. McGarvin, R. A. E. Zakia, and R. Willerman (1997). "Silent Mandibular Oscillations in Vocal Babbling." *Phonetica*, 54, 153–171.

Mendelson, E., ed. (1996). *W. H. Auden: Prose and Travel Books in Prose and Verse.* Vol. 1: 1926–1938. London: Faber and Faber.

Mendelson, M. J., M. M. Haith, and P. S. Goldman-Rakic (1982). "Face Scanning and Responsiveness to Social Cues in Infant Rhesus Monkeys." *Developmental Psychology*, 18, 222–28.

Miller, G. A. (1996). *The Science of Words.* New York: W. H. Freeman.

Miller, J. (1990). "Communication Without Words." In Mellor, D. H., ed., *Ways of Communicating.* Cambridge, England: Cambridge University Press.

Miller, P. M., and J. G. Ingham (1976). "Friends, Confidants, and Symptoms." *Social Psychiatry*, 11, 51–58.

Mills, A. E., and J. Coerts (1990). "Functions and Forms of Bilingual Input: Children Learning a Sign Language as One of Their First Languages." In Prillwitz, S., and T. Vollhaber, eds., *Current Trends in European Sign Language Research.* Hamburg: Signum Press.

Mines, M. A., B. F. Hanson, and J. E. Shoup (1978). "Frequency of Occurrence of Phonemes in Conversational English." *Language and Speech*, 21, 221–41.

Mithen, S. (1996). *The Prehistory of the Mind: A Search for the Origins of Art, Religion and Science.* London: Thames & Hudson.

Morisset, C. E., K. E. Barnard, and C. L. Booth (1995). "Toddlers' Language Development: Sex Differences Within Social Risk." *Developmental Psychology*, 31, 851–65.

Morris, D. (1967). *The Naked Ape: A Zoologist's Study of the Human Animal.* New York: McGraw-Hill.

———. (1969). *The Human Zoo.* London: World Books.

Morton, E. S. (1977). "On the Occurrence and Significance of Motivation-Structural Rules in Some Bird and Mammal Sounds." *American Naturalist*, 111, 855–69.

Moses, P. J. (1954). *The Voice of Neurosis.* New York: Grune & Stratton.

Moynihan, M. (1970). "The Control, Suppression, Decay, Disappearance and Replacement of Displays." *Journal of Theoretical Biology*, 29, 85–112.

Mulac, A. (1989). "Men's and Women's Talk in Same-Gender and Mixed-Gender Dyads: Power or Polemic?" *Journal of Language and Social Psychology*, 8, 249–70.

Myers, D. G. (1992). *The Pursuit of Happiness: Discovering the Pathway to Fulfillment, Well-being, and Enduring Personal Joy.* New York: Avon.

Naremore, J. (1989). *The Magic World of Orson Welles.* Dallas, TX: Southern Methodist University Press.

Nelson, K. (1992). "Monologues in the Crib." In Nelson, K., ed., *Narratives from the Crib.* Cambridge, MA: Harvard University Press.

Newhagen, J. E., and M. Ancell (1995). "The Expression of Emotion and Social Status in the Language of Bumper Stickers." *Journal of Language and Social Psychology*, 14, 312–23.

Noë, R., and R. Bshary (1997). "The Formation of Red Colobus-Diana Monkey Associations Under Predation Pressure from Chimpanzees." *Proceedings of the Royal Society of London B*, 264, 253–59.

Norberg-Hodge, H. (1991). *Ancient Futures: Learning from Ladakh.* London: Rider.

Norris, P. (1996). "Does Television Erode Social Capital? A Reply to Putnam." *PS: Political Science & Politics,* 29, 474–80.

Nydegger, C. N., and L. S. Mitteness (1988). "Etiquette and Ritual in Family Conversation." *American Behavioral Scientist,* 31, 702–16.

O'Gara, M., and J. Logemann (1988). "Phonetic Analysis of the Speech Development of Babies with Cleft Palate." *Cleft Palate Journal,* 25, 122–34.

Ohala, J. J. (1983). "Cross-language Use of Pitch: An Ethological View." *Phonetica,* 40, 1–18.

———. (1984). "An Ethological Perspective on Common Cross-language Utilization of F_0 of Voice." *Phonetica,* 41, 1–16.

Oldenburg, R. (1989). *The Great Good Place: Cafés, Coffee Shops, Community Centers, Beauty Parlors, General Stores, Bars, Hangouts, and How They Get You Through the Day.* New York: Paragon House.

Olds, J., R. S. Schwartz, and H. Webster (1996). *Overcoming Loneliness in Everyday Life.* New York: Birch Lane Press.

Ong, W. J. (1982). *Orality and Literacy: The Technologizing of the Word.* London: Methuen.

Packard, V. (1972). *A Nation of Strangers.* New York: David McKay.

Panksepp, J., S. M. Siviy, and L. A. Normansell (1985). "Brain Opioids and Social Emotions." In Reite, M., and T. Field, eds., *The Psychobiology of Attachment and Separation.* New York: Academic Press.

Pennebaker, J. W., S. D. Barger, and J. Tiebout (1989). "Disclosure of Traumas and Health Among Holocaust Survivors." *Psychosomatic Medicine,* 51, 577–89.

Perkins, M. R. (in press). "Is Pragmatics Epiphenomenal? Evidence from Communication Disorders." *Journal of Pragmatics.*

Perrett, D. I., and A. J. Mistlin (1990). "Perception of Facial Characteristics by Monkeys." In Stebbins, W. C., and M. A. Berkley, eds., *Comparative Perception: Complex Signals.* vol. 2. New York: John Wiley & Sons.

Phillips, G. M., and N. J. Metzger (1976). *Intimate Communication.* Boston, MA: Allyn & Bacon.

Piatelli-Palmarini, M. (1989). "Evolution, Selection and Cognition: From "Learning" to Parameter Setting in Biology and the Study of Language." *Cognition,* 31, 1–44.

Pinker, S. (1994). *The Language Instinct: The New Science of Language and Mind.* London: Penguin Books.

Plutchik, R. (1981). "Group Cohesion in a Psychoevolutionary Context." In Kellerman, H., ed., *Group Cohesion: Theoretical and Clinical Perspectives.* New York: Grune & Stratton.

Powell, J. T., and D. Ary (1979). "Communication Without Commitment." In Gumpert, G., and R. Cathcart, eds., *Inter/media: Interpersonal Communication in a Media World.* Oxford: Oxford University Press.

Powell, W. W., and L. Smith-Doerr (1994). "Networks and Economic Life." In Smelser, N. J., and R. Swedberg, eds., *Handbook of Economic Sociology.* Princeton, NJ: Princeton University Press.

Premack, D. (1986). " 'Gavagai!' or the Future History of the Animal Language Controversy." *Cognition,* 19, 207–96.

Provine, R. R. (1992). "Contagious Laughter: Laughter Is a Sufficient Stimulus for Laughs and Smiles." *Bulletin of the Psychonomic Society*, 30, 1–4.

———. (1993). "Laughter Punctuates Speech: Linguistic, Social and Gender Contexts of Laughter." *Ethology*, 95, 291–98.

Putnam, R. D. (1993). "The Prosperous Community: Social Capital and Public Life." *The American Prospect*, 13, 35–42.

———. (1995a). "Bowling Alone: America's Declining Social Capital." *Journal of Democracy*, 6, 65–78.

———. (1995b). "Tuning in, Tuning Out: The Strange Disappearance of Social Capital in America." *PS: Political Science & Politics*, 28, 664–83.

———. (1996). "Who Killed Civic America?" *Prospect*, March, 66–72.

Raffaelli, M., and E. Duckett (1989). "We Were Just Talking . . .": Conversations in Early Adolescence. *Journal of Youth and Adolescence*, 18, 567–82.

Rankin, A. M., and P. J. Philip (1963). "An Episode of Laughing in the Bukoba District of Tanganyika." *Central African Journal of Medicine*, 9, 167–84.

Raushecker, J. P., B. Tian, and M. Hauser (1995). "Processing of Complex Sounds in the Macaque Nonprimary Auditory Cortex." *Science*, 268, 111–14.

Redelmeier, D. A., and R. J. Tibshirani (1997). "Association Between Cellular-Telephone Calls and Motor Vehicle Collisions." *New England Journal of Medicine*, 336, 453–58.

Redican, W. K. (1975). "Facial Expressions in Nonhuman Primates." In Rosenblum, L. A., ed., *Primate Behavior: Developments in Field and Laboratory Research*. New York: Academic Press.

Reid, E. (1995). "Virtual Worlds: Culture and Imagination." In Jones, G., ed., *Cybersociety: Computer-Mediated Communication and Community*. Thousand Oaks, CA: Sage.

Rheingold, H. (1994). *The Virtual Community: Homesteading on the Electronic Frontier.* New York: HarperPerennial.

Riesman, D. (1950). *The Lonely Crowd: A Study of the Changing American Character.* New Haven, CT: Yale University Press.

Robinson, J. P., and G. Godbey (1997). *Time for Life: The Surprising Ways Americans Use Their Time.* University Park, PA: The Pennsylvania State University Press.

Rogers, J., L. A. Hart, and R. P. Boltz (1993). "The Role of Pet Dogs in Casual Conversations of Elderly Adults." *Journal of Social Psychology*, 133, 265–77.

Rose, L. (1985). "The Art of Conversation." *Atlantic*, November 1985.

Rose, T. (1994). *Black Noise: Rap Music and Black Culture in Contemporary America.* Hanover, NH: Wesleyan University Press.

Rosenberg, N. L. (1986). *Protecting the Best Men: An Interpretive History of the Law of Libel.* Chapel Hill, NC: University of North Carolina Press.

Rosnow, R. L. (1977). "Gossip and Marketplace Psychology." *Journal of Communication*, 27, 158–63.

Ross, E. D. (1981). "The Aprosodias: Functional-Anatomic Organization of the Affective Components of Language in the Right Hemisphere." *Archives of Neurology*, 38, 561–69.

Ross, M., R. J. Duffy, H. S. Cooker, and R. L. Sargeant (1973). "Contribution of the Lower Audible Frequencies to the Recognition of Emotions." *American Annals of the Deaf*, 118, 37–42.

Rousseau, J.-J. (1782). *Les Confessions.* Edited by P. Grosclaude, Paris, 1947 (cited by Lukes, 1973).

Rubin, L. (1976). *Worlds of Pain: Life in the Working Class Family*. New York: Basic Books.

Rymer, R. (1994). *Genie: A Scientific Tragedy*. London: Penguin Books.

Sachs, J., B. Bard, and M. L. Johnson (1981). "Language Learning with Restricted Input: Case Studies of Two Hearing Children of Deaf Parents." *Applied Psycholinguistics*, 2, 33–54.

Sacks, O. (1985). *The Man Who Mistook His Wife for a Hat*. London: Pan Books.

Sade, D. S. (1966). "Some Aspects of Parent-Offspring and Sibling Relations in a Group of Rhesus Monkeys, with a Discussion of Grooming." *American Journal of Physical Anthropology*, 23, 1–18.

Sahlins, M. (1974). *Stone Age Economics*. London: Tavistock Publications.

Sale, K. (1995). *Rebels Against the Future: The Luddites and Their War on the Industrial Revolution*. Reading, MA: Addison-Wesley.

Salmond, A. (1975). "Mana Makes the Man: A Look at Maori Oratory and Politics." In Bloch, M., ed., *Political Language and Oratory in Traditional Society*. London: Academic Press.

Samarin, W. J. (1972). *Tongues of Men and Angels*. New York: Macmillan.

Sapir, E. A. (1933). "Language." In *Encyclopaedia of the Social Sciences*, 9. Macmillan.

Sarason, B. R., G. R. Pierce, and I. G. Sarason (1990). "Social Support: The Sense of Acceptance and the Role of Relationships." In Sarason, B. R., I. G. Sarason, and G. R. Pierce, eds., *Social Support: An Interactional View*. New York: John Wiley.

Scaife, M., and J. S. Bruner (1975). "The Capacity for Joint Visual Attention in the Infant." *Nature*, 253, 265–66.

Schacter, D. L., and B. A. Church (1992). "Auditory Priming: Implicit and Explicit Memory for Words and Voices." *Journal of Experimental Psychology: Learning, Memory, and Cognition*, 18, 915–30.

Schegloff, E. A., and H. Sacks (1974). "Opening Up Closings." In Turner, R., ed., *Ethnomethodology*. Harmondsworth, Middlesex, England: Penguin Books.

Scherer, K. R., J. Koivumaki, and R. Rosenthal (1972). "Minimal Cues in the Vocal Communication of Affect: Judging Emotions from Content-Masked Speech." *Journal of Psycholinguistic Research*, 1, 269–85.

Schiff, N. B. (1979). "The Influence of Deviant Maternal Input on the Development of Language During the Preschool Years." *Journal of Speech and Hearing Research*, 22, 581–603.

Schilling, K. (1991). "Privacy and the Press: Breach of Confidence—the Nemesis of the Tabloids?" *Entertainment Law Review*, 6, 169–76.

Scitovsky, T. (1976). *The Joyless Economy*. New York: Oxford University Press.

Scott, S. K., A. W. Young, A. J. Calder, D. J. Hellawell, J. P. Aggleton, and M. Johnson (1997). "Impaired Auditory Recognition of Fear and Anger Following Bilateral Amygdala Lesions." *Nature*, 385, 254–57.

Seabrook, J. (1997). *Deeper: My Two-Year Odyssey in Cyberspace*. New York: Simon & Schuster.

Sennett, R. (1973). *The Fall of Public Man*. Cambridge, England: Cambridge University Press.

Settle, M. L. (1977). *Blood Tie*. Boston: Houghton Mifflin.

Shaming, Blaming and Flaming: Corporate Miscommunication in the Digital Age (1997). A report commissioned by Novell UK and Ireland and conducted by RONIN Research.

Shannon, C. E., and W. Weaver (1949). *Mathematical Theory of Communication.* Urbana, IL: University of Illinois Press.

Shenk, D. (1997). *Data Smog: Surviving the Information Glut.* New York: Harper-Collins.

Sherzer, J. (1990). *Verbal Art in San Blas: Kuna Culture Through Its Discourse.* Cambridge, England: Cambridge University Press.

Shipp, T., and H. Hollien (1969). "Perception of the Aging Male Voice." *Journal of Speech and Hearing Research,* 12, 703–10.

Short, J. F., and F. L. Strodtbeck (1965). *Group Process and Gang Delinquency.* Chicago, IL: University of Chicago Press.

Shostak, M. (1981). *Nisa: The Life and Words of a !Kung Woman.* New York: Vintage Books.

Simkins-Bullock, J. A., and B. G. Wildman (1991). "An Investigation into the Relationships Between Gender and Language." *Sex Roles,* 24, 149–60.

Simmel, G. (1950/1903). *The Sociology of Georg Simmel.* Glencoe, IL. The Free Press. Edited and translated by Wolff, K. H. (from *Die Grossstadte und das Geistesleben Die Grosstädt.* Dresden: Jansch).

Simpson, M. J. A. (1973). "The Social Grooming of Male Chimpanzees." In Michael, R. P., and J. H. Crook, eds., *Comparative Ecology and Behaviour of Primates.* London: Academic Press.

Sirica, J. J. (1979). *To Set the Record Straight: The Break-in, the Tapes, the Conspirators, the Pardon.* New York: W. W. Norton.

Slater, P. (1970). *The Pursuit of Loneliness.* London: Allen Lane.

Slobin, D. I., S. H. Miller, and L. W. Porter (1968). "Forms of Address and Social Relations in a Business Organization." *Journal of Personality and Social Psychology,* 8, 289–93.

Smith, P. K., and K. Connolly (1972). "Patterns of Play and Social Interaction in Pre-school Children." In Blurton-Jones, N., ed., *Ethological Studies of Child Behavior.* Cambridge: Cambridge University Press.

Smith, W. J. (1977). *The Behavior of Communicating: An Ethological Approach.* Cambridge, MA: Harvard University Press.

Smith, W. J., J. Chase, and A. K. Lieblich (1974). "Tongue Showing: A Facial Display of Humans and Other Primate Species." *Semiotica,* 11, 201–46.

Smitherman, G. (1986). *Talkin and Testifyin.* Detroit, MI: Wayne State University Press.

Smolan, R., and J. Erwitt (1996). *24 Hours in Cyberspace: Painting on the Walls of the Digital Cave.* New York: Macmillan.

Social Trends 26 (1996 ed.). London: HMSO.

Solano, C. H., P. G. Batten, and E. A. Parish (1982). "Loneliness and Patterns of Self-disclosure." *Journal of Personality and Social Psychology,* 43, 524–31.

Sommerville, C. J. (1997). "Surfing the Coffeehouse." *History Today,* 47 8–10.

Soskin, W. F., and V. P. John (1963). "The Study of Spontaneous Talk." In Barker, R. G., ed., *The Stream of Behavior.* New York: Appleton-Century-Crofts.

Speer, S. R., R. G. Crowder, and L. M. Thomas (1993). "Prosodic Structure and Sentence Recognition." *Journal of Memory and Language,* 32, 336–58.

Stallones, L., M. B. Marx, T. F. Garrity, and T. P. Johnson (1988). "Attachment to Companion Animals Among Older Pet Owners." *Anthrozoos,* 2, 118–24.

Stanislavski, C. (1990). *An Actor's Handbook: An Alphabetical Arrangement of Concise Statements on Aspects of Acting.* London: Methuen Drama.

Stark, R. (1980). "Prespeech Segmental Feature Development." In Fletcher, P., and M. Garman, eds., *Language Acquisition*. Cambridge, England: Cambridge University Press.

Stedman, L. C., and C. F. Kaestle (1991). "Literacy and Reading Performance in the United States from 1880 to the Present." In Kaestle, C. F., H. Damon-Moore, L.C. Stedman, K. Tinsley, and W. V. Trollinger, eds., *Literacy in the United States: Readers and Reading Since 1880*. New Haven: Yale University Press.

Steinfield, C. W. (1986). "Computer-mediated Communication in an Organizational Setting: Explaining Task-Related and Socioemotional Uses." In McLaughlin, M. L., ed., *Communication Yearbook 9*. Beverly Hills, CA: Sage.

Stevenson, R. L. (1897). "Talk and Talkers." *Memories and Portraits*. New York: Charles Scribner's Sons.

Stiles, W. B. (1987). " 'I Have to Talk to Somebody.' A Fever Model of Disclosure." In Derlega, V. J., and J. H. Berg, eds., *Self-disclosure: Theory, Research, and Therapy*. New York: Plenum.

Stoll, C. (1995). *Silicon Snake Oil: Second Thoughts on the Information Highway*. New York: Anchor Books.

Strathern, A. (1975). "Veiled Speech in Mount Hagen." In Bloch, M., ed., *Political Language and Oratory in Traditional Society*. London: Academic Press.

Street, R. L., and T. J. Murphy (1987). "Interpersonal Orientation and Speech Behavior." *Communication Monographs*, 54, 42–62.

Stross, B. (1989). "Speaking of Speaking: Tenejapa Tzeltal Metalinguistics." In Bauman, R., and J. Sherzer, eds., *Explorations in the Ethnography of Speaking*, 2nd ed. Cambridge, England: Cambridge University Press.

Sugawara, K. (1984). "Spatial Proximity and Bodily Contact Among the Central Kalahari San." *African Study Monographs*, 3, 1–43.

———. (1990). "Interactional Aspects of the Body in Co-presence: Observations on the Central Kalahari San." In Moerman, M., and M. Nomura, eds., *Culture Embodied*. Senri Ethnological Studies 27. Osaka, Japan: National Museum of Ethnology.

Suls, J. M. (1977). "Gossip as Social Comparison." *Journal of Communication*, 27, 164–68.

Symmes, D., and M. Biben (1985). "Maternal Recognition of Individual Infant Squirrel Monkeys from Isolation Call Playbacks." *American Journal of Primatology*, 9, 39–46.

Tanford, J. A., D. B. Pisoni, and K. A. Johnson (1990). "Novel Scientific Evidence of Intoxication: Acoustic Analysis of Voice Recordings from the *Exxon Valdez*." *Research on Speech Perception, Progress Report No. 16*. Bloomington, IN: Speech Research Laboratory, Indiana University.

Tardy, C. H., W. R. Thompson, and M. T. Allen (1989). "Cardiovascular Responses During Speech: Does Social Support Mediate the Effects of Talking on Blood Pressure?" *Journal of Language and Social Psychology*, 8, 271–85.

Tartter, V. C. (1980). "Happy Talk: Perceptual and Acoustic Effects of Smiling on Speech." *Perception and Psychophysics*, 27, 24–27.

Tartter, V. C., and D. Braun (1994). "Hearing Smiles and Frowns in Normal and Whisper Registers." *Journal of the Acoustical Society of America*, 96, 2101–07.

Temple, T. (1995). "Marching Bandwidth: Advancing Information Exchange at Stability's Expense." *Journal of Contemporary Legal Issues*, 6, 409–33.

Tew, B. (1979). "The 'Cocktail Party Syndrome' in Children with Hydrocephalus and Spina Bifida." *British Journal of Disorders of Communication*, 14, 89–101.

Thomas, J. (1992). *Forty Years of Steel: An Annotated Discography of Steel Band and Pan Recordings, 1951–1991*. Westport, CT: Greenwood Press.

Thornton, T. P. (1996). *Handwriting in America: A Cultural History*. New Haven, CT: Yale University Press.

Toffler, A. (1970). *Future Shock*. New York: Bantam Books.

———. (1981). *The Third Wave*. New York: Bantam Books.

Tranel, D., A. R. Damasio, and H. Damasio (1988). "Intact Recognition of Facial Expression, Gender, and Age in Patients with Impaired Recognition of Face Identity." *Neurology*, 38, 690–96.

Trevarthen, C. (1993). "The Self Born in Intersubjectivity: The Psychology of an Infant Communicating." In Neisser, U., ed., *The Perceived Self: Ecological and Interpersonal Sources of Self-knowledge*. Cambridge, England: Cambridge University Press.

Turing, A. M. (1950). "Computing Machinery and Intelligence." *Mind*, 59, 433–60.

Turkle, S. (1984). *The Second Self: Computers and the Human Spirit*. New York: Simon & Schuster.

———. (1988). "Computational Reticence: Why Women Fear the Intimate Machine." In Kramarae, C., ed., *Technology and Women's Voices*. London: Routledge & Kegan Paul.

Turow, J. (1997). *Breaking Up America: Advertisers and the New Media World*. Chicago: University of Chicago Press.

van Hoof, J. A. R. A. M. (1962). "Facial Expression in Higher Primates." *Symposia of the Zoological Society of London*, 8, 97–125.

———. (1967). "The Facial Displays of the Catarrhine Monkeys and Apes." In Morris, D., ed., *Primate Ethology*. London: Weidenfeld and Nicolson.

Van Lancker, D. (1987). "Nonpropositional Speech: Neurolinguistic Studies." In Ellis, A., ed., *Progress in the Psychology of Language*, vol. 3. Hillsdale, NJ: Lawrence Erlbaum.

Van Lancker, D. R., J. L. Cummings, J. Kreiman, and B. H. Dobkin (1988). "Phonagnosia: A Dissociation Between Familiar and Unfamiliar Voices." *Cortex*, 24, 195–209.

Van Lancker, D., J. Kreiman, and K. Emmorey (1985). "Familiar Voice Recognition: Patterns and Parameters. Part 1: Recognition of Backward Voices." *Journal of Phonetics*, 13, 19–38.

Van Lancker, D., J. Kreiman, and T. D. Wickens (1985). "Familiar Voice Recognition: Patterns and Parameters. Part 2: Recognition of Rate-Altered Voices." *Journal of Phonetics*, 13, 39–52.

van Lawick-Goodall, J. (1975). "The Chimpanzee." In Goodall, V., ed., *The Quest for Man*. New York: Praeger.

Verba, S., K. L. Schlozman, and H. E. Brady (1995). *Voice and Equality: Civic Voluntarism in American Politics*. Cambridge, MA: Harvard University Press.

Wagner, K. R. (1985). "How Much Do Children Say in a Day?" *Journal of Child Language*, 12, 475–87.

Walter, R. (1994). *The Secret Guide to Computers*, 19th edition.

Walton, J. H., and R. F. Orlikoff (1994). "Speaker Race Identification from Acoustic Cues in the Vocal Signal." *Journal of Speech and Hearing Research*, 37, 738–45.

Warwick, C. (1983). *Princess Margaret*. London: Weidenfeld and Nicolsin.

Waser, P. M. (1977). "Individual Recognition, Intragroup Cohesion and Intergroup Spacing: Evidence from Sound Playback to Forest Monkeys." *Behaviour*, 60, 28–74.

Watson-Gegeo, K. A., and G. M. White, eds. (1990). *Disentangling: Conflict Discourse in Pacific Societies*. Stanford, CA: Stanford University Press.

Wayne, H. (1995). *The Story of a Marriage*. Vol. 1: *The Letters of Bronislaw Malinowski and Elsie Masson*. London: Routledge.

Wechsberg, J. (1966). *The Merchant Bankers*. London: Weidenfeld and Nicolson.

Weir, R. H. (1970). *Language in the Crib*. The Hague: Mouton.

Weiss, R. S. (1969). "The Fund of Sociability." *Trans-Action*, 6, 36–43.

Weiss, M. J. (1988). *The Clustering of America*. New York: Harper & Row.

Westergaard, G. C., M. Champoux, and S. J. Suomi. (1997). "Hand Preference in Infant Rhesus Macaques" *(Macaca mulatta)*. *Child Development*, 68, 387–393.

Whiten, A. (1993). "Social Complexity: The Roles of Primates' Grooming and People's Talking." *Behavioral and Brain Sciences*, 16, 719.

Wiessner, P. (1981). "Measuring the Impact of Social Ties on Nutritional Status Among the !Kung San." *Social Science Information*, 20, 641–78.

———. (1982). "Risk, Reciprocity and Social Influences on !Kung San Economics." In Leacock, E., and R. Lee, eds. *Politics and History in Band Societies*. Cambridge, England: Cambridge University Press.

———. (1983). "Style and Social Information in Kalahari San Projectile Points." *American Antiquity*, 48, 253–76.

Wilkinson, R. (1995). "Aphasia: Conversation Analysis of a Non-Fluent Aphasic Person." In Perkins, M., and S. Howard, eds., *Case Studies in Clinical Linguistics*. London: Whurr.

Wilson, P. J. (1969). "Reputation and Respectability: A Suggestion for Caribbean Ethnology." *Man*, 4, 70–84.

Wittgenstein, L. (1973). *Philosophical Investigations*. New York: Macmillan.

Wordsworth, W. (1971). *The Prelude: A Parallel Text*. Edited by J. C. Maxwell. London: Penguin Books. First published in 1805.

Wrangham, R., and D. Peterson (1966). *Demonic Males: Apes and the Origins of Human Violence*. London: Bloomsbury.

Wurtzel, A. H., and C. Turner (1977). "What Missing the Telephone Means." *Journal of Communication*, 27, 48–57.

Wuthnow, R. (1994). *Sharing the Journey: Support Groups and America's New Quest for Community*." New York: The Free Press.

Yankelovich, D. (1975). "The Status of Ressentiment in America." *Social Research*, 42, 760–77.

Zajonc, R. B. (1980). "Feelings and Thinking: Preferences Need No Inferences." *American Psychologist*, 35, 151–75.

Zuckerman, M., and R. E. Driver (1989). "What Sounds Beautiful Is Good: The Vocal Attractiveness Stereotype." *Journal of Nonverbal Behavior*, 13, 67–82.

Zuckerman, M., H. Hodgins, and K. Miyake (1990). "The Vocal Attractiveness Stereotype: Replication and Elaboration." *Journal of Nonverbal Behavior*, 14, 97–112.

Index

DATE DUE

HIGHSMITH #45115